Dear Joy —
I'd have given
it you before
but you weren't
serious.

Love DK '92

For Max from Joy
with love 2004.

BRAZILIAN JOURNAL

P.K. Page

LESTER
&ORPEN
DENNYS
PUBLISHERS

FIRST EDITION

Canadian Cataloguing in Publication Data

Page, P.K. (Patricia Kathleen), 1916–

Brazilian journal

ISBN 0-88619-166-1 (bound). — ISBN 0-88619-180-7 (pbk.).

1. Page, P.K. (Patricia Kathleen), 1916–
2. Poets, Canadian (English) – 20th century –
Diaries. * 3. Ambassadors' wives – Canada –
Diaries. 4. Brazil – Description and travel –
1951-1980. I. Title.

PS8531.A43Z53 1987   C811'.54   C86-094167-1
PR9199.3.P33Z463 1987

Map by Jonathan Gladstone, j.b. geographics

Typeset at FTL systems Inc. using the Pages system by McCutcheon Electronic Publishing Systems, of McCutcheon Graphics Inc., Toronto

Printed and bound in Canada by
Imprimerie Gagné Ltée for

Lester & Orpen Dennys Limited
78 Sullivan Street
Toronto, Canada M5T 1C1

For A., of course

I would like to thank Michael Ondaatje for his suggestion that I write this book; Arthur Irwin, Irene Lampert, Ivy Mickelson, Constance Rooke, and Linda Spalding for invaluable help along the way; Gena K. Gorrell for her painstaking editing; and members of the staff of the University of Victoria Library and the Greater Victoria Public Library for their unwitting research assistance. Good friends all.

Sections of the book have appeared with minor differences in *Canadian Literature*, *Descant*, *Views from the North: An Anthology of Travel Writing*, and *Brick*.

And in that tasting,
taster, water, air,
in temperature identical
were so
intricately merged
a fabulous foreign bird
flew silent from a void

lodged in my boughs.

Foreword

This is a period piece.

It is based, mainly, on letters to my family and extracts from my journal, written during the privileged years, 1957–1959. Where necessary, I have clarified; here and there I have fleshed out what were merely notes.

More than thirty years have passed since the events described took place. The official residence that we lived in and loved has been torn down. Our last contact with Brazilian friends has ended.

In the interim, language has changed; Brazil has changed; I have changed.

But for me—then—this is the way it was.

Victoria, B.C.
1987

BRAZILIAN JOURNAL

THE BRAZIL OF P. K. PAGE

VENEZUELA
COLOMBIA
GUYANA
SURINAM
FRENCH GUIANA
60°W
40°W
Negro R.
Manaus
Itacoatiara
0°N/S
Belém
Alcântara
São Luís
Equator
Fortaleza
Solimões R.
Amazon R.
Caxias
B
R
PERU
A
Araguaia R.
Recife
10°S
Z
BOLIVIA
Brasília
Salvador
Ilhéus
I
Belo Horizonte
Itabira
Ouro Preto
Poços de Caldas
Campos
20°S
PARAGUAY
São Paulo
Congonhas do Campo
Tropic of Capricorn
Rio de Janeiro
Campos de Jordão
Santos
Paraná R.
CHILE
ARGENTINA
Curitiba
Florianópolis
Pôrto Alegre
Bagé
30°S
URUGUAY
Pelotas
Rio Grande
70°W
50°W
J8G87

Foretaste

It was 1956 and we were in Lae, New Guinea. A. was collecting information for a report on the feasibility of independence for the territory, which at that time was governed by Australia.

I had just pressed a dress wrinkled from travelling. Perspiration dripped off my nose. Outside, the world throbbed with green. *"Verde, como te quiero verde."* This colour throb was the only movement. In such heat nothing was stirring. Not even birds.

I draped the warm dress over my arm and returned to the bedroom. A. was opening mail. An electric fan whirred. I lay naked on the bed listening to the noises—new noises: the fan, a gecko creaking somewhere in the room, that green throb.

A. said, "We're posted to Brazil."

(Nuts. There's an awful lot of coffee in.) "Brazil?" I said, unbelieving.

"Brazil," A. repeated.

"Oh, no," I said. I wonder why it seemed so impossible?

"Send a letter to Jules," I offered, "refusing. I'll draft it:

> For some
> It is surely a plum.
> Give it to thum."

A. laughed.

"Tropics," I said. "Like this?"

But it wasn't.

I find it hard now to remember why Brazil fell on my heart with so heavy a thud. Perhaps it was the memory of the Latin-American diplomatic wives in Ottawa who had looked like a cross between women and precious stones; perhaps an unformulated wish for a European post after Australia; perhaps...who knows? At any rate I didn't view the prospect with particular cheer. Yet, curiously, all that I was loving about New Guinea—the marvellous fret of tropical vegetation, the moist, hot air, the extraordinary brilliance of bougainvillea and hibiscus against the rank and thrusting green—all these were to be given to us even more abundantly in Brazil. All these and heaven too.

We left Ottawa, on the first leg of our journey to Brazil, on a bright, bitter, sub-zero morning—cars and pedestrians crunching and smoking on the snow-packed streets. Friends seeing us off, in their karakul hats and ankle-length topcoats, looked like characters from a Russian novel.

During the preceding weeks we had tried, not very successfully, to shop for cottons and learn the rudiments of Portuguese from gramophone records. In spite of books, the post report (a confidential report on conditions in the post), and endless talk about "the residence", I could form no very clear picture of the life ahead. Leaning on the rail of the S.S. *Brazil* and watching the skyscrapered skyline of New York recede, diminish, fade into the horizon, I felt that everything familiar was receding with it.

"Aren't you *afraid* of going to Brazil?" the wife of one of our senior diplomats had asked me, shortly before we left. And I had answered honestly enough that, no, I was not afraid. "Well, I would be!" was her rejoinder. I hadn't enquired why. I didn't want to add her fears to my doubts. Already I wondered if I would master the language—I, who had never properly mastered French. And I was appalled by the grandeur of the house we were to inhabit.

As it had only recently been acquired by Ottawa, we were to be the first Canadians to occupy it. We learned that it was beautiful; that it had been built by a wealthy Portuguese and modelled on his *palacete* in Portugal; and that its private chapel had been deconsecrated with the intention of leaving it empty (although Brazilians in Ottawa complained they had heard we were going to use it as a bar!)

Members of Parliament had criticized the cost of the furnishings, and the price of two eighteenth-century Chippendale mirrors for the entrance hall had caused apoplexy among taxpayers. Gossip had it that Brazilians in Rio were angry over the interior decoration—ceilings originally "marbled" in the traditional Portuguese manner, by craftsmen specially imported from Portugal for the job, had been painted over.

Further intelligence: there would be workmen in the house when we arrived; the embassy had hired a Spanish couple to keep the place clean until we could hire staff; the gardener who worked for the original owner was still in charge of the grounds; and—crowning touch!—Brazilians were so fashion-conscious that when the ladies of the Portuguese court had arrived in Rio in 1808—heads shaved because of the lice they had caught on the voyage out—the ladies of Brazilian society, thinking it was the latest European fashion, had lost no time in shaving theirs!

"Our palacete is on a valley slope facing two mountains known as The Two Brothers."

January 21

Although midsummer, it was overcast the day we arrived.
From the ship, Rio lay before us like a dog's vision of it—
monochromatic—the grey light making it two-dimensional. A flat,
platinum city. The long arc of Copacabana sand was pale silver
and the apartment blocks that encircled it were silver, pewter, and
steel. From a distance the strangely bright *amêndoa de praia* (beach
almonds) were blobs of green enamel—the only colour.

We had been told that Rio is the most beautiful city in the world,
and it *is* beautiful. As tropical as New Guinea or Singapore, with
carefully tended parks. But mildew and wet-rot eat away at its modern
buildings—more modern than anything at home—buildings which
rise, daring and astonishing, pastel or patterned, into the soft air.
Often, too often, from shanty towns at their feet. A legacy from the
past: the elegant colonial architecture of delicately symmetrical twin-
towered churches, the grave plaster façades of public buildings. And
all this set among forested mountains, *au bord de la mer.*

Our *palacete* —and it is indeed that—is in one of the city's western
suburbs on Estrada da Gávea (Street of the Square Sail), on a valley
slope facing two mountains known as Os Dois Irmãos (The Two
Brothers). For three days after we arrived, low cloud and a relentless
rain made it impossible to see over the tops of the trees at the bottom
of the garden. But now, like a backdrop, the two blunt brotherly peaks
are unveiled against a blue sky.

From street level, the house is hidden behind a high wall—
hot pink, and stained with continents of the mildew and mould
which flourish in this steamy climate. Approaching from the city,
if you drive in through the second of the two street gates you pass
the gatehouse where the gardener lives; peer through the garden's
fretwork of tree ferns, the ruler-straight trunks of palm trees, and
the intense black of their shade; cross a little stream over a bridge;
and there—beyond a lotus pond and a stretch of quite extraordinary
lawn—stands the equally extraordinary house: rectilinear façade, hot
pink again with chalk-white trim, three-layered, with two tiers of
rounded arches.

As you proceed up the U-shaped drive, you round the now empty
chapel at the corner of the house and arrive at the main entrance or
front door, if a door at the back can be so called. Only the width of
the driveway away, a forested mountain rises steeply. Its trees we

have never seen before and its floor is covered—the way an English bluebell wood is covered—with a low, red-flowering plant, *Maria sem vergonha* (Shameless Mary—for it will grow anywhere).

Continuing on, the drive passes the garage-cum-servants' lodge and turns past the house into the U's other arm, and there again is the garden and its lawn—"quite extraordinary" for having been hand-planted in tropical grasses of different shades, pale green meeting darker green in a great sinuous curve. And beyond: the stream, a sluice-gate controlling a waterfall, and the other street gate leading back into Estrada da Gávea.

The sound of water—running, dawdling, or rushing, depending on the rains—is always with us. A heavenly sound. Soothing. Cooling in the heat.

A marble-floored patio, with changing rooms and bar, stretches the length of the house on the garden side and abuts on a swimming-pool—also the length of the house—which because of low water pressure takes days to fill.

The main entrance is guarded by two vast, barred, plate-glass doors—heavy and silent as vault doors—which swing open onto a pale pink marble hall. Immediately inside, a central marble stairway of the same pink leads down to the kitchens, cloakrooms, storage rooms, and servants' bedrooms. To left and right, rising flights of stairs—marble again—end at the famous and elegant antique mirrors—flawlessly preserved even to the glass, which reflects an element seemingly denser than air. Between the mirrors, double doors of thick, black, carved jacaranda wood open into the main reception room—a great, cold, white-walled, green-ceilinged room with a grand piano, beautiful glittering chandeliers, and formal French chairs upholstered in green silk. Pale yellow brocade curtains flank the French doors and are splayed on the floor a good twelve inches in carefully arranged pleats—a custom which must have originated in a cold country, to combat drafts.

On our arrival, this room was filled with flowers in such enormous quantities that I couldn't help looking about me for the coffin. Flowers on every table, flowers on the floor, flowers doubled in the highly polished surfaces of tables or in glimmering marble. Fantastic flowers—fluorescent, artificial-looking—some in lidded wicker baskets through which they appeared to have forced their way to the light, there to bloom much as the magical Chinese "flowers" of my childhood bloomed when submerged in a glass of water.

To the right of this room, a smaller sitting-room; to the left, the dining-room, large enough to seat forty. All three open through French doors onto an uncovered terrace which overlooks the swimming-pool, the garden, and the Two Brothers. Off the dining-room, a dining patio, its furniture of pale green wrought iron and glass almost as transparent as air; and off the reception rooms, an outdoor sitting-room with rattan sofas and chairs. A library, two washrooms, a pantry, and a butler's pantry complete this floor.

Upstairs—the stairs not marble this time, but built from some nameless wood golden as amber—are six bedrooms, four bathrooms, a linen room, an enormous family sitting-room, a pantry, and back stairs. The family sitting-room is dark and furnished rather in the manner of a second-rate German liner. It is the only ugly note—partly redeemed, however, by a small balcony which juts out from it over the front door, close to the mysterious forest on the mountain behind us.

A.'s bedroom and mine adjoin, their bathrooms of milky grey marble with gold fixtures. French doors in each bedroom lead to a balcony overlooking the Two Brothers. There, hanging above the green garden, we are brought strange fruits and superlative *café au lait* for our breakfast.

There is one other feature—an elevator. I almost wrote "elephant", not because of its size but because of its ponderousness. It runs—if such a word can be used to describe its progress—from the top floor to the pool, with a stop at the main floor. You would have to be a child or very ill or very old to use it.

We were met by a German housekeeper who speaks seven languages—none of them mine. I can see that she will have to go. In addition we have a Spanish couple, Guillermo and Maria, who speak a little Portuguese; a Brazilian chauffeur, Nildo, who is currently living over the garage with his wife and children in a space designed for four servants; a Portuguese gardener, Ricardo—a minute gnome of a man who sleeps in the gatehouse and spends much of his waking time weeding the dark green grass out of the light green and vice versa; a coal-black gardener's helper, Manuel; a cook from Bahía and her coal-black assistant; and a laundress who has elephantiasis. The correct manner of staffing this place will, I hope, sort itself out in time. Considerably more staff is needed here than in non-tropical countries, partly because the heat slows everyone to a crawl and partly because, with the high humidity, everything has to be aired and brushed every day. This morning, for instance, I inspected the furniture with a view to reporting to Ottawa on the state in which it arrived a month ago, and found long beards of mildew growing from the undersides of all the chairs.

I have done little since arriving except unpack and inspect and try to get things working. And study Portuguese. And draw long breaths.

But we did have one eventful night when we were wakened by what I thought were pistol shots ringing out in the garden. Silence. Then they rang out a second time. As no voices were raised and there was no further noise, we presumed the revolution had not really begun. But about five we were wakened again by another volley, and this time I could see flashes through the curtains. Peering over the balcony, A. reported that our personal policeman was marching imperturbably up and down the terrace. Then we heard drums and strange singing in the nearby hills and realized, with a mixture of relief and disappointment, that my pistol shots were the fireworks of a *festa* in the neighbouring *favela*.

That is our most dramatic adventure to date.

The second-most was the arrival of what looked like a large cockroach but turned out to be a more talented creature. When asked to leave, he turned on two brilliant green headlights—all the better to blind you with!—which slowly dimmed and went out when he thought the danger was past.

Attended our first Brazilian party. In an immense apartment on Avenida Atlântica, which opened onto a veranda overlooking Copacabana beach and a bay that glistened with the lights of a distant shore, thirty people sat down for dinner and were waited on by half a dozen footmen in white gloves. I sat with my host, who is reading *The Cocktail Party*; a young Frenchman—the *enfant terrible,* I would guess, of this particular group; and a pale and cerebral young man from Brazilian External Affairs.

"Where were you before Brazil?"

"We were in Australia."

"Did you like it?"

"We loved it."

"I'm afraid, if you loved Australia, you will hate Brazil."

"I can't agree," said our host. "If they loved Australia, they will *adore* Brazil."

After that the conversation, in English, was almost entirely of sex. Our host, a small, lively Brazilian of great charm, began it by saying that his wife claims women are attracted to him only because they know he sleeps with her—anyone she sleeps with must be a good bed-fellow. She is glamorous, I allow, but I think she flatters herself.

Half-way through dinner all the lights in the city went out. Darkness everywhere—inside and out—except for the myriad points of light on the bay, floating now in so vast a night. But how afraid we still are of the dark! At once all the footmen fumbled through the blackness in their white gloves and returned with lighted candelabra. Beautiful too.

February 3

How could I have imagined so surrealist and seductive a world? One does not *like* the heat, yet its constancy, its all-surroundingness, is as fascinating as the smell of musk. Every moment is slow, as if under warm greenish water.

The flavour is beyond my ability to catch. The senses are sharpened by *that* smell—a vegetable polecat called jack-fruit which when fallen looks in size and contour like a black porcupine, and when ripe is picked from trees in our jungle; by *these* sights: Niemeyer's bridges, for instance, built over the canyons of this remarkably mountained city—long, sinuous, low bridges on pylons, white as platinum against the green of the *mato*—with bright glimpses of the sea both above and below; recurring couples—on the street everyone is paired—in love, embracing or half-embracing, whatever the heat; and the solitary figure in the window, usually female, framed by a mat of hot air and gazing off into a kind of languor, as if all time were designed for that purpose.

It is hard to get anything done. It is hard to focus. A thought is barely born before it melts, and in its place so lovely a void one could hardly have guessed emptiness so attractive. We swim now, in the great hot pool—not cooling off, merely drowning our wetness in a greater wetness—while next door the Sisters sing their Aves in the totally dark convent. The other night we heard the giggles of a host of small girls, and leaning on the balustrade in what must surely be the classical Brazilian pose, found—instead of a children's party as we had thought—the Sisters themselves, those whom we have seen at dusk, silently reading their breviaries under the cassia trees, now swinging on the swings, black robes flying. A wonderful subject for

Pegi Nicol, had she been alive to momentarily lay aside her bright jujube colours and try the inky ranges of blues and greens.

I think of her now, perhaps, because her joyful, bright oils, bursting with life, somehow parallel all this tropical exuberance. And once reminded of her, I see again her posthumous show at the National Gallery of works painted when she was dying—beautiful, brilliant, large canvases, filled to overflowing. It was as if the lethal, proliferating cancer cells within her had been transformed into a multitude of life-giving images which made dance the grey air of the gallery.

And because our reception rooms are like the shell-white grottoes where mermaids might sober up after a drunken night, a large Nicol of girls gardening and bending in a profusion of colour would shed a warmer light in all this green and white. A Nicol, a Lillian Freiman, and a great Bonnard.

The Goodridge Roberts in the small *sala* —and all my life I've wanted to live with a Goodridge—is dark and totally without movement. Its pines against the sky are characteristic as a signature—but it might be forged. Sky, trees, water—his best ingredients—lie locked on the canvas. What would I not give for his large still life from the National Gallery—the fruit, the bottle, the plate, painted as if he had suddenly descried a world in which all objects glow.

A. is spilled on his bed like warm milk, and the frogs, treetoads, cicadas, and whatever else cut, saw, bang, and hit the black tropical night. Around and around the driveway the armed guard in his sand-coloured uniform strolls, like a succession of men. In the darkness between the pools of light shed by the lamps he is totally lost. The frogs sound like dogs, like hens, like drums, like strings, and when they stop—which they do occasionally, as if obeying a conductor—one hears the other drums and the weird singing from the *favela*.

It is from the *favelas* that the sambas come, according to our host of the other evening—a small Brazilian of Italian origin. He is, he claims, a true Carioca (citizen of Rio): loves the heat, the movement, the noise, the Negroes; and he loves the sambas and takes pride in having published many of the best, which he claims to have found when visiting the hills.

February 6

The heat is over for the moment. During the weekend the temperature soared above the century and no breeze moved among the smallest leaves of the maidenhair. But, dramatically, Sunday night, a storm blew up and the house seemed to rise like a flight of wooden eagles, wooden wings flapping, as every shutter banged and swung. You could almost see the cooler air as it streamed through the rooms overturning photographs, riffling papers—a manic housekeeper on the loose.

Last Sunday, a day as sunny as looking through a topaz, we set off for O Corcovado (The Hunchback)—one of the highest peaks in Rio—to which we climbed through forested mountains by a series of switchbacks. (Brazilians are great road-builders. They think nothing of going up mountains, down mountains, or even through mountains, where necessary.) Part-way up the actual peak, the road ended in a parking lot, and a winding footpath led us up to an assembly of kiosks selling postcards, dolls, and butterfly-wing pictures. Small boys, like acolytes, swung smoking braziers and peddled skilfully twisted, cone-shaped packets—some edible, but what? Then a climb up endless flights of steps with lovers—brown, black, white—loitering and being photographed in their Sunday best. And finally, at the top, the Christ, arms outspread—fifty metres tall—and the lovers now being photographed at his feet by young men popping under black cloths.

Below us, Rio: Guanabara Bay, large enough to float the navies of the world on its celestial blue waters, its narrow entrance between two peaks—the conical Pão de Açúcar (Sugar Loaf) and the Pico de Papagaio (Parrot's Beak); mountain spurs reaching for the sky, their valleys seemingly filled with an avalanche of buildings—red-roofed and white colonial buildings, modern skyscrapers—spilling onto the coastal plain to be brought to a sudden stop by the ocean's sandy shore. If there is a more beautiful setting for a city, I can't imagine it. *Cidade maravilhosa!*

February 13

Notes on flora and fauna: in the garden a bird like a yellow-bellied flycatcher. Trying to find it in the inadequate bird books we have acquired, I discover that Brazil has a marsupial duck! Why baby doesn't drown while mother swims, I don't understand.

Yesterday, when Maria, the Spanish maid of all work, was cleaning the veranda, she found a very blond frog asleep on the lintel above the door to the *sala*. Giving it a good peasant swipe with her broom—the kind she would in affection give to her husband—she brought it to the marble floor with such a resounding smack I'd have thought it dead. Instead it leapt through the door to the sitting-room and straight onto an upholstered French chair, with all the authority of the transformed prince. Finally, finding Maria's persistence with the broom too much for it, the poor thing clung with both forearms to a veranda railing and gave a great wail like a Siamese cat.

For the first and quite unforgettable time, we have seen a Brazilian blue butterfly—as large as a flying hand—the upper surfaces of its wings an iridescent Mary-blue, the underside soft as the colour of snuff. And these are the butterflies that are made into pictures for souvenir hunters!

Reports received before we arrived told us that the water pipes are corroded and that there would be "inconveniences as regards hot water and the use of toilets on the third floor". Too true! Also, as Canada was moving in with more electrical appliances than had been used previously, the electrical wiring was overloaded and would be another problem. It still is.

The lift van containing our pictures, books, *objets d'art*—sent from Canberra, via Durban—arrived before us and was unpacked to prevent its contents from mildewing. I have been finding a place for them in this vast green and white house. Thank goodness we have paintings. The Jori Smiths look wonderful here, and the small Surrey. I like to think they were warmly received by the resident Lemieux, the de Tonnancour, and the Roberts—Quebeckers all.

Despite generous help from embassy staff, moving into a fifty-seven-room house never before equipped as an official residence requires endless patience—doily-counting patience. I check inventories, make lists of needed supplies—those to be purchased locally, those which can't be obtained here and must be requested from Ottawa. I write endless letters to the Supplies and Properties Division.

Our blanket count is as follows:
8 Ottawa Valley Ivory 72 x 90 (in reasonably good condition)
2 Ottawa Valley Green 72 x 90 (old and much shrunken)
4 Hudson's Bay (two fairly fresh, two shrunken and matted).

(I wonder who thought of sending Hudson's Bay blankets to a tropical post?)

> We need vacuum cleaners, most urgently. Also our three thermos jugs have broken stoppers and as we use boiled water in the bathrooms for drinking and cleaning our teeth, with the present equipment we cannot look after guests, let alone ourselves.

(Our water comes from wells in the cellar and it tests three times the maximum allowable coliform count.)

> A shipment arrived the other day, containing irons, etc. Such a relief. We've been borrowing the iron of the chauffeur's wife.

(Now I know why you learn that kind of sentence in all good foreign-language grammars!)

Then there are the difficulties of language. I spend an enormous amount of time trying to communicate with the servants and an almost equal amount trying to disentangle the misunderstandings I have created. "Don't buy any more young girls," I say to the cook. Hours later I realize I meant *maçãs* (apples), not *moças*.

Ho hum!

A. presented his credentials last week. I wish I had been able to see the ceremony. I was only allowed a second-hand view, as it were.

At 10.30 a.m., four members of the embassy staff assembled at the residence—not unlike a comic chorus in their variously tailored morning-suits. Having not yet acquired a *copeiro* (waiter), we hired one for the occasion, and he arrived handsomely attired in white jacket and Mickey Mouse gloves.

At 11.45 the deafening blast of a motorcycle escort announced the arrival of the member of the Foreign Office delegated to accompany the Canadians to the Catete (Presidential Palace). We drank traditional *cafèzinhos* (smaller than a demitasse, blacker than tar, and thickened with curiously grey powdered sugar, less sweet than ours) in the green *sala* and the morning-suited sextet departed in three black cars. The motorcycle troops were in jungle-green uniforms, their white helmets emblazoned with red paint. As they roared down the long drive through our tropical garden, they might have been a painting by Rousseau the *douanier,* known to me alone.

A. reports that a large military parade and band were massed in the square outside the palace, that he presented his credentials to the president in carefully rehearsed Portuguese, and that the band played a rousing rendition of "O Canada" followed by umpteen verses of the Brazilian national anthem—an impossibly difficult tune to sing.

A blast of motorcycles returned the six men to the residence for champagne. Pleasantries exchanged.

The credentials, incidentally, are two letters of credence on parchment paper carrying Canada's coat of arms, in which Elizabeth the Second "Sendeth Greetings!" to the President of Brazil. One announces the recall of A.'s predecessor, and the other presents A., "Our Trusty and Well-beloved...to reside with You in the character of Ambassador Extraordinary and Plenipotentiary of Canada." Both letters are signed, "Your Good Friend, Elizabeth R."

"Your Good Friend", what marvellously simple language! And the Queen's signature is large and strong—unexpectedly so—like a banner flying from a fine Greek E.

February 18

Is the house controlled by poltergeists? Keys here yesterday have vanished today, elevators mended yesterday break down today. Lights suddenly fail. And taps.

The plumber came again. It took me more than an hour to show him the jobs that need doing. I am amazed at the number of times I have demonstrated the deficiencies of a bidet for the edification of strange men!

Today I fired the laundress with elephantiasis. Hated doing it but she was not a very good laundress and eighteen sugar bananas and five kilos of beef unaccountably disappeared on Saturday. Unfairly, perhaps, I suspect her. Yet I am sorry to see her go. It is unlikely I shall ever again employ a grotesque: elephantiasis of the legs and breasts and a strange little beard which hangs straight down under her chin and curls only at the end. In a book I was reading the other day, the author said Baudelaire was the poet of the Brazilian jungle... and certainly Lourdes, for that is her name, is pure Baudelaire. Ready for the clothes-line, her great brown arms full of white sheets, rows of clothes pegs clipped to her dress like rows of nipples on some gargantuan sow, she was a truly awesome figure.

In the garden one tree has four great sprays of tree orchids growing from it—white with purple centres; another has a yellow orchid with a rust centre; still another, an indescribable flower of bright cerise with cerulean blue tips on its large heather-shaped flowers. I wish I knew how to describe the vegetation, or indeed how to paint it. It is so excessive. Every tree puts forth some flower in clumps or sprays or showers of yellow, purple, pink, white, or red—and almost every trunk bears orchids. Nature doesn't seem to know how to control itself! For instance—the other day a yellow-bellied flycatcher flew out of a cassia tree heavy with yellow blossom, the tree growing in a flowerbed massed with yellow day-lilies, and caught, if you please, an immense yellow butterfly.

In my bedroom at this moment there is a flying creature about two inches long. A cricket? A locust? Black lace wings and a green brocade head and a noise like a DC-3 revving up. Just as the crisp air, the warbling of magpies, and the smells of gum smoke and daphne will for ever conjure up Australia for me, so will immense wet heat and thousands of night insects—*bichos*—conjure up Brazil. And too, tremendous lengths of sand, blinding white in the sun; the façades of white buildings which, for all their contemporary design, look somehow like the ruins in a John Piper painting; pedlars with eagle-shaped kites under a barrage of bright balloons on the boulevard by the sea; black-eyed children in pony carts with coloured nurses in starched white; the faded patchwork of the houses in the *favelas*; women balancing parcels on their heads; crowds at the beaches in the midday heat, minus sunglasses, minus hats, beating out samba rhythms on the blistering hot radiators of their cars. This is Barbados and Paris. But there is more—and other—as well.

February 23

It is cool today—seventy-five degrees, with the humidity at a hundred. The air coming through the windows is like sheet rain. Everything is mildewing. We burn lights in our clothes cupboards and place bags of salt among our shoes, but the mildew grows. I have just found, stashed away in the basement, some bottles of Mildu-Rid. Plan to plaster it on everything.

During the day I sometimes feel I am under house arrest. Our personal car has not yet arrived and first thing in the morning A. leaves for the Chancery. Despite its formal name, it is in a modern office building in downtown Rio on Avenida Presidente Wilson. It houses the embassy's political, trade, consular, and cultural offices. At this particular period it is also, in effect, a properties office, trying to cope with the problems of the residence—problems which range from contaminated wells and malfunctioning pumps in the basement to leaks in the roof, not to mention the more domestic matters which are my responsibility.

I fire and hire—write receipts in Portuguese for departing servants to sign. They come and go, an itinerant population, moving beautifully and dreamily through my house, my life, often leaving chaos behind them.

One black-skinned boy we employed as a cleaner was so affected by my difficulties with Portuguese that he became totally mute—able only to point and gesticulate. The first day that he actually *did* understand something I said, he underwent a vocal catharsis—releasing a great flood of mellifluous speech. This was accompanied by a kind of ballet in which he mimed—of all things—his love for the Canadian flag! He hung his duster from the top of a closed patio parasol, then saluted it with immense gravity. I found myself baffled by the finale in which he placed his head on folded hands and shut his eyes. Did he mean he wanted to sleep with the Canadian flag over his bed? When, next day, I was able to produce a small flag for him, his face lit up like a child's and slowly filled with the solemnity of an overwhelming love. He crossed both hands over his breast and bowed deeply. This latter action was repeated every time we met.

Our newly acquired second cleaner, André, is a Russian. He reminds me so much of Hymie Kaplan that I fear I shall call him that. Yesterday, when he arrived for duty, he rushed at me and kissed my hand! Today he is getting about his business. He and Guillermo working together are a comic act.

> Me (to Guillermo, who is using the vacuum to little effect): Do
> you think the vacuum needs emptying, by any chance?
> Guillermo opens it and triumphantly holds up a bag that is nearly
> bursting.
> André (rushing forward and taking it): Let me! Let me!

So we continue our one step forward, two steps back. Lavatories, record-player, telephones *não trabalham*—don't work yet. But it is all very lovely and, praise be, we have had a reprieve from the heat.

February 24

Went to our first formal reception the other night, given by the Venezuelan ambassador to decorate President Kubitschek with some Venezuelan order. The women were smart but I was not dazzled. I am told they really dress only during the season.

February 26

What a terrible fate to have no interest or conversation other than servants. For the time being it seems to be mine—although I have made a solemn vow not to talk about them unless asking for specific advice. But it is exactly like having a house full of monkeys. Maria, the Spanish girl who now looks after the upstairs, has been told, every day since we arrived, to do my room as soon as I am out of it, so that I can get back to my desk. Yes, she understands, finish it first. But she is there all day. Short of locking my door, I cannot keep her out. She returns like smoke.

We have acquired, at considerable expense, a French cook whose references are excellent. At his request we hired an assistant for him, reputed to be a good cook herself. She is the wife of hand-kissing André. They cook for the servants—eleven, counting themselves—who eat lunch here. Eight of them eat dinner here, and seven breakfast. They cook for us, when we are in. If not entertaining or out, we are one for lunch, two for dinner. Breakfast, tea, and late snacks are the responsibility of the *copeiro* in his *copa* (pantry).

Yesterday, cook's day off, I found André, the cleaner, busily preparing vegetables for his wife. I suggest to him that his job is that of cleaner. Yes, he replies amiably—other days. Today he help his wife.

> Me: I cannot have an assistant to the assistant cook! There is too much cleaning to be done.
> André (his face alight at my reasonableness): Yes, too much work. Must get more servants. Yes?
> Me: Must get more servants, no. Get more servants and you say, "Too much work in kitchen." What do we do then?
> André (pleased that I have caught on): Get more servants to work in kitchen.
> Me: !!!!!

Notes on fauna: yesterday, flying over the lotus pool, dragonflies of bright cerise with blue wings. A friend once said that cerise was hideous and not a true colour. When I asked what she meant by "true" she said it was not found in nature. She had certainly not observed nature in the tropics, where bougainvillea and dragonflies deck themselves with it.

Last evening a bird like a ballerina—tiny, black, dressed in a white tutu—flew out onto mid-stage, did a fabulous *tour en l' air*, and disappeared before I could further observe it.

February 27

Today the house is full of painters, electricians, and plumbers—*bombeiros* in Portuguese, which also means firemen and spies. This afternoon I have been de-mildewing books. Each day it's dry enough, I remove the books with the longest beards and put them outside in the sun. Today, however, I got caught with my books down: in one minute flat the sun had turned to torrential rain.

This is a very public house—in part because we are over-run with workmen, but it is also something to do with Brazilian life, I think. I remember an Indian friend in Ottawa complaining how lonely she was in a Canadian house; in India she did nothing alone, she was always accompanied by others—in everything, as far as I could make out, from cooking to making love. The bliss for me of a house where I see no one all day!

Curiously, even though I speak of the house as public, at the same time I wonder about its "emptiness". For it *is* empty, psychologically. Built for de Braga, reported to be a cousin of the King of Portugal, on a dramatic site, with imported marble for the floors, imported artists to paint the ceilings, it is architecturally beautiful. A long three-storey house of terra-cotta pink with white trim, wrought-iron railings, terraces, verandas, and arches; double and triple French doors with shutters and charmingly designed transoms. Lighted, at night, it is like a birthday cake waiting to be blown out; while doubled upside down in the swimming-pool, its pinkness melts and slides in the dark water, and the seven frosting-white arches of the lower terrace reflect in shimmering U's.

To lay out his gardens, de Braga employed Burle Marx, Brazil's leading landscape architect. He used a stream with a waterfall, a lotus pond, flagstones, and three different-coloured grasses planted in sweeping curves, to make an abstract painting of the land.

Here in this *palacete*, set in a jewelled garden, de Braga lived with his beautiful wife until one day she was missing, then found dead. Sometimes Maria, eyes large, says, "The *senhora* walks tonight, Madammy." And occasionally, when I've been wakened by the heat and unable to sleep again because of the drums from the *favela* or the frogs or the tree-toads, I wonder if the *senhora* does walk. But I have never felt her presence. If anything, it is her absence that I feel—a sense of her having walked out, taking the essence of the house with her. And it is this emptiness that the walls guard, as if it were a trust.

March 2

A hundred hirings and firings. Will it never end? We have hired an Italian *mordomo* (major-domo), Salvador, and his Yugoslav wife, Mary. We have fired the Russian hand-kisser and his wife. If the *mordomo* arrives tomorrow as scheduled, we should enter a new phase.

Fauna continue to be interesting. Tonight a small lizard, five inches from nose-tip to tail-tip, scurried about importantly with a green leaf-insect in his jaws. The lizard was naked and pale as a plucked chicken. Yesterday, out of our jungle, walked an altogether different fellow—a lizard too, but two to three feet long, black and green, with a head so shiny it looked armoured, and perhaps was. Large insects shaped and coloured to resemble leaves—flat and brilliant green—join us after dinner. And the other morning a long, pale green slug—three inches of suction—clung to the wall over the chesterfield.

March 6

All of Rio is sleeping off the orgy of Carnaval. Nothing now but hangovers and fatigue—hospitals and prisons bulging. For the rich there was a series of balls, all fancy dress—a ball a night, we are told. The Municipal Ball had a mere 7,400 attend! Many thousands of *cruzeiros* are spent on costumes and the dancing goes on all night. For the poor in the *favelas*, this is the event of the year. Months in advance they join "samba schools" and practise night after night. Just what they practise I am not sure, because their "dances" to the samba beat are a kind of mass walk, arms in the air. Each school has its own group attire—one group of about forty were all in diapers and bonnets, and sucking bottles.

Virtually everyone dresses up. In mid-afternoon we saw two adults, male and female, in Grecian costume, earnestly conversing on a downtown street. And a man mounted on a papier-mâché horse in the manner of an ice comedian, "riding" it along a sidewalk all by himself—and having considerable difficulty keeping it from throwing him. Here and there a ghastly-looking female (male, I suspect) carrying a placard: "Miss Portugal 1957", which bears out what we have already been told, that the Portuguese are one of the favourite butts of Brazilian humour. No baby so small it could not wear a paper hat, at least; and one, only months old, was, in all that heat, dressed as a white rabbit. Tiny, tired Spanish noblemen in black velvet were lifted to rest on the radiators of cars. And everyone, large or small, carried the golden spray bottle of scented "ether" which is said to provide the energy to keep going. A very small boy sprayed A. on the legs, so we came home smelling of carnival.

In the evening, on the invitation of the mayor—Negrão de Lima—we went to the Teatro Municipal to watch the parade of floats sponsored by the Tourist Department. To my surprise, we were able to fight our way through the crowd and up the wide stone steps through a mass of people—flexible, good-natured…rubberized, almost, and so able to contract and expand at will. The mayor, looking a little like a Brazilian clerk because of his double-breasted white linen suit, greeted us with champagne. Below, one of the most extraordinary sights I have ever seen: a wide river of people samba-ing up and down the Avenida Rio Branco, thousands of them moving in such a way that if you half-closed your eyes you lost entirely the sense of them being people at all. A great illuminated multicoloured pattern, pulsing to the beat of the samba. As far as we could see, there was nothing but people—the tropical night sitting fat and black on herds of zebras, families of leopards, tiny ballerinas no longer on their points, and other enthusiasts who had done nothing more than sprinkle talcum powder on their heads. One indefatigable equilibrist whom we had seen in the afternoon, standing on a narrow sloping ledge and knitting a red woollen garment with frantic speed, was still there three hours later, knitting with the same frenzy.

Nature notes for the day: after one of the worst days domestically I have ever been through, I went out to get flowers for the dinner table and something moved in the high branches of the trees. I promised to forgive the whole day if it was a monkey. And it was! But the wretched little thing swung away from me into the jungle. It was small, only slightly larger than a squirrel.

Trees: in the garden there are varieties of what the Australians would call rain-trees—with composite, finely fretted leaves, and clusters of flowers, pink, red, white, or yellow. There are numerous palms: one with a pointed, bladelike leaf and a massive tower of white blossoms; one like a feather duster, which throws its old leaves down—feathers shed from a giant bird. We have the elephant-ear tree, of which no more need be said, and one that grows smooth and straight as a young telephone pole, no branch below twelve feet. Then there is the dense and darkly massed foliage of the jack-fruit tree, and a spreading tree with large, deeply indented leaves and green fruits which look like mangoes. Feathery stands of susurrant bamboo. And both nearby and, as it were, echoing off into the jungle-clad hills, the *quaresmas* (the name means Lent, which is the season when they flower), blooming now with vibrant purple. And beside them, trees of pure silver, broad-leafed, and others with small clusters of flowers as yellow as gorse.

March 8

Once more the house is full of plumbers, the old electricians, new electricians, and a succession of people applying for jobs. But with Salvador between them and me, I have relative peace.

There is a flavour in Brazil I have not yet touched on—let alone come to terms with! It might be called drama. Newspapers report libellous stories, seemingly with no fear of charges being laid. Police officials are accused of corruption and perjury, and a note of despairing mockery is directed at persons in authority. A story from the morning paper:

> São Paulo. Paulo Pires Assis, inmate of the penitentiary where he is serving a term for murder and robbery, left that penal establishment on Carnival Monday, accompanied by two prison guards in civil clothes. They headed towards the house of Irineu Cintra where the prison guards waited outside while Paulo broke a window and entered the house, stealing money, valuables, and other objects. After looting the house he returned to the penitentiary with the two prison guards.

And another:

Beating up of a municipal policeman, Emirton Correia, by a
group of revellers in the Lapa district on Thursday gave rise
to a serious occurrence yesterday when some of the injured
policeman's colleagues thought they had found the man who
had beaten him up.

Thirteen policemen, headed by Inspector Fernando Garcia,
drove up in a patrol car, and shouting, "That's him," attacked
three men who were talking in the doorway. Taken by surprise,
they tried to make off inside, but were nabbed, kicked, and
generally dusted before being taken into custody.

Onlookers called the radio patrol and it was ascertained
that the three men were João da Silva, Hélio Melo, and Oscar
Camilo. It seems that João da Silva, who is a sergeant of the
military police, was suspected of manhandling Emirton Correia,
who is in a serious state in the hospital. However, according to
his statement, this was impossible because at the time of the
aggression he was on duty in another sector.

Of the sixteen municipal policemen, six were recognized by
witnesses and were charged as well as Inspector Garcia.

There has been another type of story in the papers lately, too—
about falling skyscrapers. According to one report, a ten-storey office
building collapsed in a mass of rubble six hours after an engineering
professor from the University of Rio inspected it and professed
his certain belief that, despite its fissures and cracks, the building
was completely safe. His assurances, however, meant little to the
occupants—all but five of whom vacated at once. Since then various
other buildings have come tumbling down, and some hopeful is
predicting the downfall of twenty-three more!

When I spoke to a Brazilian lawyer about this he said, "Why do
you expect a beautiful thing to last? Do you ask a flower to live for
ever?"

Drove a mountainous road last Sunday to a famous look-out built
by one Dodsworth. Was this Sinclair Lewis's Samuel who, after
concluding his European travels, ventured into the mountains of
Brazil, there to erect an impressive if stark stone bastion graced with
one small mermaid? On close inspection, I was surprised to find
she had two tails—in effect, legs with scales and finny terminals. I
obviously know nothing about the mermaid myth, for surely much

of her fascination for sailors lay in the torment of never being able to possess her. (On checking in the few reference books we have, I find the mermaid in German heraldry does have two tails.)

Shortly after our arrival, I was interviewed by a young Brazilian reporter who is also a writer of short stories. I am not much good as an interviewee, I fear—due partly to inexperience, I suppose, but mainly to the fact that I am much more interested in learning about Brazil than in talking about myself. However, at pen-point I did manage to tell him that I had worked as a scriptwriter for the National Film Board, where A. had been Film Commissioner after years of being editor of *Maclean's*, and that I have published poetry and short stories. I then told him a bit about the state of poetry in Canada and gave him the names of poets whose work interests me: Jay Macpherson, Anne Wilkinson, A.M. Klein, Earle Birney, A.J.M. Smith, F.R. Scott, Irving Layton, and James Reaney. Although his English was quite good, I realized how strange those names must sound in his ears when I saw him struggle to write them down.

Over a *cafèzinho* he told me that in Brazil's national anthem there are words to the effect that "the giant is resting". "Once," he said—indignant and nostalgic both—"there were Brazilian heroes. Now, they are resting." And I saw famous generals resting on their swords, explorers resting mid-landscape, politicians resting in Congress—and all in that position of upright rest so noticeable here: solitary figures quite simply leaning on air, as if propped by it.

Went, for a treat, to the Museum of Modern Art—one room only!—and found, to our disappointment, a show of European non-objective painters. Disappointing because of our hunger for knowledge of Brazil. There is a new building under way which should be completed while we are here. Maybe *then* we shall see.

All was not lost, however, as we bought a book on Portinari, probably the most famous Brazilian painter, containing good reproductions. Also a catalogue of a sculpture exhibition by Maria Martins—the person to whom Australia's Maie Casey gave me a letter of introduction. I can't say I like the photographs of her work—entrails, feces, the coils of fantastic tubas. But perhaps I shall like her.

March 10

Two beautiful red finches—I think—in the garden yesterday. Like two ripe fruits on a tree. A beetle, dead on its back among the leaves, larger than a humming-bird. Humming-birds in the orchid-like blossoms of the hoary old tree near our balcony—such an old grandfather of a tree, so covered with parasitic growth, I would not have thought it had the heart or the energy to flower of itself.

Awoke this morning to an immense chittering in its branches and struggled from sleep onto the balcony. Through the field glasses saw, among the cerise flowers, six different kinds of small brilliant birds: one pair, finchlike, of every conceivable shade and colour from turquoise through the jade- and yellow-greens to yellow; one minute yellow canary and his paler wife; another finchlike bird of a clear cerulean blue with a black eye-mask and throat, so neatly feathered he looked carved and polished from some mysterious blue stone, his wife dull green and blue; a charming, smooth, wrenlike pair, their base colour—chestnut—covered with a fine stipple; one sparrow-like chap with a chestnut neck, striped head, and spotted back—he an observer rather than a participant in all the activity; and in and out among them a flutter of humming-birds with emerald green breasts and glowing purple heads, while above *them*, on a higher branch, a soft dun-coloured dove, like a nanny watching the children play.

Yesterday, on the swimming-pool terrace, we found a huge moth which one of the cleaners pounced upon, claiming that it was *muito perigoso* (very dangerous). When asked why, he replied that if the powder from its wings got into your eyes...! An Englishwoman to whom I was later talking suggested he was having me on but, having seen no evidence of a propensity for teasing in Brazilians and every evidence of their great sense of drama, I am prepared to think he believed it.

Two additional bird events. One, the arrival of a pair of robins—larger than ours, and different in that the upper breast is grey. And two, the incredible sight of jumping birds. Four not very distinguished, large, sparrow-like birds with striped heads, stamping about on the lawn in the manner of robins, suddenly began jumping quite high into the air, beaks upraised—I suppose for low-flying insects, but it looked absurd.

March 12

Last night, dinner with the Dutch—a small party: the Argentines; two Shell people; Ambassador Nabuco, president of the Museum of Modern Art in Rio and one time ambassador to the U.S.; and Chateaubriand, newly appointed ambassador to London, prime mover in the São Paulo Museum of Art, a senator and owner of a chain of thirty newspapers as well as magazines and radio stations. The women elegant in black, and much jewelled. We waited interminably for Chateau—as he is called—who finally phoned to say that he would be "a little late". Ambassador Nabuco—large, warm, expansive, sophisticated—loathed Chateau and made no bones about it; said he would not have accepted the invitation had he known Chateau was invited. It was interesting to compare the two—both ambassadors, both involved in museums of modern art, both Brazilians. There the similarities ended. Chateau spoke volubly in French, which Nabuco claimed was ninety per cent error. Later, forced to speak English, he was just as voluble and the percentage of error just as high.

When the party broke up, Chateau asked A. and me if we would care to see the Cruzeiro Palace, the plant where *O Cruzeiro*, Brazil's most widely circulated magazine, is published. It seemed obvious that we should and so we drove off through the rain and darkness (nights seem doubly dark in Rio by virtue of a by-law forbidding the use of headlights; only parking lights are permitted) down into the old city, where the streets are narrow, and the buildings warehousey and undistinguished, to come at last to an enormous multi-storeyed cube, as light as foam rubber and glowing as if phosphorescent. Designed by Niemeyer, probably the leading Brazilian architect, the building is raised on pillars and the glass of its external walls if protected by a *brise-soleil* pierced with a repetitive pattern of punch-holes two to three inches in diameter. Lighted from within by a particularly white light, it seems to float, a weightless cube of magnesium burning in the black night. A half-finished mural by Portinari is in the entrance hall, and upstairs a dozen of his paintings are waiting to be hung. Strange paintings, flat, like cartoons for a mural, of groups of people—wonderful in their design, disappointing only in their surfaces, looking much as prime coating does.

As I think of the three of us—the two men black and white in summer dinner jackets, me in a black-and-white dress with streaming black ribbons—Chateau small, stocky, ill-tailored, talking execrable English, pulling us by force of will across the cobbled streets in the black rain to the cool martini of a building—it seems more like a sequence from a black-and-white movie than an actual experience. And Chateau talking on, yawning and talking through his yawns, of his masters—Caesar and Nietzsche—of the ugliness of the world, of his great marble hall in São Paulo "for the people". The photo of him in the front of the book about the São Paulo Museum is a wonderfully good portrait. It is a snapshot of a small, squat man in a crumpled suit, wearing on his head a child's newspaper hat. The accompanying wooden sword is not there. He doesn't use one—of wood.

Manuel, our gardener's assistant, has planted a new lawn at the side of the house. This is done in the manner of planting seedlings: a little hole is made in the earth and a small shoot of grass popped in. The effect, at this stage, is of a candlewick bedspread, brown with green tufts, the whole as if measured and ruled.

March 14

Further notes on jumping birds. There are new jumpers on the lawn today, smaller than the first, but jumping with them. Through the glasses they are seen to be small finches—donkey-coloured, with paler undersides and brilliant flame eyelines and beaks.

The larger jumpers have grey heads marked with many black stripes, black eyelines, and two black frownlines between the eyes. The head markings stop abruptly at the neck, giving the impression that the head of one species has been glued onto the body of another. They scuffle and scratch in the manner of hens. Bound, too, after bounding insects. And jump.

Our lawn has sprouted, here and there, tall grass stalks with seed heads. Are the birds jumping for the seeds? Ricardo is scything the lawn. We shall see.

Dinner with the American Episcopalian Bishop of Rio. Much unction. His wife told A. not to bother to learn Portuguese. There is no need, she said.

March 17

How crippled one is by the lack of a language! Not only do I talk a kind of baby talk, with an appalling accent, but the things I actually say are often quite different from what I mean to say. This confuses the household no end. I give orders to the staff and yes, yes, they say, and I feel fine, on top of things, in control. Then nothing happens. Yesterday, listening to A. talk to the *mordomo,* I began to understand some of the reasons. With great thought and care A. said, clearly and slowly, "Salvador, I think I have been two keys." And, "Yes, Excellency," said Salvador solemnly.

March 27

Reading Ortega y Gasset's *The Dehumanization of Art* and Hugh MacDiarmid's poetry. Curiously, the two go together rather well. MacDiarmid's

> ...and the principal question
> Aboot a work o' art is frae hoo deep
> A life it springs—and syne hoo faur
> Up frae't it has the poo'er to leap

might almost be an epigraph for Ortega's book.

Formal Portuguese lessons have begun at last—three a week, first thing in the morning. A pretty, stern girl, a textbook abounding in irregular verbs, and homework.

March 30

Went, in intense heat, to see the Museu de Arte Moderna in the process of construction. It is being built by private subscription and will cost in the vicinity of three million dollars. The building committee consists of Senhora Bittencourt, wife of the owner of one of the largest newspapers; Ambassador Nabuco, whom we met at dinner; the elegant young chief of the Department of Tourism; and Henrique Mindlin, architect and editor of an interesting and well-produced book about modern architecture in Brazil. We know his book, and I had noticed among his acknowledgements the name of Elizabeth Bishop. When I asked him if she was still in Brazil, he said yes. The next thing is to meet her.

The maquette of the museum is impressive, and standing in the dust and brick of the actual foundation, on recently reclaimed land, we were struck by how immense the building will be and how wonderful the site—overlooking, as it does, an arm of the bay punctuated by the Sugar Loaf.

"... the dining-room, large enough to seat forty."

March 31

Have paid my first official call. *Finally* managed to get an appointment with the wife of a senior Cabinet member, one of the three
Brazilians whom protocol advises I call on. As she was said to speak
French and Portuguese but no English, I took with me Henriette, the
wife of one of our officers, who speaks all three.

We set off, much dressed up, for our appointment at six—I feeling
exactly as I always do on such occasions—that the whole thing
is make-believe and that I am dressed up in my mother's clothes.
Arrived at a great towering apartment block on the beach of the
inner harbour. As we approached the elevator, what can only be
described as a slovenly-looking woman opened the door for us, not
very graciously. This apartment block, like many here, has only one
apartment to a floor, and as we stepped out of the elevator into our
hostess's vestibule the door opposite opened cautiously to disclose
an even more slovenly-looking woman, dish-towel around her waist,
who ushered us into what might have been a second-hand store for
Roman Catholic artefacts. One entire wall was a window overlooking
the harbour, and with the lights starting to come on the view was quite
beautiful—but the room had been arranged to ignore it, obstruct it
even. The furniture consisted of a small two-seater Victorian sofa and
matching chair, occasional chairs and a glass cabinet of spindly gilt,
and a flowered rug with a table in the middle of it. All flat surfaces,
cabinets, tabletops, were covered with badly made plaster casts of
the Virgin and Christ Child, and the walls with ugly oleos. Propped
against one wall was a wicker basket containing some rather formal
greenery and two large evil-looking purple orchids. A telegram was
pinned to one of the petals. Behind a drawn curtain we could glimpse
what looked like the reading-room in a library—long bare tables
covered with newspapers.

All of this was contrary to everything I have come to expect. The
Brazilians we have met have all been chic and contemporary, and
their houses—whether modern or baroque—elegant, so I was totally
unprepared for this tasteless apartment.

We had a good ten minutes to examine our surroundings before our
hostess appeared. She was in her fifties, short, pear-shaped, dressed
in a badly cut navy blue dress that showed a bit of underwear at the
neck. She had a face like some of the women Maxwell Bates paints—
running away at the chin. When she spoke, her voice was like wind

in pine-needles—high and soughing. She said how beautiful Canada was—Niagara Falls, Toronto, Montreal; how she liked Canadians— they were not as hard as Americans. We, of course, countered with how we liked Brazil. In a room at the end of the world, we exchanged any number of compliments, interrupted only by the arrival of a thin, pathetic-looking woman in dark glasses introduced as *"minha filha"*.

Our desultory exchange of courtesies continued, in French, Portuguese, and back to French again, while in the next room birds sang. I asked about them. *"Canários,"* I was told. "Their song makes a house *alegre*, does it not?" Of all houses, this, it seemed, could do with their help.

Another untidy servant brought us glasses of lemonade which we drank as the chitter of praise and pleasantries continued. I was *"muito jovem"*, *"muito bonita"*, *"muito simpática"*.

We left with great protestations of thanks and appreciation. As I shook hands, our hostess gave the kind of tug that precedes a kiss. Unprepared, my mind rejected the possibility, and my body the tug. With Henrietta, who had not met her before either but who is an older hand at Brazilian ways, the kiss was exchanged. This too is a language.

April 1

Portuguese is fascinating. In a country which, to us, seems to place small value on life, there is little difference between "to live", *morar*, and "to die", *morrer*. So far I have been unable to find any expression for "how funny"—perhaps because the Brazilian finds everything funny. One learns *muito bom* —"very good"—immediately; it is used about almost everything that is not *muito bem*, "very well", or *muito mau*, "very bad". And the ubiquitous *muito* is said with such feeling that the most ordinary events become dramatic.

Interesting the differences between language texts and the spoken language. Servants are no longer *criados* —a word originating with slavery, when a small child would be brought up in the house of the master and, in effect, "created"—but *empregados* or "employees". But they are still addressed as *você*, the second person, as a child or an intimate would be, and not with *o senhor* or *a senhora*, the more formal third.

As to the small value placed on life, one has only to read the newspapers to learn of the number of people who carry guns and fire them. Just the other day a member of the Chamber of Deputies fatally shot a traffic policeman who had stopped him for speeding. This is but one of many such incidents. If one can believe what one is told, the law itself places a low value on life. In a traffic accident, for instance, responsibility for the injured lies with whoever calls an ambulance or obtains medical help—with the inevitable result that a victim may lie neglected in the roadway for hours.

April 2

Have begun my calls. There are more than fifty diplomatic missions in Rio and we have to call on all of them—A. on the ambassadors, I on the wives—nor can they entertain us until we have so announced our presence. Then they have to pay return calls! This is an odd sort of international two-step, but it has its uses. They are all sources of information of one kind or another, some of it invaluable. Also, it's a means of meeting *tête-à-tête*.

The first on my list—for no particular reason—was the German ambassadress. (A misnomer, this; she is simply the wife of the ambassador. But it's a Brazilian custom to make us all *embaixatrizes*!) She is Swiss, I think, and prettyish. She speaks English quite well but I suspect understands it less well, as she looked deaf whenever I spoke and made a point of doing most of the talking herself. I know the signs.

The German embassy is large, with attractive gardens and patios which overlook the harbour. They employ fourteen servants, and when I asked what they all did her cynical reply was that each was employed in watching the others to make sure they did no work. They keep three dogs who sleep by day and roam all night, as they don't trust the guard supplied by the Brazilian government, and—more to my taste—a toucan with an electric blue eye, a bill like an idealized banana, a body of sculpted soot set off by a white onyx collar and gorgeous red drawers. Splendid fellow!

In the afternoon I called on the Argentine *embaixatriz*. She is an attractive, intelligent, rather brittle American who met her husband when he was *en poste* in Washington. Their residence is a square wedding cake, icing-white and very formal. Inside are marble statues, gold leaf, and tapestries. I am incapable of knowing whether or not I like it—probably not. Our house is a bare shack compared with this museum.

They have been here a year and a half and she claims it is their hardest post—partly due to climate and partly because she cannot get good servants. They feed twenty—twenty-two including the police guards.

She advised me to have my ice made from bottled water, which freezes white; that way you know at a glance if it is safe. All foreigners here seem to express dissatisfaction with staff, and apprehension over food and water.

The Spanish wife, who has been here almost three years, lives on the beach in an untidy-looking house badly in need of paint on the outside, but elaborate enough inside, God knows. Oriental rugs and tapestries and gilt. How modest is our *palacete*! She claims to be growing increasingly blind but takes a fatalistic attitude to it: "I may be short of vitamins."

April 5

Many calls and *muitas dificuldades* since last writing. The temperature has been in the eighties, the humidity close to a hundred for weeks now. Everything is mildewed, damp and smelly. Shoes, books, gramophone records suffer most.

Called on "Mrs. Greece" this morning. Our only common language was Portuguese—very comic. We were both so intrigued by the extraordinary means of communication that we couldn't stop. Her practical advice was to do my own marketing and buy everything at the Suco where the prices are clearly marked. I doubt that I shall be so good a housewife.

Two nights ago we gave a dinner for the air minister, who is about to leave for Canada—all Brazilian guests, with the exception of an embassy couple. I was apprehensive of a hundred things beforehand. Various diplomatic wives have told me of their first dinners, when they sat down eleven at a table set for twenty-four. Brazilians, they say, often don't turn up or bother to let you know. On the dot, however, the guests arrived: the air minister and his entourage, the economist, the banker, etc.,—everyone, in fact, but one man from the Protocol Division of the Foreign Office, who turned up punctually at 8.30, twenty-four hours late!

Service passable, at last! Food still leaves something to be desired. Totally ice-cold tournedos. But perhaps, in this heat....

A. returned today saying he had bad news.
"About whom?" I asked.
"Herb Norman."

"He's committed suicide," I said.

"How on earth did you know?"

"I didn't know—I just...."

We are rocked by it. Relieved to see how solidly everyone at home is behind him. But there is such stark horror in it all: the difficult time in Egypt—Irene hanging on—not leaving with the other wives—the second libellous attack....

The whole maze of tropical life and its complications continues, and has to be dealt with, but Irene and Herbert block my way; insist on being thought about *now*.

Nature notes: saw one other kind of bird in the hoary old tree— a creeper-cum-woodpecker—small, mottled, yellow-headed. And heard a bird like a whippoorwill who calls in the morning. No birds have jumped since Ricardo scythed the grass.

Last night we attended the launching of the first Spanish-language edition of Chateaubriand's magazine *O Cruzeiro*. That lovely glowing building was phosphorescent against the night sky, and from its flag-bedecked roof salvo upon salvo of fireworks was fired— the stipple of their sounds echoing the stipple of light from the *brise-soleil*.

Inside—the cruciform lights of television; a dance band, a Negress swaying her hips and singing; the president making a speech; champagne, food wrapped in silver and gold leaf and served from blocks of ice with patterns frozen into them, or from small glowing braziers; orchids; heat; a hundred men, a few office girls in organdy, and— through some misunderstanding—me! Only husbands had been invited but I am glad I went.

All the Portinaris had been hung—quite wonderful colour, but flat. So many strange heads, chins tipped up, faces acutely foreshortened. One painting of—madmen, I think, with musical instruments and a half-opened umbrella. Positions extraordinary.

April 6

Went with A. to see some contemporary tapestries by a young man from Bahía—Genero de Carvalho. Very sharp, as if seen through some medium other than air—isinglass perhaps. Colours brilliant. A great sense of the flora and fauna of Brazil, abstracted.

April 8

Called this morning on the Israeli ambassador's wife. She is young and pretty. She said she found Rio difficult at first, but now, after nine months, she finds it easier. (Like a pregnancy?) Her husband is a painter—Arie Aroch. And a good one.

The word for "parrot" sounds like "pappa guy". I wonder if that is what my grandfather meant when he said, "dressed up like a real pappa guy"? Did he know Portuguese? Was he really saying *papagaio*?

Quite cool today. I am actually wearing linen.

What to do about writing? Is it all dead?

April 14

Just returned from a luncheon where we met a number of press, radio, and theatre people, plus one poet—Cecília Mereles. A biggish party, and enjoyable.

The men and women were seated separately at table. Not a bad idea as the sexes will *not* mix—they are worse, if possible, than Australians. I had thought, at previous parties, it was perhaps because the women had no intellectual interests, but in this group that was not the case. Odd that in a country where sex plays so large a role, there is this kind of segregation.

Likewise the other night, at an immense dinner for us given by the Gallottis—he the senior executive in Brazil of the Brazilian Traction Company—all the women sat together before dinner. I am told that this group is the very cream of Rio society and I can well believe it. The women are a cross between flowers and jewels—beautifully made, perfectly groomed, extravagantly dressed. "But where," one asks, "are all their handsome brothers?"

Despite the fact that the party was for us, and that the guests could all speak perfectly good English, they spoke Portuguese at table. One man did stop speaking Portuguese long enough to tell me, in English, how important it was for me to learn Portuguese. Of course it is. I'm learning as fast as I can.

Calls. Calls.

The wife of the Yugoslav ambassador said that all foreigners here wear light cottons suited to the climate, whereas Brazilians wear mostly black. When I asked if she knew why, she replied, "Because

Paris does." I must say, I have been astonished by black velvet hats and feather cloches.

As I stepped from the small box of an elevator into the apartment of the Swiss minister, I entered a Matisse painting. It was a brilliantly sunny day, with Niterói shining white as an Arab city across the ultramarine bay, and there in a light-filled apartment, in a blue-and-white striped blouse, Madame—youngish, dark, attractive, on a yellow-and-white striped chair. On a veranda like a high wharf above the water, under a coral-coloured umbrella with white fringe, we drank excellent coffee from tall thin cups. Below us were four lanes of traffic which we neither saw nor heard.

She told me you can make friends with Brazilians easily if you let them know you like them. This contrasts sharply with the point of view of the bishop's wife, an Episcopalian cleric's wife, and the wife of a gin representative—all of whom have been here twenty years and seemingly know only each other. They tell me there is no point in trying to get to know Brazilians—that the rich live in a rarefied world that is out of reach and all the others within a bourgeois concept of family that is impossible to penetrate. When I say, "But...," I am met with ominous noddings and "You'll sees".

On the other hand, Her Highest Serenity the Princess Mechtilde Czartoryska, resident for seventeen years, tells me that she adores Brazil and that its people open under your approval, like children. She also offered me a piece of advice—everyone who has been here a day longer than I is full of advice—which was never, never to pull up plants in the jungle "because your fingers will be painful, filled with pus, and next day you will find a beast under each fingernail." Shades of Gulliver! I shall take *her* advice, certainly.

April 15

The beach yesterday so white and blue—beach umbrellas of every colour, as close together as space allowed. And all the boulevards full of balloons and kites. We stopped and bought a kite like a large eagle. They are called *papagaios*. By the time we returned to our green garden, though, there was not enough wind to lift a postage stamp.

April 22

Our personal car has arrived—a great relief. I can now, if I wish, get away from the house. Took off for Copacabana this morning—my first shot at Brazilian traffic. Eight lanes. Fast!

Such a morning...the sea beautiful, and miles of beach. I swear every child in Brazil has a kite and manages to get it airborne no matter how tiny the piece of ground on which he is standing. The sky jerks and bobs with them. One, a candy-pink heart on a string, leapt and spurted its joy.

I walked among the shops, just looking. Prices high, even for tropical fruits—custard apples, *caquis*, and *mamãos* (papaya). In a workman's shelter on the side of the street a group of men was solemnly playing dominoes.

Saturday and Sunday of Easter weekend we drove to Petrópolís. Elizabeth Bishop lives there and I understand why: it is a small hill town set in beautiful country with a wonderful climate, and light-hearted enough to make you light-headed.

We were there for the São Paulo–Rio Golf Meet—an annual event in which Canadians from both cities participate. Pretty dull, too.

We stayed at the Quitandinha Hotel—an extraordinary structure—half Swiss chalet and half seven-minute frosting, blown up to vast dimensions. It's the largest hotel I have ever seen. One section is domed, and the span of the dome is said to be greater than that of St. Paul's. When first built, it was the world's largest gambling den. Now that gambling is abolished it is run, after a fashion, by the state. It is sleazy, dirty, bereft. Small parcels of dwarfed people move about in it like groups of tourists in a museum without exhibits. Pretty Brazilian girls, following the fashion, show off their sensuous, hippy figures in toreador pants.

We had barely arrived in our room, which was far from clean and very cold, when the desk called to ask if we were satisfied with it. I replied that we were without linen. They said they only provided that when they knew the guests were satisfied. Very circular.

The altitude and cold air made us sleep. Fourteen hours!

Strange and wonderful parasitic plants for sale at roadside stalls on the way back. Dozens of different kinds of bananas—from tiny and smooth to large and angled—varying in colour: yellow, green, white, and even red. And behind the stalls, blue and mauve *hortênsias* (hydrangeas) apparently growing wild.

Incidental intelligence: the Brazilian labourer usually wears wooden clogs—a wooden platform with toe-strap. You can hear him approaching from a great distance. Those who wear oxfords and loafers cut the backs out so the shoes can be donned and shed easily. All workmen leave their shoes outside and enter a house barefoot. Despite the heat, I have never known them to smell. This, I am told, is their inheritance from the Negroes or Indians—I've forgotten which!—who taught the Portuguese to wash. On Sundays one sees men, women, and children, like a stream of ants, climbing perilously steep mountainsides carrying old gasoline cans filled with water on their heads. In the circumstances of *favela* life I think I would revert to Portuguese ways.

April 25

Episode of the goat. Yesterday Morel, the cook—who is slim and rather effeminate with a peroxided streak in his hair, and who looks absurdly young in his white uniform and chef's hat—asked if he might bring his goat. He is, he said, an orphan with no relatives, and Negrinha is his only family. I agreed on one condition: that he obtain the consent of the gardener.

Today the goat arrived. I was taken up the hill at the back of the house to meet her. Negrinha. She is indeed black and female, as her name implies. And she is most comely. She was tied to the little abandoned house up among the wild mango trees, safely beyond the reach of all valuable plants. If she was excited by the sight of me, she was nothing like as excited as Morel was by the introduction. I asked if she was noisy. He assured me she was almost mute.

A great bleating began in the *mato* just as A. returned from work. In the hope that his attention would not be drawn to it, I pretended to hear nothing. He, thinking that it was some kind of wildlife, was intrigued to see how long it would take before I showed some interest. Finally his curiosity overcame him. What, he asked, did I think that noise was? "O that," I said, making it nothing at all, "is our goat." And so we climbed the hill in order that A. too could meet her.

When I suggested to Morel that she was far from the mute animal he had described, he assured me, "It is only because she feels strange here. She will soon get used to it and then you will never hear her."

Returning from an ambulatory tour of the garden before dinner we caught a glimpse of a slim dark silhouette by the kitchen door and, catapulting through the same door as if shot from a cannon, José, our *mulato* cleaner, and Morel in his chef's hat. The chase had begun.

But Negrinha was too quick for them. The three nimble-footed, fleet young things leapt flowerbeds, crashed through shrubs, and made an all-out dash around the swimming-pool and across the lawn until they were brought up as if against a brick wall by the stream. Negrinha, wily and fast, made a lightning turn and headed for the driveway leading to the gate. There she was caught by a triumphant armed guard and led away by a flushed and pleased Morel—who told us as he passed that he would like a picture of her by the swimming-pool!

April 26

Episode of the goat continued. This morning I was wakened by unbroken bleating—not from the *mato* at the back of the house, but from somewhere in front. Negrinha, it appeared, had escaped during the night and been caught, this time, by Ricardo the gardener, who had shut her up in his gatehouse. It was reported by Salvador's wife, Mary, who brought our breakfast, that Ricardo liked Negrinha very much—so much, in fact, that he wanted to buy her. But Morel would not sell. Negrinha was no ordinary goat. She had travelled with a circus. She was an artist.

Later this morning, when I went down to the kitchen to talk menus with Morel, he told me, nearly in tears, that Negrinha had escaped from the gatehouse. Had he my permission to go in search of her? Of course he had, and when last seen he was hurrying down the drive, a length of heavy wire in his hand, in search of the wilful circus artist.

His crestfallen and empty-handed return in the afternoon made me so sorry for him that I suggested we search for Negrinha by car. "Have you seen a black goat?" we called to pedestrians as we passed. "*Uma cabra? Uma cabra negra?*"

Occasional leads took us to the tops of hills and down again to the beaches, but nowhere did we see the least flick of her black tail or hear the least whisper of a bleat.

Morel, in a voice filled with emotion, told me, "Madammy, if we find her, I will give her to you. She is yours." And I, protesting his generosity, told him I couldn't dream of accepting the only member of his family. But that afternoon the present was not his to offer nor mine to refuse. Despite the bright day, Negrinha was as invisible as if it were night.

I assured a downcast Morel that we would advertise for her. But before there was time for the ad to appear in the paper, an animated Morel announced that a man had phoned saying he had found a black goat at Ipanema—an enormous distance for her to have travelled. He understood it belonged to the Canadian embassy.

Morel's final announcement: that Negrinha is once again shut up in the gatehouse. And that she is mine!

April 27

Conclusion of the episode of the goat. Wakened again this morning by Negrinha's song to the dawn. Mary, bearer of breakfasts and the latest news, told us that what is now known as the "goat of the *embaixatriz*" had twice escaped during the night to the convent next door, and twice been returned by two unamused Sisters of God.

Too much, too much, I complained to Morel. We wanted no more songs outside our bedrooms at five a.m., no more chases, no more.... But as we were discussing her, Negrinha escaped again. This time, starved from so much time in the gatehouse, she was on an eating rampage—day-lilies, anthuria, the tenderest buds of the peacock plants and the rose grape. Now the gardener gave chase, and the *mordomo*, Salvador. Ricardo, a tiny Portuguese like one of the Seven Dwarfs, and Salvador, a tall, elegant Italian in a white sharkskin jacket, were a kind of tail to her kite—zigzagging and darting as Negrinha made her split-second turns and sudden leaps. Here a bite, there a bite. Black Negrinha ravaging the garden. Now Manuel with his rake and Morel in his chef's hat joined the breathless trio just as Negrinha made a wild dash for the gate. But this morning there was no guard to stop her, and as I watched Morel and Salvador and José and Ricardo streak after her in their various attires, I vowed that never again would I aid in her search.

After a long time they returned, flushed and goatless. This was the moment for which Ricardo had waited—the moment when Morel, nonplussed, worried, fed-up, would be willing to be rid of Negrinha. It is a point one has seen reached in human relationships—when the scale finally tips, the situation can no longer be borne. Ricardo was now ready with his offer: two hundred *cruzeiros* for a vanished goat. And willingly Morel accepted, as if Ricardo were doing him a favour, and altogether forgetful that Negrinha was mine!

Later I was told that Ricardo, by some alchemy, found and caught Negrinha without delay and led her straight away to his weekend shack on the outskirts of Rio.

Peace reigns once again on Estrada da Gávea.

April 30

To produce small boys quicker than you can say "kite", fly one. We went on Sunday with our *papagaio* to the beach at Ipanema. A strong wind tossed it up and flung it down again, its right wing always leading. All the small boys on the beach were kite doctors. Each took it as his right to tie another knot in the harness to "restore" the balance. After each "restoration" the kite descended, right wing leading. The small boys made us offers for our "poor kite". Many negotiations.

The beach was beautiful—slightly hazy. Black, brown, white Brazilians in *futebol* sweaters, kicking the ball about in the thick, soft sand; the curving façade of apartment buildings—whites, pinks, blues; the odd-shaped mountains—how describe their shapes? elongated cones? the top joints of thumbs?—making the sea look like a surrealist painting; and the waves tumbling in—riding in green and high, their plate glass cracking and breaking and pulverizing into crystals and white powder.

We drove back with our wounded bird to the young man who had sold it to us and he undertook to mend it. A long, thin, tight young man with one leg swinging at an unusual angle and a face like a Modigliani. He ripped off the kite's harness and, from a spool of string, measured exactly from wing-tip to shoulder, shoulder to beak, wing-tip to beak, knotting as he went and hanging the strings around his neck; checking further measurements by the length of his palm plus one, two, or three fingers—all his actions quick and certain.

We squatted with him on the boulevard, beneath his row of coloured balloons bobbing in the wind, as the light failed suddenly and the street lamps came on and traffic increased and the balloons bobbed more wildly. His small helper, wearing shorts and the top of an old bathing-suit which came just below his nipples, ran to his bidding as he shouted orders—the two of them serious and intent beneath the balloons.

By the time *papagaio* was completed, the wind was too strong for kite-flying, and the night too near. But the young man gave him a trial flight, letting him out over the traffic, almost losing him in a perilous drop over the telephone wires in a sudden calm, then fighting as if he had a trout on his line, using all his skill and cunning to edge the bird into whatever wind he could find until, coaxing, beguiling, he finally eased it up and over the wires and, miraculously, safely back. I thought then, as all kite flyers must, that this strange childish sport which holds so great a fascination is really fishing in reverse.

May 1

Drove into the depths of the city yesterday alone for the first time. Took as my route the whole length of beach. Beautiful, beautiful. I shall never get used to it.

May 12

On the first we left for São Paulo on our first official visit. Went by plane, returned by car. One world to another. One planet to another. Between the two cities a difference much greater than between Montreal and Toronto.

From Rio's downtown airport you can catch a plane to São Paulo every half hour, like a bus. The airport buildings, designed by M. M. M. Roberto, are not my cup of tea—columns too heavy and a kind of de Chirico–like desolation about them. We were given numbered discs upon arrival and boarded the plane according to number. Very orderly and neat. *Café* and *biscoitos* served on board.

Capital of the state of the same name, São Paulo is situated on a plateau at an altitude of 2,300 feet, about forty miles inland from the coffee port of Santos. Its population has increased five times since 1920, according to A., and today it has topped the three-million mark. Good agricultural land, its strategic location, and a relatively bracing climate, together with large quantities of hydro-electric power— Canadian-engineered—have made it the heart of the largest industrial complex in South America—the Chicago of South America, the Paulistas call it—when they are not calling it the locomotive state, dragging a reluctant Brazil behind it.

Stepping off the plane one senses the difference. People move faster. The air feels positively crisp by comparison with Rio's.

On the drive in from the airport, São Paulo looked more like my idea of a Scandinavian city than a Brazilian one. The houses on the outskirts are mainly two-storeyed, white and austere. Our hotel, the Jaraguá—a mixture of North America and Australia in flavour—is the upper half of a skyscraper, the lower floors of which house the largest newspaper in São Paulo. Much use is made of tile inlaid in floors and walls and forming planters filled with tropical vegetation. From our window we might have been visiting a higgledy-piggledy New York—skyscrapers everywhere, and as if without plan.

Our room was full of those extraordinary baskets of flowers—*cestas*, they are called, and I hate them. Each flower head is cut off and wired. Within a day they are all dead. One *cesta* was of camellias—six dozen, I should think—and one of incredible flowers like pale mauve anemones with a great brush of striped stamens. Orchids and red roses from the wife of the governor.

The first day we went to see the school run by the Canadian Fathers of the Holy Cross. I was presented with an enormous bunch of flowers by a minute child, and A. made his first speech in Portuguese. The children sang "O Canada" and "Alouette"—*Gentee Alouettee* sounded quite funny. For a finale, two little creatures samba-ed to the carnival hit of the year, "Eu Vou". It's a delightful song about a man who has decided to go to Maracangalha, come what may. *Se Anália não quiser ir, eu vou só*—should Analia not want to go, I shall go alone. "*Quiser*" if you please—future conditional in a popular song!

Next day A. made his three speeches in Portuguese—the first in the Chamber of Deputies. I am told there were many *deputados* in the halls when he began, and some in the Chamber were talking or reading, but when they heard Portuguese those in the halls returned to listen. The aide said there have been four ambassadors here recently and A. was the only one to use Portuguese. The Japanese spoke in Japanese!

Later we went to the Museu de Arte Moderna. (It is housed in the same building as Chateaubriand's Museu de Arte. Very confusing.) There, A. presented the museum with thirteen Norman McLaren films, three of which were screened, *Rythmetic*—which we had not seen before, based on numbers and absurdly and beautifully funny—*Blinkity Blank*, and *Hen Hop*. Over drinks I met a woman whose husband had just finished writing a book on Jean Vigo. She was astonished, I think, to find I had heard of Vigo, let alone admired him.

Saturday, a lovely day, we set off in a large party for the Brazilian Traction hydro-electric installations at Cubatão in the Serra do Mar—between São Paulo and Santos. Here water which would naturally flow inland is diverted and dropped 2,300 feet from the crest of the *serra* to the coastal plain below. Brazilian Traction, Light, and

Power, popularly known as The Light, is the Canadian company that provides light, power, gas, streetcar services, and telephones to São Paulo, Santos, and Rio de Janeiro, as well as light and power to many smaller communities. It began as a mule-drawn tramway in São Paulo in 1899. Today it provides something like sixty per cent of the power for the entire country.

Our Brazilian host, Sr. Lutz, had a head full of ideas and concepts and knowledge about flora and fauna. His wife was a schoolteacher before she married. These are the first middle-class Brazilians we have met—quite different from Rio's café society.

An immense lunch at a company house on the edge of the escarpment, with Brazilian fruits for dessert. A. and I both chose *caquis*. These must be persimmons, but so different from the ones that find their way north. Marvellous to be confronted by fruits you know nothing about—taste, texture, whether they have stones or small seeds, are soft or hard. Advised by Sr. Lutz, I cut mine north and south. A., unadvised, cut his east and west. "A natural error for a citizen of an east-west oriented country," was Lutz's comment. After lunch we plunged down the escarpment in the front seat of an incline-railway car with a plastic awning and nothing but a knee-high barrier between us and space. It was like being in an oversized roller-coaster that went on dropping straight down from the top of a mountain.

Sunday was the best day of all. We visited two early nineteenth-century *fazendas*. The first, a colonial house, light pink with white pillars, and lacy black grilles on the windows. Its present owners have modernized the plumbing but left everything as much as possible in its original state. The downstairs hall, with its honey-coloured stone floor and rough-beamed ceiling, was decorated with three beautiful cherubim and four flat candelabra from old churches, wooden, painted cream with gold leaf. Off the hall, a room full of trophies and slave relics, and off that, the slaves' room. I asked Senhora Meireles if it was haunted and she replied that there was a little old lady, very nice, full of good will. Upstairs was a mixture of modern and old— beautiful church carvings, a Gobelin tapestry which covered an entire wall, and, oddly, a Vlaminck. On a deep veranda, dark from creepers with pink bells, were birds in cages and a white tasselled bridal hammock. She said Chateau had given her an antique white one and her Doberman puppies had eaten it!

Her husband, a rich industrialist who is now a rich farmer and who gave up riding some years ago in favour of a jeep, still wears the shiny chestnut boots, spotless white breeches, white shirt, and chestnut tweed jacket of an equestrian. He is blond, bland, blue-eyed. She—dark, with long thin hands and immensely long scarlet nails—was wearing plaid slacks and a white twin-set.

We drank a Brazilian cocktail—made from *pinga*, a sugar-cane liquor—which tasted very like a daiquiri. Then lunch. On the dining-room table, and running its entire length, was a narrow, flat dish crammed with every kind of yellow, red, and orange flower the garden produces—flowers only, no leaves. Brilliant, startling. The meal began with what looked like a bowl of potato soup with a poached egg staring from its centre. (*Bem te vi!*) This was *cará* soup; the *cará*, I would guess, is a variety of yam. It was followed by roast pork and black beans mashed and made into a roll—garnished with little sausages and sitting on a bed of what looked like cooked grass and tasted bitter and pleasant. For salad, sliced cucumbers and cold, sliced marrow. Dessert was candied pumpkin and fried bananas served with farm cream. And coffee. Everything a product of the *fazenda*. Everything traditionally Brazilian. And very good indeed.

After luncheon we saw the coffee plantation. Bright, shiny green bushes with scarlet berries—birds in a bush, beads of fire. As far as the eye could see, coffee bushes stippled the lovely, undulating land. And the coffee courtyard floors where the beans were dried. In the dairy we visited the calves, which sucked your fingers as if they were udders when you put your hand out to stroke them, and saw the elaborate forecasting, month by month, of the number of calves to be born. *A senhora* looked after the coffee and *o senhor* the dairy; he preferred, he said, his cows to his textile workers!

The second *fazenda*, smaller than the first, was equally old. The house was slave-built, of adobe. The material is still in use today—bamboo canes are placed horizontally, about a brick-depth apart, and the spaces between packed with the red earth. At this stage, and from a distance, it looks like a brick structure. Then the whole is plastered with mud and whitewashed.

The main room downstairs was shaped like a dumbbell with a tiled fireplace taking up one entire wall. Flowers, in a child's small bunches, without leaves—one of daisies, one of red roses, one of zinnias—pushed tightly into mug-shaped vases, were perfectly placed by a painterly eye.

Our hostess, well dressed, attractive, was polite but cold. I after-wards learned that we were an hour and a half late arriving, and even in a country where time is measured by slower clocks, that is going a bit far. Our host, warm and charming, who looked as if he had In-dian blood, drove us to a height of land to see the young green wheat pushing its frail little spears up through the almost blood-red earth. He said that some kind of bean grown mainly in Spain, wheat, corn, and milk are his interests. His dairy was completely without flies—due, he said, to keeping the floors washed down so they never dry. This was a contrast to the previous dairy which, while equally clean and sweet-smelling, was filled with flies; they were a source of great concern to its owner, who claimed that as the flies were now immune to sprays, he knew no answer to the problem.

We also saw the equipment used for artificial insemination—and there, under a microscope, for the edification of the men, some semen.

After the semen, the chapel, with a beautiful Nossa Senhora, and on the altar, as in the house, the same child's tight fistful of flowers—marigolds this time, against the red velvet backcloth.

On our return to the house we were taken upstairs to a surprisingly large dining-room where we were offered coffee and cake and whisky and fruit juice. The dining-room ceiling was painted with black and white stripes simulating beams, naive and utterly charming. And traditional, according to our hostess.

A Brazilian who drove us back to São Paulo talked compulsively of divorce, or rather its lack. He said that our second host was "divorced" from his first wife and "remarried" to his current wife, a widow. I asked about the chapel and the fact that they had had mass there this morning—could divorcés attend mass? Yes, he said, they could attend mass but not take communion. He claimed that much of Brazilian society was in a similar position. His point: if people were going to "remarry" anyway—and they *were* —how much better for the Church to allow them to do so decently.

Next day the cobalt bomb which A. was to inaugurate was still firmly in the grip of customs officials, and no *mordida*—the little bite or bribe which usually makes everything possible—would release it. So we went, A. and I, to visit the park that was built to celebrate the fourth centennial of the foundation of São Paulo—its gardens laid out by Burle Marx and its buildings designed by a group of architects headed by Niemeyer. What a desolation is this architecture! Every bit of it seemed wrong—which just shows how inconsistent I am, because there are times when I find it so wonderfully *right*! Perhaps it needs sun. The building which houses—but does not show, for I think it is rarely open—the aeronautical exhibition and the Santos Dumont artefacts (Dumont was a Brazilian claimed by his fellow countrymen as the first man to fly—even before the Wright brothers)—is a long, low, two-storey structure of glass and pillars. Seen under a grey sky, with the nose- and hand-prints of a thousand A.'s attempting to peer in, it looked simply shoddy. From our peering position it seemed unsuitable for the display of aircraft, the ceiling being so low that the top of even a small plane all but touched it. The nearby Palace of Arts, built exactly—but exactly—like an igloo with the addition of a row of port-holes around its lower edge, really depressed me. Why transport a form dictated by materials and weather conditions of the Arctic, put it down in Brazil, and then blow it up to a radius of 250 feet?

Disturbed and excited by Brazil. Why? What is it all about? Does place alter person? It's like falling in love—with the country itself.

Am reading Yeats' letters. He complains that George Eliot had morals but no religion and that if she only had had a bit more religion she would have had less morality. He writes, too, of his dislike of reasonable people whose brains suck all the blood from their hearts. And how he disliked moralists with neither spirit nor imagination enough for a good lie. How he would have loved Brazilians—and how, indeed, do I!

Drove to Santos, the coffee port, late in the morning and took the ferry to Guarujá, an island summer resort. Going down the escarpment from São Paulo the weather was clear, so we could see the sinuous double road with its tunnels, the narrow strip of flat coastal land, and the sea. Very lovely. Arrived finally at a totally unspoiled beach on a wild and beautiful coast and, unfortunately, an all too Hawaiian-appearing restaurant. More interesting was an absurd trio of small monkeys in a cage—the ones with tufted ears—their tiny fingers, trying to remove my rings, felt moist and limp as the stems of violets. Four *araras* —the large macaws—wing-feathers cut to prevent flight, sat on perches and cracked sunflower seeds. Their black, dry, ill-fitting tongues moving about in their mouths looked as if each had bitten off the little finger of a Negro which they were now trying unsuccessfully to spit out. Nearby, two green parrots, chained and aggressively bad-tempered, screamed at each other and everyone else.

There was a clean and pretty aviary where I had a chance to identify some of "our" birds—for their keeper, a truly Conradish man with a week's growth of beard and a long, wistful face, was kind enough to understand my Portuguese and let me understand his. As he stood in the cage peeling bananas and fixing them onto the bars, cutting oranges in half and impaling them on pointed branches, placing sunset-coloured arcs of *mamão* on the ground, he told me the names of the birds around him. We saw "our" tanagers in the cage, and the little jumping birds with striped heads were identified as *tico-ticos*. The *sabiá* was there too—like the North American robin, only larger—and the dove, and a dozen pairs of lovebirds all freezing and huddled together.

After a long wait, a fine lunch: fresh shrimps from the sea and good Brazilian beer. Afterwards I followed a row of bright pink shells along sand almost as firm as turf. Returning, in the distance, beyond the curve of the shore—appearing like shafts of distant rain—we saw the skyscrapers again, surrealist in such a setting. Their vertical lines a reaction against the horizontal lines of colonial architecture, perhaps. Or more likely—A.'s theory—that Copacabana has become the symbol of all things lovely and so is being duplicated everywhere. In Santos this argument is certainly borne out. There, like Copacabana's twin, the curving Santos beach is rimmed with skyscrapers, its sidewalks patterned with black and white stones.

We drove to the port—the largest coffee port in the world—and visited the aquarium, where we saw the terrible Amazonian carnivore—the piranha which, in seven minutes flat (I think that's the number), can reduce a horse to a pile of bones. I had imagined something the size of a shark and found, to my astonishment, a little fish no more than a foot long. This remarkable creature can smell blood a great distance off, and will come in a flash to attack anything already wounded. Saw, too, the inevitable sea-horse, which never fails to amuse me—why should it want to stand upright, like a man?—and those poor blind shrimps with their wide-ranging antennae, looking half like a caricature of a guardsman, half like a nervous pianist, their anxious white front legs like fingers uncertainly playing the same music over and over. At one tank of striped yellow-and-black fish, as bright and flashing as anything you could wish, a minute child gazed mutely until an inch-long colourless guppy swam into sight, whereupon it set up a great howl of excitement: *Pequeninho, pequeninho!* (Little one, little one!)

Next morning I had the good red São Paulo earth washed out of my hair, gazed at some Brazilian tourmalines which, when well cut, might easily be emeralds, and in the afternoon had tea at the Canadian consul's. Saw Sra. Lutz once again, who had by now sent us a bird book and a fabulous basket of *fruta de conde, caquis*, tangerines, and oranges; and met Sra. de Souza, one of the smartest women I have ever seen, dressed in a black-and-brown checked tweed suit cut very wide at the neck so that she could wear a long rope of pearls wound around her throat about five times. She looked a bit like Merle Oberon and talked about Rilke, Faulkner, Camus. I wish she and Sra. Lutz lived in Rio.

Took the Canadians from the consulate to dinner and then on to the *futebol* game—São Paulo playing Palmeiras—where A. was to kick off. This was not without its drama. Attended by a military aide, we were escorted by motorcycle police through a dense traffic jam and a sea of pedestrians. From our seats we watched A., the consul, and the aide march like toy people into the middle of the playing field—the tier upon tier of bleachers apparently suspended from the starry sky. A stupefying arena without pillars or posts—a great elongated flying doughnut. The crowd of some fifty thousand stamped and roared and clapped and those tiny figures mid-field moved about, intent upon something obviously important to them, which to us was too small to see. We were giants suddenly, intent upon ants. Why did we become large because they became small?

A. finally kicked the ball. What followed was soccer—a very pretty game. Look Ma, no hands! Rockets and fireworks went off whenever a goal was scored and the crowd roared like an exultant or wounded beast.

The next morning's newspaper included a photo of A.'s *pontapé* apparently being intensely studied by Mazzola, the captain of the home team, who had been under heavy criticism for losing too many games. Typically Brazilian, the caption read, "Mazzola pays close attention—but he never learns."

While A. went about his business, I spent the next morning visiting churches and museums with Sra. Lutz. A real tourist. The cathedral immensely domed, gothic, with a strangely austere interior for a South American church—for a Catholic church, come to that. Row upon row of gothic arches—a glade of grey stone trees. On to an older and smaller church with God in a blue cloud painted on the ceiling above the altar. Both churches crowded with people praying—mostly young girls, praying, I suppose, for husbands. So many touching the feet of carved saints. Sra. Lutz says that Saint Anthony never fails her and that most Brazilian women love him.

I saw someone go through a door by the altar, so I followed, hopeful of finding the room where supplicants leave models of those parts of their bodies in need of a cure, but all I found was a grille with guttering candles and some rather smelly latrines.

In the Museu de Arte Moderna we saw what they called a "didactic show", rather badly hung. A collection of slightly grubby prints with one or two paintings by da Silva, one of their primitives, whom I like. But they didn't seem to have a collection—or if they had, there was nowhere to hang it. Yet this is the group that organizes the Bienal at which countries from all over the world exhibit their best artists.

The Museu de Arte, Chateaubriand's collection, was still enjoyable, even with most of its notable paintings on exhibition in the States. The Brazilian section includes a whole roomful of Portinaris—large, strangely grey paintings full of pain; some Segalls and di Cavalcantis, and a fair collection of da Silvas. In the international section there is an El Greco of St. Francis; two enchanting little Renoirs; a number of early religious paintings; and then, almost alarmingly, about five hundred small Degas statues, looking rather like the black notes on the piano. The much larger ballerina in her real tutu is there as well, with her hair tied back. But the little ones lose any impact they might have. Quantity definitely diminishes quality— the eye blurs. The figures are reduced to the stick-men children draw on the upper corners of the pages of their schoolbooks, which make a "moving picture" when riffled.

Lunch with A. at a French restaurant and then to the natural history *museu* with Sra. Lutz to see the birds. We began by having coffee with the curator, a man with a face just like a dog's. Most extraordinary. As I looked at his eyes, they were dog's eyes—pale eyes, honey-coloured—and I thought, "Nonsense, look at his nose," and his nose too was a dog's. And so I switched to his teeth—pointed, white, dog's teeth. Uncanny. But such a polite dog. Wouldn't cock his leg just anywhere.

I don't really like stuffed birds; nevertheless I learned a good deal. "Our" lovely little blue bird with its black mask is the *saí-azul* (blue-skirt). Upstairs—preferable to those in the cage below simulating life—was the result of one man's field trip: twelve hundred birds lying on their backs, stuffed with dried grasses. So light! And like a rainbow. Drawers full of them. The *alma de gato* (soul of a cat) is a variant on our mangrove cuckoo, or yellow-billed or black-billed. Rufous above, grey beneath.

I asked about the marsupial duck. It is true enough; Brazil has a number of marsupials. I said, "Australians think *they're* the only ones who have," and our guide replied morosely, "It's not the business of Australians to know about Brazil. And we will never tell them because all we think about is football." He showed us a large, blond, marsupial rat with four babies in her pouch. And a skunk, just like ours only brown instead of black. We saw a balleen in his bones, long-fingered hands at his sides.

> I Cannot tell who loves the Skeleton
> Of a poor Marmoset, nought but boan, boan.
> Give me a nakednesse with her cloaths on.

And I had a long, slow look at the sloths, with their loofah fur and their Henry Moore faces.

Sra. Lutz told me of a bird, *João de Barro* (Clay John), which used to build, from clay, a single room at the end of a tunnel. It is evidently becoming more sophisticated, because recent "nests" are found to consist of as many as three storeys. This same bird has also been known to seal his wife inside with clay. ?!?!

On our last day, in a party of three women and two small children, we went one morning to the *Museu e Instituto Butantã,* home away from home for snakes from all over the world, where antitoxins are made. We gazed over walls and into grassy pits where the snakes lay like dried cow-dung. By great good luck, a keeper in white jacket and leather spats arrived with new snakes for the pasture. With a specially constructed stick he hooked them from their boxes and, on discovering he had an audience, "milked" a rattler of its venom—the colourless poison squirting out in a fine spray—and handed me the nozzle tooth through which it had squirted. In the manner of the bee and its sting, the rattler loses a tooth with each squirt. But unlike the bee, he has six spares. The keeper also showed us a coral snake—small, coral-coloured with rings of black and white—very pretty and very poisonous—which rarely attacks because its mouth is so small it has great difficulty biting! And he showed us a false coral snake—which is not poisonous—almost exactly the same except that its black and white rings are less regular and its mouth bigger. But who would stop to measure mouths when meeting on a walk? He passed it to me to hold, and little Sally, emboldened by my action, held it too. He then produced a larger black snake, remarkable for being able to eat poisonous snakes without itself being poisoned. Once again he passed it to me to hold, but little Sally, apprehensive this time, only touched it. I must say I had to overcome a decided reluctance.

I am confused by much we were told, as I understand only snatches, but I *think* he said that non-poisonous snakes all lay eggs while the poisonous bear live young, and that only non-poisonous snakes can climb trees. Sr. Lutz, whose business is engineering but who knows more about natural history than many specialists, told me this last is not true. He cited an island off Brazil inhabited by a poisonous snake which is also found on the mainland. As there is none of the snake's natural food on this island, it has in desperation learned to climb trees in order to find other food. So do we adapt.

I was amused to discover that Brazil, which we Canadians consider to be filled with dangers, is also filled with Brazilians who are more alarmed by the rattlesnake we in Canada take pretty well in our stride.

To reward little Sally, I gave her the nozzle tooth from the rattler. She promptly put it up her nose.

The drive back from São Paulo was beautiful—rolling country culminating in mountains as we approached Rio—a climb and then a tortuous drop to sea level. We passed coffee plantations, citrus fruit farms, cattle. Saw oxen hauling carts and burros with wicker baskets and Negroes in bright colours and *flamboyantes* in flaming flower.

We passed one little town built on a knoll from which every tree and blade of grass had been meticulously depilated, the whole red-earth structure of houses and hill rising like an Australian ant-hill—while crowding at its perimeter, the lush, tropical growth of Brazil. One day I hope to return and go into the church, for it was here that a miracle occurred, so the guide book says—but my Portuguese is not quite good enough to understand what the miracle was. O Glory be!

May 16

An unearthly silence for the last week from the children at the convent. Either a sick Sister or a ghastly punishment. The schoolyard full of little mutes reading or sewing. Uncanny.

On our return from São Paulo we found a box of bird whistles, over thirty in all, in appearance a cross between a chessman and a small woodwind. And accompanying them, a record of birds' songs, so you can learn to play them correctly. They are made in Espírito Santo for—I regret to say—hunters. Are there really so many birds worth shooting?

The poinsettia bushes (*bicos de papagaios*) are in full flower and reflected in the lily pool.

For my sins, attended a fashion show put on by the YWCA—an enormous affair in the restaurant of one of the large department stores. They had equipped my table with a Canadian flag and we were all given samples of toothpaste and face powder. Clothing interesting: so many heavy suits—really heavy. These are apparently luxury items in tropical wardrobes. All skirts skintight—tighter than anything I've ever seen. From my point of view, the worst possible design for Brazilian women, who have tiny waists and large bottoms. But they like to show their curves and their men like to see them.

May 18

Nature notes: I saw a spider with a golden web. (It sounds like the start of a riddle poem.) This spider has a torso about the size of the top joint of my thumb and of the same general shape. In colour it is dark grey with gold spots. The web matches the spots. I would have thought it a trick of light except that, no matter what the light, the gold was unchanging, and on the spider's abdomen was a clot of golden thread—like the clot formed by a sewing machine on the underside of the stitching if the tension has not been correctly adjusted.

I had believed, without knowing much about spiders, that they spin webs as invisible as possible in order to deceive insects into thinking they are flying through air. If that is so, then what is this spider up to? And still what, even if it *isn't*? Does it eat only those it can lure by beauty? Do flies have an aesthetic sense? Why do I imagine it is the property only of "manunkind"? Is stupidity justified by anything less than beauty's trap?

"From our window in São Paulo . . . skyscrapers everywhere, and as if without plan."

May 20

Bought a *figa* as a present for one of the girls at the office. The literature that accompanied it cannot be paraphrased:

> *Figa* is one of the oldest charms against evil eyes and spirits: the human hand with the thumb between the indicator and the middle-finger, it's the symbol of reproduction which annuls the negative influences of sterility and adversity in life.
>
> *Figas* or phalus were hung from the necklaces of women and children in ancient Rome. Dante mentions it in the *Divine Comedy (Inferno XXV),* so does Shakespeare in *Othello.*
>
> Made in copper, bronze, brass or pottery, designed or carved out, the *figa* appears in every antic collections, on frescoes, mozaics, or on offering pieces, found in Pompei and Herculanum, and in the Mediterranean world.
>
> It is the material gesture of despise, scorn and contempt, when figured against someone.
>
> Pistoia (Italy) built a giant marble *figa* on the heights of the Carmignano Castle, defying Florence, which declared war immediately.
>
> The *figa* as a jewel, watch-trinket, tie-pin or charm has always persisted and kept its credit of older times; black ones (jet) to get rid of evil eyes; red ones (Guinee wood) for good luck; the yellow for good memory; the pink for remembrance or recollection; the green ones for hope.
>
> It is the popular belief to not look after a lost *figa,* for it took away all the evil that would fall on its owner; some people believe that they must be given to you as a gift in order to work as good luck charms, besides they must be always the left hand.

Many small girl-children in Brazil wear *figas* round their necks. It is believed to be good luck—and of course, in a peasant community fertility *is* good luck. What, then, is the variant—the hand with the key? I couldn't help teasing a rather worldly acquaintance when she asked me what it meant. "Surely," I said, "you know all about *that* perversion."

Apparently Jean-Jean, two-year-old son of the Canadian First Secretary, had the maids hysterical the other day when he played "I've got your nose". They thought he was making *figas* at them.

Went to an enormous dinner at the Italian embassy the other night. Almost all the senior diplomats there—British, American, Dutch, German—plus a raft of elegant Brazilians. I found myself amused.

Reading a novel by Daphne du Maurier in Portuguese. I can manage it with the help of a dictionary, but it bores me. That is the trouble: what interests me I can't read; what I can, doesn't.

Last night in my room, a leaf insect—a dead leaf. During the summer when the world was green, the air was full of green leaf insects. Now—in winter when the world is still green (although, in fairness, the few deciduous trees have shed), this brown leaf walked in. I didn't like him much. He had, I thought at first, a head like a "pushmi-pullyu"—but the long undercarriage, the "lumpjaw" as it were, was a pair of folding legs which he let down when necessary, thus making the head end of his body very mobile. He must be related to the praying mantis.

May 30

Extremely bad attack of inner ear trouble—Ménière's syndrome. Life itself tilted and tried to slide me off.

The departure of Chris and Henriette Hardy (the First Secretary and his wife) has brought to our door a pair of parakeets. She is mainly green with some blue in her tail-feathers, he more handsome, with much yellow and orange to set him off. Their screams sound like silk being torn and they are unfriendly and fierce. She would bite you to the bone. I don't much like them, for all their fine looks, but I am interested in them. He behaves as if he is ashamed of her. If she approaches him when you are watching, he flies into a rage and drives her away. But if you come upon them unexpectedly, he is always cuddled up against her at *her* end of the perch. The instant he hears or sees you, he edges away, and by the time you have reached their cage he is at the extreme opposite end of the perch. I have yet to discover any different behaviour.

Am struggling to read a book on Portinari in Portuguese—more difficult than the du Maurier which boredom forced me to abandon, *and* more interesting. What an extraordinary man! Still under the spell of his grandmother, and almost a prude: the only nudes he has ever painted were in art school. Of Italian extraction, he was born in 1903 to a peasant family in the small Brazilian town of Brodowski and there, aged eight, he helped whitewashers paint stars on the ceiling of the little church. His paintings and drawings of children playing in Brodowski are more moving by far than the great murals depicting the suffering of the workers. Those little running kids in a vast space, scattered like grains, go through me like needles.

Today and yesterday actually chilly. Wore wool and a fur and will again tonight. Winter rain here makes your bones ache. There is no way of drying anything and your clothes feel like chain mail.

June 1

Beautiful Brazilian women take their beauty very seriously. Innocently having my hair cut, as I look about me I see women, hair on end, white froth at the roots, white froth on their upper lips, skirts above their knees while they are depilated, pedicured, manicured. No privacy. One immense female, her large arms spread and one gross leg extended, was having her toenails painted scarlet by a small pedicurist. With his free hand he was taking large gulps of tea.

On the way home saw a hearse out of a René Clair film—all gold pillars and wheels. Like the last car—embalmed and dressed in its best.

June 6

Returned this morning from a quick trip to São Paulo. Our trips there are uncommonly amusing and I come back, veins full of air. The reason for this visit was the delivery, in Campinas, of the first six of twenty-five Canadian-built General Motors diesel locomotives. Accompanied by General Motors brass from Canada and the States, we set forth on the hour-and-a-half drive from São Paulo—I, covered with orchids and maidenhair.

The first to arrive, we disembarked at an old-fashioned railway station—exactly like a small-town railway station in Canada—and watched the local population turn out. A brass band lined up in the tile-walled vestibule of the station and played vigorous and spirited music. We were asked to stand inside with the band but it was simply not bearable—the decibel level made your heart reverberate behind your rib cage. Outside in the square, a bright sun shone on a Portinari painting of Brodowski: his church, bull, and dog all there. But most *particularly* "Portinari", the immense amount of air—great high arches and naves of it. We waited and waited—for what?—enjoying the square in the sun as the tricycle battalion arrived and the sense of excitement mounted. Then buses pushed in with movie crews and guests from Rio, and we all trooped into the station. The remarkably pretty Brazilian wife of one of the Americans from General Motors set off for the ladies' room. Such a triumphant march along the crowded platform! Forcing herself through the dense throng, she was greeted with little cries of joy by friends and acquaintances. The men kissed her hand, the women kissed her on both cheeks, she must stop and talk and stop again. How far that lavatory became!

Camera-men hung from the rafters or sat in strategic positions on the tops of walls and we, solid as a meat pie, jammed the platform, brasses blaring. Then a rocket was fired, or a pistol, and a kind of drawn-in breath sounded from the crowd, and down the track— reminding me of the ice-cream streetcars of my childhood—came the first diesel, a fantasy in yellow and blue. I felt it should be decked with balloons, so removed from reality was I. It roared as it passed— a lion of an engine, solid and strong. And then another roared in; and another; and another; and still another; and one further still. Yellow and blue—and each with a flag—and each roaring. And Brazilian women wept and the mob surged back and forth and A. was told he must make a speech—just a few words. Now, he had a speech prepared for the luncheon to follow, and—not yet at the stage where he can ad lib in Portuguese—he and one of the General Motors officials scribbled a few lines onto a piece of paper. But as an eloquent Brazilian speech flowed on, rising and falling, it became clear that "a few words" would not do, and so A. decided to burn his bridges and give his luncheon speech.

Then someone suggested that I unveil one of the diesels by pulling down the Brazilian flag that was tied across it. A. said, "She cannot pull down the Brazilian flag!" and once said, although no one had thought of it before, it was plain as plain that I could not. A. made his luncheon speech; the women cried. By lifting the flag in an ungainly upward throw, I unveiled the *Jânio Quadros*, a *bispo* blessed it and threw holy water on it, the band played the Brazilian national anthem. The women cried. Then a kind of madness took over and nothing would do but I unveil all the diesels, and so—in a dream that was not a dream—I continued to lift Brazilian flags and find diesel engines. Meanwhile, in an ever-milling mob, people greeted each other and shouted and embraced, and the band continued to play. Finally, when everyone had yelled at everyone else and all the kissing was done and the band had blown its last note, we got aboard a 1914 carriage with cleanly laundered white slipcovers on leather seats, grateful simply to sit, as the great diesel pulled the little carriage through coffee country where, at each station, the locals came out, bright in their pinks and yellows and whites, to see the circus pass.

After some three-quarters of an hour on board we were taken to a restaurant luncheon for course after course of food. Exhausted, fulfilled, full, we were a bedraggled bunch, we North Americans. The wife of one of the General Motors men from the U.S. was talking about her pill schedule and what her doctor would have to say about her forgetting it. But the Brazilians, most of whom had been dancing until two the night before, still looked fresh and happy.

Back in São Paulo, we took the Canadians up to our hotel room and, dazed, poured Scotch and tonics, threw them down the wash-basin, and tried again, growing hilarious on whisky and anecdotes of the day.

All night long I lifted larger and larger Brazilian flags over my head.

June 13

Much preoccupied with the visit of President Lopez of Portugal. A splendid parade on the day he arrived tied up traffic from ten in the morning until five in the afternoon—sure sign of a good parade. First, on foot, a scattered collection of newspaper reporters and camera-men, taking notes, taking pictures, running ahead of the open car in which the president sat. Accompanying it, scarlet-clad troops mounted on black horses; from their helmets streamed what appeared to be the scalps of long-haired brunettes. And smart as Flit soldiers, the ceremonial infantry in cream flannel with very tight trousers, jackets trimmed with red, red feather dusters sprouting from the headgear of the officers, red bullrushes from those of the men.

June 15

Two days ago I gave notice to Salvador, the head servant, and his wife. The house feels like a powder keg. I am sorry about it for all our sakes, but perhaps most especially for her. This must have happened to them before: he beautiful and lazy; she efficient and madly in love with him.

Have been drawing with a felt-nibbed pen. A totally new concept in pens; I bought one in Ottawa to mark our boxes and trunks, and duly unpacked it here and put it on the desk in the library. It was on the desk when I gave Salvador his notice. My Portuguese still leans heavily on the dictionary. I was nervous. He was grand. It took me a long time. I doodled as I talked and I fell in love with the nib, which is very black and totally indelible.

"What's all this?" A. asked later, picking up the doodles from the desk. "That's me firing Salvador." "You could draw," said A. "Surely, if I'd been going to draw, I'd have drawn by now." "No," said A. firmly. "You could draw." And the next day he returned with a roll of drawing paper so beautiful in itself that there was no way I could put a mark upon it. But since then I've been trying to draw, to recreate the wonderful shapes of the leaves and the intricate patterns of mosaic tiles. I think I might be able to draw if only I could...what? If only I *could*.

There is a phrase used here—*amigo da onça*, "friend of the panther", meaning someone who is not your friend. Heard the origin of it today. One man said to another, "What would you do if you were chased by a panther?" "Why, I'd run, of course." "And if the panther was gaining on you?" "Why, I'd climb a tree." "And if the panther climbed the tree after you?" "Look here, who are you, anyway? Are you my friend or the friend of the panther?"

June 17

Our marble floors are like sliced brawn—or is it head cheese?— lots of gelatine and veal and pork with occasional bits of fat. A cold-buffet chef's dream.

And the royal palms are truly the elephants among trees. Their trunks are to the trunks of other trees as the elephant's leg to all other legs.

Went the other day with a young artist to see the equivalent of our "spring show". It was hung in the very beautiful Department of Education. The prizes are handsome—a year in Europe, for instance. Another prize is jury-free submission next year...more like a punishment, to judge from last year's winners. It seemed to have taken away their talents. But there were many things I did like—a monotype of stylized fish in a kind of rainbow; and some splendidly royal fruits: pillarbox-red strawberries with gold sepals as if wearing crowns. Among the black-and-white section so many drawings I feel I could do if I had a bit more control—semi-doodles. And one man, d'Horta, doodles with a scalpel. Where others tattoo, he makes incisions.

June 28

A long blank space—but, *so busy*—so Portuguese President Lopez's visit has been neglected. I regret it, as the reception given by Itamarity was worth describing, and now the edge is off my memory. But I shall try.

The reception began at ten in the evening. Because of the length of the guest list the traffic jam was tremendous and we were a long time on the road. It would have been bad enough had everyone had cars that functioned, but Brazil is a country where many reverend old vehicles take to the road and occasionally break down altogether. They must all of them have been out for this event.

Itamarity, the equivalent of our East Block, headquarters of External Affairs, goes back to imperial times. It is built around a rectangular courtyard lined with imperial palms—in its centre an ornamental pool with swans. The setting could not be more lovely. The night of the reception it was brightly lighted and jam-packed.

We met a young Jewish couple, new to the Israeli embassy, who had previously been in Canada and who had known A.M. Klein. They told us he had had a complete breakdown. I can hardly believe it. Looking back to those days when we were all together in Montreal, collaborating on *Preview*, I would have thought Klein safer than most of us. When I asked if they knew the cause, they looked at me accusingly, I thought, and said it was due to the anti-Semitism in Montreal. "But we all *loved* Abe," I said, vehement, hurt. "How could he have misread us?" But of course, he didn't. It wasn't *us*.

This conversation was interrupted by a request that we go upstairs to watch the ballet. It was danced on a floating stage at the far end of the pool. I had a pillar in front of me—like the materialization of Abe—blocking my view. The visibility was further reduced by a fountain between us and the stage, so we watched through a screen of water, which might have been my tears.

How can I take in the fact that Abe is so seriously ill? Abe so funny, so witty, such good company. Abe so—legal, is that the word? So established in his suit and tie with his wife and family and reputation. Abe invincible, as a parent is invincible. But why did I not listen to

"Portrait of the Poet as Landscape"? "And some go mystical, and some go mad." How poignant now:

He suspects that something has happened, a law
been passed, a nightmare ordered. Set apart,
he finds himself, with special haircut and dress,
as on a reservation....

Did he foresee it all?

June 29

The next "gala" connected with President Lopez was the reception he gave in the palace of the Brazilian president. We had dinner at the Argentine embassy beforehand, and then by car at a slow crawl—which took over an hour instead of the normal ten minutes.

Brazil dressed up is truly something to see. Such jewels! Such hairdos! Such high fashion! If tight skirts are in, here they are tighter. One elegant creature had to lift her ankle-length sheath above her knees in order to ascend a flight of stairs.

Next morning to the president's stand—all too well named!—on Avenida Atlântica to watch the final parade in Lopez's honour. Avenida Atlântica, which parallels the coast, is a wide avenue with, in its Copacabana section, skyscrapers on one side and the beautiful beach and sea on the other. The day was perfect—soft and hazy at 9.30, the hour we arrived—but clearing as the morning wore on, so when the parade reached its climax all the destroyers and submarines and naval craft on the water suddenly became apparent as if a gauze backdrop had been unobtrusively raised.

July 5

So busy since last entry. A shortage of servants and the Canada Day party combined have kept me hopping. Salvador and his wife, who had agreed to stay until after July 1st, walked out two days before as a result of a fight with one of the cleaners. That added to the work. Luckily, a friend helped me with the flowers—a massive job in a house this size. The party was further complicated by the fact of it being the first large reception—five hundred people— given in a house all Rio is curious about. We were under more than the usual scrutiny. And we were setting up, for the first time, lights in the garden, tickets and a loudspeaker system for the cars, police to manage the parking, special cloakrooms in case of rain, etc., etc.

Well, it didn't rain. Couldn't have been a more beautiful day. The garden looked gorgeous, the house at its shining best, and the staff worked cheerfully and well. Only three minor disasters: one admiral had to wait a long time for his car—his chauffeur had fallen asleep; one woman fainted; one had a weeping jag.

Somewhere in between Lopez's visit and July 1st, I was summoned to call on the president's wife in the baroque palace. We had coffee in a tiny anteroom, she—young, easy, attractive—and an interpreter whom I didn't use. I can now do a social call in Portuguese.

I go on playing with that felt pen. Have done a large drawing of one of the *cestas* sent us for July 1st. It amazes me how easily and quickly I draw—just start right in with my heavy black nib.

July 6

Last night we dined with Maria Martins, the Brazilian sculptress to whom Maie Casey had given me a letter of introduction, and her diplomat husband. An extraordinary party full of beautiful women, immaculate men, and noise. The apartment is wonderful—Renoirs tucked away in corners, a group of nudes by Rouault, a Picasso. Also a new acquisition by that Portuguese woman, da Silva, entitled *The Circus*, that was like an intricate and mysterious crossword puzzle in more than the usual number of dimensions, mixed with a feeling of circus tents and the checked clothing of Pierrot, the patches of Harlequin, and the corridors of dream. My felt pen could have done such a thing...I cannot blame the tools!

The rain has stopped, after two days, and today is a dream of a day. Sun drawing the moisture upwards makes the air diaphanous, as if the earth were breathing. I have spent all of it, felt pen in hand, attempting to draw the garden and the mountains. Difficult in black and white. And how can I catch that texture of the air?

Tonight a concert with the Israelis. Pray I may stay awake but doubt it. Too many late nights. Too much fresh air.

July 14

Here I sit waiting for Madre Cecília, the Mother Superior of the neighbouring convent—she who was unamused by our goat. A. suggested I invite her and her assistant for a *cafèzinho* and they are due any minute now....

They arrived in their starched white coifs and black habits. When they left I walked to the foot of the garden with them to see them off. I was no sooner back at the house than what should appear but another pair—*their* coifs folded in more elaborate ruchings—entering by the self-same gate and following the route of the previous pair. I began to think that, through some error, I had invited nuns from two different convents to come for coffee. This pair, however, passed round to the back of the house and there…evaporated. Was one of them related to a member of the household staff and taken in for a meal? On enquiry I am told that no one here saw them. Am I mad? Have I taken to seeing pairs of nuns in pairs? My final conclusion: that they had been meaning to go to the convent next door and, seeing "my" two nuns going out our lower gate, thought this was the convent. But where they went nobody knows, or if they know they don't tell.

Almost totally preoccupied with drawing. It is like an illness—anything beyond its radius is blurred. I tell A. that before we leave he and I will have a joint show at the Cultura Inglêsa and, for the *vernissage*, serve fig biscuits and cocoa. The only show we have seen there—dismal premises smacking of the "Y"—depressed me utterly. Work by an amateur—a large woman in wrinkled stockings. A good object lesson for all us other amateurs.

Am reading *Sons and Lovers* for the first time. What a writer he is, and you know it from the first page, the first sentence. He makes me remember the great mystery of people—a perfect counterweight to having seen too many people too superficially for too long. I feel a return to grace, a state I had almost forgotten. But this may not only be Lawrence. I think the ground was prepared by Brazil.

The other night, dining with Brazilian friends in their elegant, modern apartment, looking out over the harbour to the lights on the other side, I felt overwhelmed by beauty.

It was such a funny Brazilian party—the men and women separated—and rather muted. The two daughters of the house with us before dinner, composed like a drawing. The fifteen-year-old, already mature, with a dark and heavy beauty and awake to her own womanliness—her eyes held as if by a bright globe none of the rest of us could see, her hands curled in her lap. Close at her side, the younger one, still a child, flat-chested, her blonde hair pulled high to

the back of her head and falling long and straight down her back—
leaning slightly towards her sister, *her* hands curled in her lap too,
and her pale and rather pointed face full of an intellectual eagerness. I'd have loved to have my pen with me. And the guests: the
thin man beside me, his hands raw from some terrible allergy, saying, "It is not only the architecture and the vegetation of Brazil that
are baroque—it is the people too." And the father of our hostess, a
tall almost-Englishman who had been educated at Harrow and, when
I stupidly asked had it been worth it, replied, "Yes. When I arrived,
along with other small boys of less than fourteen, the headmaster,
who later became an archbishop, addressed us thus: 'Gentlemen, I
bid you welcome to Harrow. I hope you will be happy here. We have
no intention of trying to teach you anything. We merely hope that you
will learn how to learn.' I am an old man now, yet I still remember
that opening speech." He was an extraordinary old boy, a real Ed-
wardian who, if my Portuguese served me correctly, lived high and
well at a time when it was perhaps a bit vulgar for a gentleman to
have a social conscience. "Education," he said, "was considered to
be merely one of the attributes of the gentleman, it was taken quite
naturally." And his wife in green velvet, the third woman in Brazil to
drive a car, had something of the emerald's fire in her.

Something mad is happening to me. I seem to be falling in love
with the world. And something in me is afraid. It is hard to know joy
from pain—just as it is hard to know hot water from cold, if either is
hot or cold enough.

July 18

Went the other day to see the charitable organization As Pioneiras
in action. Started ten years ago, it now has branches all over Brazil,
and provides varieties of help to anyone who asks: sheets, pillow-
slips, and operating-room linen for hospitals; clothes for the poor;
milk and reading lessons for children; and for women, information
on nutrition and how to use a sewing machine. Its headquarters
is in Guanabara Palace, the only building in Brazil which, due to
some oversight at the time the royal family was exiled to Portugal,
still belongs to the princes. It is a beautiful building, embracing a
courtyard.

I was taken by Dona Helena—whom I had not met before—
a small, dark woman, hair greying slightly, whose straightforward,
blunt manner was strangely un-Brazilian. I liked her very much. She

introduced me to the other workers—vigorous, attractive, friendly women—and then set me to work cutting factory cotton into specified lengths for operating-room sheets. We formed an assembly line and worked fast for two and a half hours. I spoke Portuguese all that time—or listened to it.

It turns out that Dona Helena paints. I am to go next week to see her work. I wouldn't be surprised if we became friends.

July 19

Dinners, ballet films, art shows. One, at the Museu de Arte Moderna, by two Uruguayans—very contemporary, but the pictures without mystery, going through you and leaving no trace, direct as bullets. Many were laminated and a young Brazilian, explaining the process to us, claimed that it was very dangerous. When we asked why, he said, "Imagine what would happen if it got into the hands of people who are not artists." I wanted to ask him about the pencil.

Just back from a reception at Itamarity for the Conference for Girl Guides. We have five delegates, one of whom was president. We are told she did an excellent job—cool, collected, fair, and to the point. From her face I am sure she did; it is all those things. I prefer Brazilians—hot, uncollected, unfair, etc., etc. What is this revulsion in me against all the values I was brought up to respect?

Had Thomas Bata, the shoe manufacturer, and his Swiss wife to luncheon. She, one of the delegates to the conference, is a lawyer, quite beautiful, very young, and I am sure she is as efficient as a Swiss watch.

The army has moved in with tanks on one of the *deputados* who, as earlier reported, shot a traffic policeman who stopped him for speeding. Two machine-guns which he kept for "his personal use" were captured in the raid on his "fortress". This may be what kept half the women away from As Pioneiras yesterday. The organizer for the day said in explanation, "*A situação,*" but I didn't know what the situation was.

July 21

Bitterly cold and a nasty wind. All Brazilians are shivering in their shoes. And so am I. Tried to draw the house today but the wind drove me in.

Went yesterday to the Jockey Club. The buildings are like the palaces of Indian princes and the thumb-shaped Rio mountains rising around us made the scene something out of fantasy. But the horses looked real enough and quite splendid. I was filled with wonder at the shape of a racehorse. Am I only really seeing it for the first time or is the new racehorse a different shape? At any rate, I lost my money twice on two shapely horses.

July 22

Still cold. And I am restless as the cold winds. Have just finished drawing the house and chapel—long view. Very difficult.

July 24

The cold has lessened a bit, but flannel nighties and woollens and furs have been the order of the day. Dinner last night at the Iranian ambassador's. The British there. I do not grow to like them better. They bring out the worst in me.

July 29

Beautiful weather again. Today soft and misty and infinitely mysterious. Yesterday beautiful too, I am told, but I was sick of a fever and so saw nothing. Right as the weather today, but weak.

The other night we went to an elaborate concert and supper at the Spanish embassy to hear the guitarist Yepes. He was very clever and could make his instrument imitate anything—drums, footsteps, etc. Played Scarlatti purely and well and more to my taste. No sign of flamenco in his playing which, of course, I would have loved, having cut my guitar-teeth on Montoya. The food was fabulous. Marvellous Brazilian *doces* (sweets)—surely among the world's great culinary creations. They look and taste like food from another planet. Even their names are strange: *fios de ôvos* (strings of eggs), *ôlhos de madrastas* (stepmothers' eyes).

August 1

Have felt very *mais o menos* for a week now but have managed to keep going and today, I think, I am on the mend. A busy week.

Wednesday we had dinner with a famous Brazilian judge who has the largest private library I have ever seen—like the stacks at McGill. Books to the ceiling on steel shelves, all bound in leather to his taste, and tended by a servant whose job is solely to keep them from mildewing. The guests at dinner included the wife of a defeated presidential candidate (her husband is now in some deep-sleep clinic in Switzerland), an ageing and distinguished judge who is a member of the Brazilian Academy (this is modelled exactly on the French Academy and no women allowed!), and an intelligent and amusing newspaper editor.

Next day another session with As Pioneiras and then cocktails with members of the North American community. Very, very tiresome. It's as if they have no eyes. For them Brazil is nothing but a series of smells—all unpleasant! One encounter, however, amused me. A tall fellow, who liked talking, told me he had gone overseas in World War I with an Alberta regiment. I said my father had gone overseas in World War I with an Alberta regiment. But the man didn't listen. He said he had fought with the 50th Battalion. I said my father had fought with the 50th Battalion. Still he didn't listen. Then he said, "I had a wonderful colonel. His name was Page." I said, "I had a wonderful father. His name was Page," whereupon he did a double-take and said, "Would you be embarrassed if I kissed you?" Well....

August 4

On Friday, dinner with Helena. An incredible evening. The only other experience here that compares with it was that first *fazenda* outside São Paulo.

Helena's house is large. The seating arrangement, laid out on cards in the hall, showed four round tables with eight people at each. In the living-room were four of the most beautiful eighteenth-century paintings. They nearly covered the four walls and appeared more like tapestries than paintings in their size and the softness of their colours. The artist, a Chinese who had been influenced by Watteau, painted quite lovely trees, each leaf separate. Helena discovered them last year in a castle in France and simply bought them! The room in some way—a Brazilian way, perhaps—was perfect. We drank champagne and I talked Portuguese until my head split. The atmosphere was unlike anything I have seen before—a certain formality and dignity coupled with tremendous warmth and spontaneity. This was professional Brazil: a leading woman novelist, asked by Vargas to go as ambassador to Spain; a noted criminologist and his wife; an ex-president—Doutra; a famous chest surgeon, etc., etc. An enchanting young guest played a guitar after dinner—folk songs of Brazil. A particularly haunting one had romantic lyrics about *favela* life—how the sun shining through the holes in the roof made stars on the floor—and "my man walks careless among the stars at his feet".

Outside, the floodlit garden. There, as if under a black dome, every conceivable kind of leaf—green with white stripes or white splotches; green with red; pure red the colour of blood; of all shapes, all sizes; and anthuria—miniature white ones, large patent-leather pink ones, deep red ones, shining from the depths of Rousseau's green.

This seems to me what life *should* be like and as if something in me has always known it—just as one knows, before one has ever been in love, what love is like.

Asked A. on the way home what he thought of Helena, whom he had not met before. He said, "She has perfect taste in everything, including her four daughters-in-law."

The following evening we went, in a party—our hostess in a Dior evening dress of yellow satin, looking astonishing with her flat Indian face and immense mouth (a tigress, A. says, and I'm sure she is)—to the annual sweepstake dinner dance at the Copacabana Hotel. It is held every year, the night before the great race. The evening began at ten, when we had drinks as guests of the Jockey Club, and then on to the enormous hotel dining-room and samba-ing on the tiny dance floor of blue and gold glass squares, lighted from beneath.

And today, Sunday, the great race, the men in grey toppers and we in our finery. The day was beautiful and the strange mountains stood clear as stage cut-outs for all Rio to parade in front of in varying degrees of best dress. Such hats! Never knew there were such shapes!

The house continues on its immensely complicated course. One thing is solved and another raises its head. But for all that, I adore it here and hope the Conservatives don't decide that somebody else would like the post; they so easily mightn't. I am one of the few diplomat wives who do. Most get swamped with the problems. Heaven knows, I do too, but some indefinable element in the air gives me a happiness I have never known before.

August 13

Today, suddenly, it is very hot and I am searching out a thin dress to wear to luncheon—seven Canadians, two local and five visiting firemen.

I still don't feel very well. Must have had a kind of grippe. Would prefer to be left alone. Have spent some time in bed, quite pleasurably, reading Henry James and Trollope and Simone de Beauvoir. Yesterday I bought some ochre gouache and a large brush and now I can make my white paper cream. Tried to draw a clump of bamboos yesterday but they look strangely like giraffes.

On Sunday A. took me for a drive and we followed the sea and took photographs. I await with considerable eagerness the arrival of the colour film, for now that A. has a new camera, I shall appropriate his old one and take the beautiful patterns of *brise-soleils* and vegetation and haunt the *feiras* (markets) with their colourful stalls—the underwear stalls blowing with pink satin bras; those that look decorated with strung popcorn which on closer inspection turns out to be lace; those selling multicoloured hammocks and baskets—nothing you really want when you see it close up, but from a distance it looks gay and pretty. And then the more ordinary stalls selling staples—rice and black beans carefully displayed in striped sacks, the tops folded neatly back. And the fruit and vegetables, like harvest festivals.

August 14

A wild Rio wind in the night shook the house as if it were a matchbox and the *pau mulatos*, tall, slim trees covered with smooth bright ochre bark and minus branches until near the top, are shedding their bright ochre and standing there in green, as vivid as the grass. They slip out of their old skin almost all of a piece, like a snake.

August 15

A very good party here last night—among others: Maria Martins and the Mindlins—he an architect and she an engraver. Maria asked me to show her my drawings and was high in her praise of them. She said she would organize a show for me and when I said, "Oh no!" she thought that I was shy about showing here and said, "All right, I'll organize one for you in Paris." Crazy woman. She urged me not to take lessons, just to follow my own direction—which, at the moment, is drawing *everything I see.*

The evening went well. All the guests interesting and a group of people, luckily, who liked each other and had something to say to each other. (New to a place, one can't always be sure. My great fear is to seat ex-husbands beside their ex-wives!)

They are so warm, Brazilians—touch you, flatter you, kiss you, love you. Forget you next day, of course. But while they are with you they are whole-hearted. This rather suits me. It frees you from having to know them for ever just because you've enjoyed their company once. I think I could like most people—really like them—if I felt I never had to see them again. At any rate, I greatly enjoyed talking to Maria. Her head is full of poetry and, like the *pau mulato,* she has clearly shed many skins over the years.

August 17

Two beautiful *cestas* today from guests of the other night. One I drew—and, daring, used some colour. Unfortunately muddied up the drawing by filling too large an area with an imperfectly saturated nib. The other is beyond me—a straw hat, the brim folded up on two sides, packed with orchids no bigger than your thumbnail—yellow mottled with pinkish mauve. (If I have changed my mind about *cestas* it is because not all have the flower-heads cut and wired in the manner of the first I received.)

We drove today up over the hills and through the *favela*, which should make any sensitive, decent person devote his life to social reform, but I'm afraid my initial reaction was one of fierce pleasure in its beauty. Turning a corner we saw a group of vividly dressed people standing against a great fortress of square gasoline tins painted every conceivable colour. Water, of course. And socially distressing. But my eye operates separately from my heart or head—or at least in advance of them—and I saw, first, the beauty.

Following the beach, the great roaring green waves rising and smashing, the roadside edged with a low-lying palmlike plant which is putting forth small ears of golden corn, we came finally to Bandeirantes (Explorers') beach, where a high conical rock joins the sea to the sand and a disreputable-looking inn is located. But I love the inn, straight out of a rather sordid short story, and its round tower and tile roof and untidy paling fence, and the herds of munching goats and the sheep that tried to eat our picnic basket.

In front of the inn, two men were involved in what appeared to be a minute survey. One, black, dressed in a spotless pith helmet and white shirt, carried a knife with a blade long enough to disembowel you. The other, white, pant-legs tucked into ankle-high boots, made his calculations beneath a violet beach umbrella. Drugstore cowboys riding delicate little motor scooters arrived by the half dozen, wearing lilac and yellow shorts. And a dusky *brasileira* in a linen suit of so bright an orange that it almost hurt your eyes walked along holding the hand of her sweetie, whose pale green slacks made her the ripest orange on the tree.

Following an irrigation ditch on our return brought us to new ground—flat, market-garden country where canals covered with green scum ran past small shanties. Some large black birds flapped about in a rather sinister fashion—their uncommonly long spatula-shaped tails made them clumsy on the ground and their short, curved black beaks made them look vicious. On a tree in the distance some even larger birds appeared like pendulous black fruit as they sat motionless among the leaves. From the nearest shanty an elderly and very dignified woman and a little girl of about seven walked down to the irrigation ditch, squatted on their haunches, and began their laundry. Farther down, two men in large straw hats were fishing with a circular purse-net. As they pulled it in empty, one called out to us good-naturedly, "*De nada.*"

We crossed the ditch and drove up towards the hills into what might have been New Guinea. Bananas and market gardens growing beets, corn, and swedes. Densely populated and densely overgrown with trumpet plants and bougainvillea; a wonderful nameless plant we have in the garden with vivid scarlet flowers which are as silky and fine as poppies but hang forever asleep from their green calyx; and the crimson flowers that grow on a high bush and look like rosettes made by children out of crêpe paper. (In our garden at this moment there is a wild plant from the *mato* which puts forth a white lily at the end of twigs like old man's thumbs; the flower is as chaste as a Rossetti woman and dies almost as you look at it. And the red banana-flower, heavy as male genitals.)

The houses in this area are mainly of wattle and their gardens, like those in New Guinea, are cleared of all vegetation but trees and sizeable shrubs, the hard-packed earth swept as if it were a floor. Perhaps to keep poisonous insects away. We watched as vegetables were packed into baskets and loaded onto *burros,* or into cases covered with banana leaves to await the coming of the truck. We saw the truck farther up the road, painted with a myriad of stars like the ceremonial saddlery of cowboys.

Home by the beach road again—the pounding sea on one side, the lagoon on the other, and an evening mist giving the impression that spume illuminated the dark land. Earlier it had been bathed in a smoky blue, translucent and luminous. I grow to love Brazil more each day—even the wide flat corner with some rather awful houses and no vegetation but grass cover. That to me, now, is so like a Portinari painting that I greet it with a special kind of eye. In fact, I think much of my pleasure is a literary pleasure. Had I read nothing and seen no pictures, what *would* I see?

The frogs are beginning again tonight and the marmosets are back in the breadfruit tree.

How do I write my love song? It is as if I were wired and someone (Someone?) had a finger on the buzzer all the time. *Can* one fall in love with a country?

August 18

Luncheon today with the Nabucos—a handsome, aquiline couple who might almost be brother and sister—he a cousin, I think, of Ambassador Nabuco. Their house, in the heart of Rio—a high heart, for it's up a steep hill from the centre of the city—is an old coffee *fazenda*. It overlooks the bay and has a vast garden, a swimming-pool, and a guest-house.

Portinari has painted the dark-eyed family. We were shown, with pride, the first Portinari they commissioned—the Sacred Heart, which hangs in a golden frame. In their dining-room are three enormous murals of Brazilian fauna—monkeys, parrots, anteaters.

The party was entirely family—dozens of young people—girls with immense eyes and young men with brandy snifters. Highly baroque mirrors with frames of gilt and mirror "tears" let in, like eyelet embroidery. In the library, the books are all bound in gorgeous leathers. We ate Bahíana food—ground rice cooked to look like snow, fish with shrimps and blistering hot sauce full of tiny peppers.

This morning I drew the jacko tree—attacked it like a crazy woman to get it onto paper before we went out. It's not very good but I shall do it again. And I shall buy a full range of gouaches and see what happens.

August 19

This wild Rio wind is tearing at the house again. Last night it blew and blew and blew. Blew through my dreams. Awakened as if I had been tossed about all night.

It dropped in the morning and I drew with Helena, after lunch, in her garden. Did a view of the *lagoa,* mountains and palms and apartment blocks visible through an opening in the trees. And then I looked through a ravine and saw a tile-roofed house with shutters and banana trees and a jacko towering overhead. Helena's style is quite different from mine—curlier. Her house and grounds still astonish me with their beauty.

Reading the letters of Robert Louis Stevenson. What a darling he was. How extraordinary of him to set off for the South Seas with his wife and stepson and mother when, at any moment, a haemorrhage could have ended his life. And what a life in Samoa! It would suit me fine. Every day a new vegetation for my constantly hungry eyes.

August 21

Last night dinner with the British—a Commonwealth party and what a deadly bunch we are! I feared it might be dull so wore my most marvellous dress with train, and as much green eye-shadow as I could get away with, to cheer myself up. Was amused—albeit sadly—by the young Pakistani wife who has been here two months. She said that when she says to her maid, "Madelina, make the beds now," Madelina replies, *"Depois."* "Madelina, *por favor*, clean the kitchen," and Madelina replies, *"Depois."* "I don't know what is this word *depois* and have to wait until my husband comes home to learn it means 'later'." She drags the word out in such a funny way—*dee-poy-is*— making it sound so sad.

Started out this morning with Helena. She was full of confusion and concern—we must go to São Antônio's Church to draw because she owed São Antônio money. She had lost her diamond clip and had promised him a lot of money if he found it. Later, when she discovered the clip on a dress, a friend had told her that as it hadn't been lost after all, she no longer needed to give the money. But might this not be São Antônio's way of showing her that she hadn't been giving enough to the poor? She must go at once, today, before she forgot. But first, could I drive her to her dentist, as she had broken a tooth.

It was terribly hot, even at nine—the air coming in through open windows was like a furnace—but the sun was shining and the day beautiful. We parked the car outside the Teatro Municipal and, acting against all previous plans, went straight to São Antônio's. It's an exquisite church with a simple, putty-coloured façade, plain except for the lovely curlicues on the towers and the stonework around the windows. Inside we stayed only long enough for Helena to drop to her knees, scattering drawing blocks, paints, a folding chair.

São Antônio himself wore a halo of baguettes of mirror. Through a room like a formal drawing-room, with floorboards a foot wide and dark with years of polishing, jacaranda doors, and a white ceiling with simple mouldings of burnished gold leaf, we entered the chapel. Pure gold—every inch—every half inch. Dazzling. It reminded me of the day when I was a child and my father stopped the car and asked me to go and get some information from a man working in a field. When he opened his mouth to reply, it was as if he had the sun in his mouth—uppers and lowers of gold. That mouthful of gold is the only thing comparable to the excess—but in this case the beautiful excess—of this chapel.

Standing on the black and white marble squares outside, we overlooked a clutter of roofs moving in a dozen different directions—high gables, low gables, wide gables, narrow gables—all red tile. Spent two hours drawing like someone demented. Helena draws with great sensitivity. She drew the façade of São Antônio's with its curlicues delicately, elegantly—rather the way she writes.

Then through the crowds to the dentist, sambas blaring and the whole world light-hearted. One particularly light-hearted fellow above us dropped a paper cone full of coffee which landed, bang, on my head, point first, before spilling its contents over my dress.

Ended the morning at a shop that sells paints. I bought some gouaches. On reaching home I put some dirty red paint on all those tiles and felt very content.

Bedtime. My first day of paint. As well as the aforementioned dirty red on the tiles, I have added putty colour to the façades and laid a thin and mimsy sky. There is now a pale ochre wash on the jack-fruit and the house is pink. I like these gouaches. The colours are vivid, they mix easily and are what you will—transparent or opaque. But I am overwhelmed. I hardly have time enough to draw. How will I have time enough to paint?

August 23

Yesterday I painted in the morning and worked with As Pioneiras all afternoon. On the way back, Helena and I stopped to collect her cousins—two women who are daughters of the ex-president. They are in the process of decorating a house they have just built. It is right in the heart of Rio—pale blue plaster with red tile roof. The banisters on their inside stairs, taken from their old family house, might be by Wedgwood. What I liked best was the back of the house—all glass, modern glass—which overlooks a flagstone court, a small garden full of anthuria and *comigo ninguém pode* (literally, "with me nobody can"), and towering white windowless walls—the sustaining walls, I suppose, of houses on a higher level.

August 27

The other night I was talking about São Antônio's Church with a Brazilian, and he told me that São Antônio has the rank of colonel in the Brazilian army and that one of the Brothers goes monthly to the paymaster to collect his pay. They made him a corporal a long time ago, in a moment of great military need, and he did so well that he was promoted to sergeant. Since then he has gradually worked his way up. It is this kind of behaviour that makes me love these people.

We spent last weekend in Teresôpolis. The drive up was beautiful—over two heights of hills with strange trees beginning to flower. One with blobs of yellow sherbet on its boughs—no leaves. The really healthy ones were a cloud of lemon sherbet. Incredibly lovely. *Ipê* by name. But the trees I liked best were altogether more cart-horsey and put forth isolated white flowers—more a collection of white stamens—against soot-black boughs. I'd have loved to draw *them*.

August 28

Drawing with Helena in her dream garden. Words cannot describe it, which is perhaps why I draw. Anthuria ranging from white to deep red, those great red rockets bursting out of banana-like leaves; an *ipê* in full flood of yellow, its flowers seen middle distance like yellow hydrangeas. Against a blue sky it is unbelievable.

Helena says, among other things, that the Brazilian woman lives always in the shadow of her husband. And as lunch time drew near she bore this out, becoming anxious, eyeing her watch to make sure she would not be late. Her husband is a handsome man, a hunter, and his cages are full of birds whose calls he can imitate exactly. "Good eating," he says.

August 31

Sunday, and the last day of a wonderful month. I have painted all day. Began by doing the grand piano with the chandelier over it. Last night did a long view of the dining-room with chandelier, and the other day I did the chandelier alone. I love the chandelier! Then a series of abstractions—more exciting than realism. Realism I do very fast and am only excited when I finish and see how accurately I have drawn. It always surprises me. But in an abstraction, I can hardly breathe. And it is much slower—each line coming from a long distance. This evening listened to the *Messiah* with great pleasure and drew A. extended on the sofa.

Yesterday was a bad day on the whole—though nothing more serious than frustrations. I tried to get into the city for more paint, and ran out of gas in the busiest section of Rio when the traffic was at its height. Also we acquired a Welsh terrier, Duque (pronounced Dooky), who hates everyone but Graciano, the *mordomo*, and follows him like a shadow. He is a grown dog who belonged to some Canadians who left. They say he is a good watchdog, and he is quite sweet, but to operate only at the end of an imaginary string attached to the *mordomo* is not very engaging for anyone but the *mordomo*.

September 1

The dog, who has been almost ugly in his unhappiness, really began to look handsome today when A. and I took him in the car and then for a walk. When we returned, he thanked us most gratefully and looked happy. Poor fellow, how confused and frightened and heart-broken he must have been.

We climbed in search of the Gloria Church up winding cobblestone streets, the houses tight against the cobblestones. Such colour even without sun—Portuguese blue and rose and yellow and green. But we passed a gate where stood the dog with "eyes as big as saucers". I have never seen such a dog. Barely recovered from the sight of him, when we passed the back gate of the same house and there was a dog with "eyes as big as millstones". I didn't have the necessary checked apron and my knees fairly turned to water. But we passed without mishap.

September 3

Social note: have never met a Negro at a party.

Social notes on politeness, Brazilian style: 1) when I said to Helena that I thought I would refuse an invitation from a woman I wasn't keen on getting to know, she replied, "Oh, no, Pat. Be nice to her. Say that *of course* you'll go. And don't." 2) when I asked her if she was going to work at her charity that week, she replied, "But of course. Do you think I treat my charity the way I treat my social engagements? If, at the last moment, I don't feel like going to a dinner, I send a telegram and don't go. But my charity is a commitment."

Drew with Helena again yesterday. Not a good day for me. It was wildly windy and we had to have a sheltered place to work and it was not until we were about to leave that I found what I wanted to draw—then drew so quickly that everything went wrong. I like the subject so much that today I tried to copy it, but the act of copying bored me and I had to stop. Went up into the *mato* instead and drew the banana-flower—pink and tender with its tiny bananas hardly more than misplaced stamens. The enchanting weed *Maria sem vergonha* covered the *mato* floor with its innocent, wide-petalled single flowers which vary in colour through all shades of red and pink—startling colours, almost fluorescent. And flying among them, a black butterfly with patches of fluorescent pink on his dark wings. Many fireflies in the garden last night, and the blacksmith frog striking his anvil. By day the mock whippoorwill calling over and over, and the lovely bird of the *mato* who whistles as if he almost can't—like a child who is learning.

September 13

So much is not getting into my journal because we've been too busy with the visit of the Paraguayan president, and a house guest— the Canadian ambassador to Venezuela—who is en route to meetings in Argentina.

Every palm tree pushes an enormous flower like a tropical bird out through its tightly plaited leaf-stalks. The travellers' palm has a flower almost as large as mine. (Interesting confusion! Do I really think of my head as a flower? But why not?)

September 16

Much excitement the other night. Real-life drama!

Initially, at dinner, it was no different from any other Sunday night at home. The house quiet, a few frogs beginning to tune up in the garden, punctilious Paulo serving our meal. Then the dog began barking in the *copa*, and when I asked Paulo what was upsetting Duque, he replied calmly that it was because there was a man out there. It was said with such sang-froid that it never occurred to either of us that it was anyone but a friend of one of the servants. The meal went solemnly on.

We had just reached the dessert stage when piercing female screams reached us from downstairs. It sounded like rape or murder. A. and I were downstairs in a flash and on arrival in the servants' dining-room found Fâtima, the upstairs maid, and Cecília, the assistant cook, still screaming. It was some time before we could get a coherent story out of them but, reconstructed, it goes like this:

Homero, one of the cleaners, was off duty and in his room above the garage when he heard a car door slam. Thinking it was Nildo, the chauffeur, he went out onto his veranda to speak to him. To his surprise he saw a Negro he had never seen before, dressed in nothing but cutoffs and carrying a knife. Recognizing a *ladrão* (robber), Homero retreated to his room and carefully locked the shutters but he kept his eye to a crack and watched as the *ladrão* crossed to the house and entered by the servants' entrance. Homero, cautious, waited a while in his room before deciding to go over to the kitchen. There he encountered Cecília in the process of dishing up our dinner. He asked Cecília what had become of the *ladrão*, but as Cecília had not seen him she thought Homero was joking and they carried on a bit—yes, there was a *ladrão*, no, there wasn't, yes, no, yes, no—before Homero continued bravely up the back stairs to phone the police. Arriving in the *copa* what should Homero find but the *ladrão* himself carrying on a conversation with Paulo. The conversation is reported to have gone thus:

> Paulo: Good evening, sir.
> Robber: Good evening.
> Paulo: What do you want, sir?
> Robber: I want to speak to the lady of the house.
> Paulo: The lady of the house is at dinner.

As this went on, Paulo was coolly arranging the dishes for the next course.

When Homero dialed the police the robber decided to make off but his only escape was down through the servants' dining-room, and there Cecília and Fâtima were quick-witted enough to lock him in.

Apparently the *ladrão* had entered the house as described by Homero, passed the kitchen, and gone up the back stairs to the third floor without encountering Cecília or Paulo. Fâtima, who had been preparing our rooms for the night, met the robber on the stairs as she was on her way back to the kitchen and drove him ahead of her. On arrival in the *copa* this time, he bumped into Paulo and they conversed as reported above, Fâtima continuing on down. So she and Cecília were ready for him when he finally descended, and while they were rejoicing over having caught the poor naked fellow, he pulled the heavy table over to a high window. And escaped.

A. in pursuit, ran into the black garden—at the back the *mato,* in front a dark world of shrubs—but of course there was no way of finding him.

After an hour the police arrived—pure musical comedy! They took endless notes, made a meticulous search of the grounds, and returned to report that "*infelizmente ele fugiu*" (unhappily, he has fled). Cigars, thanks, and as much talk reconstructing, remaking the event, as there had been silence during it. Talk, talk and laughter—relief and plain mirth.

I asked Paulo why he had not told us what was going on when he met the *ladrão* in the *copa* and he replied, serious and respectful, that he had thought we should not be disturbed at dinner!

September 20

Drew with Helena as usual Tuesday. We went to Nossa Senhora da Glória, an eighteenth-century chapel on a hill and flanked by imperial palms. Plain outside, quite extraordinarily unadorned. Inside, lace curtains at the entrance to the chapel proper; a ceiling which might have been painted by a *naif*; Portuguese tiles. The wood of the altar and pulpit the colour of cinnamon and beautifully carved. Why does it almost reduce me to tears?

Outside, behind a glass shell, Nossa Senhora herself, carved from white marble, her feet among the heads of a dozen cherubim, and looking for all the world like one of the Charleses. Absurd long curls!

We had an interesting luncheon last week at the home of Jorge Grey, a prominent surgeon. He is divorced, attractive, and lives in one of the oldest houses in Rio—rectangular, pink, with intricate wrought-iron grilles and almost as much vegetation as Sleeping Beauty. Inside, high-ceilinged rooms, beautiful Brazilian furniture— some of it gold-leafed and looking as if it had come from a sacristy, which it probably had. Many paintings by Portinari and di Cavalcanti. One of the Portinaris was wonderful—a night scene of small figures dressed in white against a dark ground. So tiny, mankind, but lighted on life's dark hill. Little sparks.

We leave tomorrow, Friday, for São Paulo and the Bienal. Paintings from all over the world. I'm told the Ben Nicholsons alone are worth the plane fare.

September 24

The Bienal was extraordinary. The Palace of Arts, designed by Niemeyer—which we had seen from the outside, *and* disliked, on our previous visit—was even worse from within. In the violent rainstorm which heralded the opening, the building was like a glass hangar in which one felt little protection from the elements. In one area the aluminum shutters had been badly damaged by a recent hailstorm and could no longer be opened. As the hail had also penetrated the roof and flooded the building, the electricity was affected too and no lights could be turned on in the shuttered section—luckily not the exhibition space.

In the two-hour wait for the president to arrive and the ceremonies to begin, we met and spoke to Alfred Barr from the Museum of Modern Art in New York, who was here as a member of the jury. A very nice man—quiet and without self-importance. He told us how much he liked the Canadian exhibit—judged it conservative but good!

Kubitschek, the president, with his bright-eyed clown's face, Jânio Quadros, governor of São Paulo, carved from a broom handle, and porcine Ademar, mayor of the city, sat at the head table with Matarozzo, the wealthy industrialist whose money makes the Bienal possible. As Harold Town had won a prize and A. was receiving it for him, we sat in the front row of seats—a really dangerous place because of the surging mob between us and the head table through which photographers pushed their way back and forth. No path was kept clear for the prize-winners and it was well-nigh impossible to hear their names called, for the crowd—like most Brazilian crowds— was there mainly for the fun of it (*is* there another reason?) and had little interest in who received prizes and even less in listening to speeches. How A. managed to hear Town's name called or how he made it through the throng to the head table and back, I don't know. But he did.

Formalities over, we began our tour of the show, beginning with the Canadian exhibit. Exhibiting were Town—our prize-winner; Jean-Paul Lemieux—friend of Jean and Jori Palardy, whose *Nun* we have in our study in Rio; and Takao Tanabe, a west-coast Japanese Canadian. Town's dreamy abstractions I liked. But I was utterly unprepared for the beautiful but badly hung Lemieux—a series of long, low-key paintings of the St. Lawrence lowlands. Almost nothing more than a horizontal line—sky above, ground below. One winter scene—grey above white—echoed with the lonely everlasting whiteness of a Canadian winter, exotic in this tropical land. From another summer-evening study of the same landscape—greyish above olive drab—emanated the great quietness of evening settling on a countryside without trees, people, or animals. A third, entitled *The Maritime Express,* was similar to the winter scene, but like a small black cinder in the distance one saw the train's engine, head on. There was nothing else to evoke the train but its tracks which, wide at the front of the canvas, conveyed a great distance between us and the train. You could almost hear the train whistle faint and eerie in all that space. It *is* a horizontal country, of course. Just as Emily Carr's is vertical.

On the whole I was disappointed with our exhibit. France had seen fit to send an entire room of Chagalls as part of their entry. The U.K. sent the immense Ben Nicholson show. Italy a large Giorgio Morandi exhibit which, incidentally, won the grand prize. (One can't help wondering if it was political.) The U.S. had, as well as an exceptionally well displayed and well handled exhibition of five contemporary painters, a whole room of Jackson Pollocks. I think we should have done better. This is an important international show. Our Eskimo sculpture looked disappointingly like the discards from the Montreal Handicrafts Show; very little variety of subject. Our architectural display might as well not have been sent: small photographs which were almost invisible beside the striking blow-ups from other countries. Our theatre arts display, however, *was* good. We were the only country to have sent actual props and costumes rather than sketches or photographs. And although Tanya Moiseiwitsch's costumes were conventional, they were elaborate, rich and beautiful.

After a slap-happy luncheon we returned to the show. One should never spend so much time on concrete floors or trying to take everything in. Crazy!

We began with Brazil's largest contribution—the Segall exhibit. Lasar Segall, a latecomer to Brazil, was born in Lithuania and studied in Germany, and his work shows a strong influence of the German expressionists. At his death a little over a month ago, he was mourned as a much-admired and much-loved naturalized son. This exhibition is in the nature of a memorial and it is very fine. A compassionate social critic, he stunningly portrays rural Brazil, painting cows and stunted peasant figures in muted colours as if the uncut jewels of Brazil—topazes, aquamarines, amethysts, tourmalines—had taken over his palette.

The Morandis—so beautiful, and profound individually—became too many, too small, too grey, and too similar. Gazing at bottle after bottle after bottle after bottle blinds you to the delicacies and subtleties of his work. Quantity does not become quality. Rather, the reverse is true. The Ben Nicholsons are clean and salty. Colour lovely. His geometry is a bit too antiseptic for me and his problems too intellectual but on the whole he was as good as a trip to the sea. Lots of ozone. The Chagalls, larger than I had dreamed from reproductions, are full of a zany poetry of shocks and horrors. I love his disregard for the laws of physics. The Pollocks impressive, vigorous, emotional. But after too many of *them,* one begins to wonder, even worry. What is it Lawrence said of Clifford Chatterley?—that he didn't have a real heart to begin with—only a lot of talk and feeling which were no good to anybody. The German exhibit was enormous, and was it there— how dreadful to see a show this way!—that we saw the pictures constructed from various meshes of wire: chicken wire, mosquito screening, etc.? Also rectangles of darned sacking. A high degree of inventiveness but an almost total lack of inspiration. I find it difficult, too, to respond to what appears to be a glacial deposit exhibited as sculpture. A. insists abstraction is an inability to face reality. It may be. But the oyster can't either.

Back here in Rio the house is a hospital. *Asiática* on the rampage. I do my rounds like a head nurse—Vitamin C for all, thermometers and fruit juice for the ailing. "Don't make me take the pills, Madammy!" Luzinha the laundress implores. "I want the sickness, Madammy. I have never been sick." Ricardo, in bed in the gatehouse, looked gravely ill. The doctor has removed him to hospital. "You don't want to go to hospital like Ricardo." Luzinha's face is ecstatic. "Oh, Madammy...!"

Will we get off to Minas Gerais, as planned?

-1957-

Our little river is suddenly a river of blood. Unaccountable and extraordinary.

The swallows are here. We can't keep them out of the house. They fly in and out the bedroom and bathroom windows before we are awake. Looking for a place to nest, they talk it over between themselves perched on the tops of doors—arguing, rejecting.

"... *one of the* cestas *sent to us for July 1st.*"

...e main reception room—a great, cold, white-walled, green-ceilinged room...."

"High gables, low gables, wide gables, narrow gables...."

"I like these gouaches. The colours are vivid...."

"Flowers on every table . . . ."

...he reception was held at Itamarity....

around the pool, tables with scarlet tablecloths and candles."

My bedroom: "The black tropical night is tangible and close."

ent Easter on an island near Angra dos Reis...."

"The stairs, built from some nameless wood golden as amber...."

October 8

My worst fears about the *asiática* were groundless. We *did* manage to get off to Minas Gerais (General Mines. Imagine Ontario being so named!) Left on Sept. 29th. And now we are back. Flew to the new capital of the state, Belo Horizonte (Beautiful Horizon), population 550,000—270 miles north of Rio—in a Convair. The hotel, also new—indeed what is old in so young a city?—is modern with the kind of ugliness to be found in Australia. Hard to understand in Brazil, where there has been a long tradition of beauty.

Hanging out the window next morning, we could see an immense double avenue stretching off into the distance, its central mall shaded by two long lines of tall trees clipped like box hedges. How? From helicopters? Skyscrapers towered above us and others clambered up, almost before our eyes—their lovely, intricate, variously coloured *brise-soleils* stippling and striping the city. The air is pure Calgary, bright as glass, and the residential districts full of new bungalows also suggest western Canada. But there is more use of colour than in any Canadian equivalent, and certainly I don't associate mosaic murals with the prairies!

The city's site is a great saucer (altitude 2,700 feet) surrounded by hills and low mountains. Sixty years ago it was a cattle ranch. The state's contribution to Brazil's national income is second only to São Paulo, for it produces almost all the country's iron ore and gold and ranks either second or third among the states as a producer of pig iron, steel, coffee, cattle, sugar-cane, citrus fruits, and bananas. The Mineiros are known as the Scots of Brazil and they are convinced that Belo Horizonte, because of their state's enormous natural resources, is destined to become one of Brazil's greatest cities.

In the morning A. called on the governor and inspected the troops in front of the governor's Palácio da Liberdade and I called on his wife, Dona Queridinha—literally, Little Darling. The palace interior is like a Hollywood set for a Middle-European costume drama. Troops lined red-carpeted stairways and foyers. I was ushered into the Sala das Jóias (Room of the Jewels) where Dona Queridinha awaited me. She is between fifty and sixty, not very beautiful, plump, dark, with crooked teeth—and a little darling! I told her how much I admired the rows of *palmitos* lining the driveway to the palace. That made her laugh, as the word is *palmeiras*. The *palmito* is the Brazilian asparagus or heart of palm.

In the afternoon, while A. continued with officialdom, I was driven to Sabará, a small nearby town where gold was once mined. The road was hilly, the earth red. Masses of bananas and palms—a landscape of feather dusters. Roofs red, of course, their tiles made from the soil. How I love this homogenization—if that is the word—and the red/green contrast! The little town is charming. Full of flat-faced bungalows tight together.

Our first church, Nossa Senhora de Conceição, built about 1710, was to me the most beautiful of all the churches we have so far seen here. Its interior has a kind of innocence about it. Rather as if a little girl had said, "Maybe I'll make a church," and so had painted the things she loved—a bunch of flowers, a ladder ending in a cloud, a sunflower. Simple and full of grace. The sunflower more like a sun-worshipper's symbol than a Catholic's, but Brazilian Catholics probably *are* sun-worshippers. In this church I saw my first black Nossa Senhora—and swallows flying in and out as if they were darning the threadbare air.

Our next church, Nossa Senhora do Carmo, contained early carvings by Aleijadinho (The Little Cripple). Born Antônio Francisco Lisboa in 1738, the son of a Portuguese master-builder and a Negro slave, he is said to have been a small, ill-made *mulato* who lost both hands—perhaps to leprosy. No record seems clear. What *is* clear is that, chisel strapped to wrist, he produced works of extraordinary sensitivity and strength. Here we saw two of his large gilded figures and, holding up columns, two brightly painted statues of Atlas. Some of his most beautiful carvings appear over church doors—lovely baroque scroll-work and the heads of cherubim. But the work for which he is most famous we saw only on the last lap of our journey, in Congonhas do Campo. There, outside the Santuário da Nossa Senhora Bom Jesus de Matozinhos—a traditional Portuguese twin-towered church, its façade putty-coloured, its double doors Portuguese blue—stood Aleijadinho's twelve apostles, life-size, carved from soapstone.

Due to a series of infuriating delays, we arrived just as the light was going—and light in the tropics goes with a rush, almost a crash, as the sun drops below the horizon. From the distance the figures appeared like a pageant. Close up, all—interestingly—have the same features but different expressions, different clothing, different postures. Quite beautiful, not only individually but as a group—as many groups, spread out over the wide area of the steps leading up to the height of land on which the church is situated. Not easy to handle so many figures and have them compose and recompose as the viewer moves. As we walked among them, it was almost as if *they* walked, their now-dark silhouettes shifting and turning eerily as the light was sucked over the western horizon. Meanwhile church bells unlike any I have ever heard—not ringing or chiming, just banging like pots and pans knocked together in a complicated rhythm—filled the near-dark with their astonishing cacophony.

How easily one jumps to generalizations! Even accepting the fact that one cannot know Brazilians on the basis of knowing a few, I find I continue to assume that I do. Why, otherwise, was I so surprised by the people we met in Belo Horizonte? My mental picture of Brazilian women perfect as jewels, smart as Parisiennes, was badly damaged when, at the governor's banquet, I met twenty Brazilian women—fat, frumpy, and full of imperfections. Like bourgeois Belgian or Dutch. But all charming.

The dining-room—and indeed the whole palace—was baroque, every inch frescoed and carved. Decorating the table were wonderful dried flowers and pods from the *mato*. The meal was poor—dreadful champagne, with the rims of the glasses dipped in crystallized sugar that cut your lips. Yet after dinner, when additional guests arrived, traditional *doces* were served, pretty as ballerinas, looking like tulle and tasting delicious.

Home about 11.30, very sober and very tired, but touched, rather, by Governor Bias Fortez's speech at dinner, in which he spoke of the good relations between Canada and Brazil and the similarity of the problems which confront the two countries. He said that Brazil was trying to achieve economic emancipation and industrial self-sufficiency, and that there was no better road to follow than that which had been so successfully pioneered by Canada. He also referred to the contribution of Canadian capital and technical skills invaluable to the development of their country.

More unexpected, perhaps, was Mayor Celso Melo de Azevedo's speech at his luncheon the following day in which he described the Canadians as an American people who, by reason of their adherence to the Commonwealth, constituted a significant link between the New World and the Old. He also eulogized the manner in which Canadians of Anglo-Saxon and French descent had achieved political unity while respecting each others' cultural characteristics. The resulting "unity with diversity" was an achievement much admired by Brazilians.

Off in a single-engine plane in the morning for Itabira, about sixty miles away, to visit a high-grade hematite mine. Itabira is a 300-year-old former gold town which now has a population of five thousand odd, dependent solely on iron ore.

Were met at the airport by what looked to me like—what? I hardly know. *Not* like a Brazilian. (Generalizations again!) A heavy-set blond man in a pith helmet. He was the engineer in charge of the mine and a very nice fellow. He drove us to the great red-purple mountain of iron where they take out only the high-grade ore—68 to 69 per cent—which can be converted directly into steel.

We lunched in a sun-filled valley at the company guest-house, a simple and attractive building surrounded by an old-fashioned garden with lizards and annuals. Lunching with us were our two pilots, un-uniformed as bank clerks, our military aide, hanging with tassels and gongs, and Vince Chapin, our Commercial First Secretary. Such food! Three meat courses: first chicken in a kind of stew; then a Mineiran dish of sausage and *feijão* (black beans) with finely shredded *couve mineira* (a lettuce-coloured cabbage); then *bife* with vegetables. And two desserts to follow! Why are they not all enormous?

Walked about in the garden and saw the *jabuticaba* tree, whose fruits, when ripe, resemble stemless black cherries growing in clusters directly from the trunk of the tree. A funny effect, almost as if the tree were diseased. The fruit is delicious but, like the flower-apple of Quebec, it lasts only a day. I learned the name of the very beautiful leaf we have in the garden in Rio—an oval leaf about a foot long with alternating bands of dark and light green, like watered silk. It is simply called *pena de pavão* (peacock-feather). Also the strange tree with the large silver-appearing leaves that I so admire is called the *imbaúba*—pronounced "imba-ooba".

The real surprise of the trip is my disillusionment with Niemeyer. With the exception of the buildings in São Paulo, I have seen his work only from the outside or—more abstractly—as architectural drawings. Either way, one is impressed. But on closer acquaintance some of the magic evaporates. For instance, one of his schools in Belo Horizonte consists of three buildings. They are unorthodox and pleasant to the eye until you realize they represent a ruler, a piece of chalk, and an old-fashioned rocking blotter. Like building a house in the form of a lamb chop, a bed, and a bath! We didn't go into the school, and it may be fine inside, but I'm put off by the conceit. We did however go into another Niemeyer building—the Iate Clube (Yacht Club) at Pampulha—where we had a three-hour luncheon with the *prefeito* (mayor) and his wife. To be fair, I must mention that the club was designed for the shore of a lake, but two years ago the dam broke leaving it sitting on the rim of a dry saucer. For all that, from outside it is a pleasant, angular building, with bold horizontal lines held in balance by the vertical patterns of its *brise-soleil* and the skilful use of tiles. But as soon as you step onto its entrance ramp, which is far too steep, you sense something wrong, and as you enter the main clubroom you become uneasy at once, feel at odds with yourself. Have you a cinder in your eye? Lost the heel of your shoe? No. It's the shape of the space you are in. And it hurts.

Niemeyer was commissioned to design four buildings in Pampulha—the Iate Clube, a casino, a dance pavilion, and a church. They are quite distinct one from the other, but a strong, clean style made possible by the use of poured concrete unites them all. I liked the idea of the Casa do Baile being circular. Imagined it filled with waltzing couples, even though Brazilians probably never waltz. The Church of St. Francis, so highly controversial that it has never been consecrated, looks from the outside like Mrs. Quonset-hut joined to two little Quonsets on her right and one on her left. The day we were there its white roof reflected a sky as blue as the dome of the mosque at Isfahan. Its façade, all in one plane, is covered with an abstract blue-and-white mural by Portinari. Inside it is abysmally bleak; an untidy scaffolding supporting an already disintegrating roof, and rain stains on the walls, do nothing to help. Portinari's altar mural of a Christ with all the burdens of mankind on his shoulders is a fine if depressing work. Happily, at the sides of the church lively tile panels of fishes and birds honour Saint Francis. Thank you, Saint Francis.

In complete contrast to this modern church, already a ruin, was the British gold mine at Novo Lima—an old wreck of a mine still functioning, although inadequately, with what must be 150-year-old machinery. We had heard of this mine with its Casa Grande for visitors and, romantically, I had imagined the sort of place Gilberto Freyre wrote of, not this Victorian manor house in which we were entertained rather as if we were in England instead of the heart of Brazil. Remarkable, the British!

Next morning, after various formalities including a farewell call at the Governor's Palace and the inevitable *cafèzinho*, we set forth on the dusty road to Ouro Prêto, which, translated, means black gold. This small town, once the capital of Minas Gerais and now protected as a national monument, dates back to the early eighteenth century and the gold rush. Narrow cobblestone streets wind horizontally and vertically between colonial houses of honey and cinnamon colour with paprika-red roofs. Their façades are multiple-windowed with beautiful *bandeiras* or transoms. Proportions perfect—healing, almost—as if those early builders knew something we have forgotten. Baroque churches, usually twin-towered, many decorated by Aleijadinho, top most of the city's hills. "I will lift up mine eyes...."

Interestingly, in the midst of all this Niemeyer's very modern hotel—long and low, standing on *pilotis*—is, quite astonishingly, not incongruous beside the surrounding colonial architecture. In its colour and in its patterns of light and shade, it is a curious twentieth-century near-equivalence. Niemeyer has been remarkably sensitive to the hidden archetypes of baroque form. Yet—step inside the hotel and you are struck once again by what seems the consistent gracelessness and awkwardness of his use of interior space, markedly noticeable here because of the contrasting "golden" ratios of the insides of the churches. (They may well not be golden, but they give one such a sense of well-being they must be silver, at least.)

Our two-storey suite—the president's—differed from the others only in size. From its main floor sitting-room—with one wall of sliding glass doors opening onto a balcony—a circular staircase leads to the bedrooms. It is too narrow to ascend carrying a suitcase unless you bear it aloft in front of you like the traditional Christmas boar's head. The two bedrooms are without cupboards; all cupboards are in the sitting-room below! An incredible bathroom provides a shower minus cubicle or curtain, its nozzle sticking out of the wall above the lavatory. (Rare, in my experience, to need both at once.) The second floor is completed by a narrow gallery which overlooks the ground-floor room. One could blame much of the interior ugliness on decorators or the lack of them, but for the actual functional failure Niemeyer alone is to blame. He is evidently interested in form at the expense of people. Disaccommodating!

After an official luncheon, while A. and Vince toured a Canadian-owned aluminum plant in nearby Saramenha, I was taken on a tour of the city. Mainly churches. So much gold, such beautiful ceilings, so much imitation marble and fabulous silver. Interesting, this simulation of marble—originating, I suppose, in a place where there were no marble quarries and at a time when transporting it was excessively costly. Yet marble painters still exist, and simulated and real marble are used in many buildings today, including our official residence in its pre-Canadian incarnation.

Most wonderful of all the churches was Nossa Senhora do Carmo—its Aleijadinho carvings and the proportions of its sacristy alone elevated it to some place above the others, beautiful and gilded though they all are. And talking of gilt—was the building and gilding of churches by the owners of those early mines a means of expiating guilt? Or is this a typically twentieth-century question? Perhaps the baroque church was a joyous offering of gratitude to a benign and generous divinity.

It is splendid to imagine Ouro Prêto in the eighteenth century, when music sounded from its churches—the music of Handel, Boccherini, and Mozart as well as that of local musicians, of whom José Joaquim Emerico Lôbo de Mesquita was the reigning genius and whose works, according to my source, "bespeak an exceptional creative power". There were few organs in Ouro Prêto at that time, but there were string orchestras and singers and, to quote the same source, "a musical movement of unusual value developed, more intense than any other artistic manifestation of the time in the Western Hemisphere...all the work of free *mulatos* and Negroes."

The only non-church of our tour was the Museu da Inconfidência (Museum of Traitors). Once a prison, it is situated in the public square—itself a marvel of proportion and baroque detail. (In fact, it was just like the movie set I was going to find it had become the following morning.) But there was no time to loiter and look, for I was urged on by my hosts to see the museum, which housed magnificent church carvings and early jacaranda furniture. An entire room was devoted to one of the first martyrs of Brazilian independence— José Joaquim da Silva Xavier, nicknamed Tiradentes (Tooth Puller). In the late 1780s he and a group of young Mineiros, fired by the recent success of the American Revolution, made plans to overthrow the Portuguese government. But their plot was discovered and the conspirators were imprisoned or exiled—with the exception of Tiradentes who, as their leader, was hanged and quartered and had his head displayed on a stake in the square that today bears his name.

That evening, a truly Brazilian dinner—hours and hours and hours of it. I sat beside the *prefeito*, a scruffy little man who would have taken me to his bed then and there, given half a chance.

The next morning, while A. and Vince went to the School of Mines, I—armed with my camera and a morning to myself—dashed off to the square only to find I was immobilized by a movie crew shooting a film on Tiradentes. Infuriating! Store fronts were hung with birds in cages, donkeys were tied to hitching posts, excitement was in the air. But the script didn't call for a twentieth-century *gringa*. So I had to content myself with the buildings out of range of the cameras, where I bought a few small beige-and-grey pots made from the local soapstone—the same stone Aleijadinho used for much of his carving. And I managed one quick sketch after lunch, before we left for Congonhas and the twelve apostles—our last stop in Minas, on our way home.

October 25

Home seems peaceful enough on our return. But it is very hot, very humid. The kind of heat that wipes my mind like a damp sponge. I barely remember anything. Is this how amoebas feel?

We had a *gambá*—a sort of small opossum—in the house today. A baby. He had rather spiky fur, a naked ratlike tail, a slightly ratty face, and immense ears that glowed like mother-of-pearl. His voice was that of a Geiger counter. Was it his mother in the big trees last night, crashing about in the blackness?

All our lilies are out—white, yellow, orange, flame. Also the agapanthus—blue and white—and a tall tree with flame flowers and some orchid-coloured orchids. Quite beautiful.

November 3

Haven't been feeling quite normal for some time, and today managed to get to a doctor. He recommends an operation. I am so given to thinking physical difficulties are psychological that I am almost relieved. He says it is not urgent, so I shall be able to accompany A. to Rio Grande do Sul, later this month.

December 4

Spent just over a week in the states of Rio Grande do Sul and Santa Catarina.

Now we are back, I have seen the surgeon who is to operate on me. He suggests that I get it over before the worst of the heat sets in, and so I go into hospital next week. I shall just have time to do my Christmas shopping and, with any luck, write my notes on the trip.

It was on Sunday November 25th that A. and I set off by Convair for the land of the *gaúchos*. We arrived in Pôrto Alegre (Happy Port), the capital of Rio Grande do Sul, in the early evening. An immense, literal mural depicting the discovery and founding of the state adorns its airport. Pôrto Alegrenses express much happiness in it—as befits their name.

Rio Grande do Sul is known as "the frontier", being the most southerly state in Brazil and bordered by both Uruguay and Argentina. It is also known as "the granary", and well it might be; it is the leading producer of wheat, wool, tobacco, wine, *mate*, and coal, and ranks second in cattle, rice, corn, and potatoes.

Pôrto Alegre is a city of half a million people on the estuary of the River Guaíba, upstream from the head of the Lagôa dos Patos (Lagoon of Ducks)—the fresh-water lagoon that parallels the coast for a hundred and twenty miles before it finds outlet in the sea. Flanked by the flood plains of five rivers which converge on the estuary, "It looks like a swamp," A. said, his nose to the window of the descending aircraft. Certainly watery.

On Monday morning A. went about his official appointments, the first of which was to call on the governor, Ildo Meneghetti, in the Piritini Palace—which he described as "a magnificent edifice which might have been built by Napoleon for Josephine". I was free to wander about the city and I loved it. An untidy Belo Horizonte— older by a hundred and fifty years. Mixed ancient and modern. Wide avenues and narrow cobblestone alleys. Skyscrapers and colonial buildings. Merchants slung their wares outside their shops as if it were market day.

The people seemed taller than farther north, perhaps on account of their diet. After all, they eat wheat here. Or perhaps on account of their Portuguese, Spanish, German, and Italian origins. Or both. At any rate, the farther south, the taller the Brazilians.

At noon we joined a long cavalade of cars headed for an unfinished school near Viamão, fifteen miles east of the city, which was to have the word Canada added to its name in honour of our visit.

The governor and his wife led the procession. They were two of a kind—of Italian extraction, short, long-faced. She without style—a small shopkeeper's daughter. He a civil engineer of an unassuming, homespun quality, not unattractive. The Minister of Education, Ariosta Jaager, and his wife, were already old friends as they had met us at the airport the previous evening. (In fact, she had actually driven back from the airport to the hotel in the same car with me and two British wives who had apologized in loud voices and in her presence for the fact that "she" spoke no English!) There were many lesser dignitaries, teachers, and a number of male students. Like a sequence in an Italian movie, we trailed across fields to a college still under construction.

On entering the building the *chefe de cerimônia* fell into a hole in the floor and disappeared utterly. This development was hailed with good humour by all, including the rescued victim himself—who, however, walked with a limp thereafter.

When the entire entourage had assembled in the large, bare dining-room—a small deal table and one kitchen chair were its only furniture—Ministro Jaager spoke in eloquent terms of the Rio Grandenses' regard and respect for Canada and asked A. to inform his government that the government of Rio Grande do Sul, as a token of friendship, was naming the new school-to-be "Escola de Mestria Agricola Canadá" (School for Agricultural Mastery, Canada). Whereupon Governor Meneghetti sat down at the little table and signed the necessary decree. A. made an appropriate reply and, after a tour of the site and much desultory chat with staff and students, we trailed once again across open fields to our first *churrasco*. This is the *gaúcho* variant of the Australian chop picnic. Trestle tables had been set up under an enormous *figo* tree and nearby, on stakes over fire-filled trenches, great haunches of beef and lamb cooked and dried.

I was interested to see that most of the women drank whisky. This is unusual in Rio. The Rio Grandenses all carried special *churrasco* knives—long-bladed, sinister-looking weapons, their blades beautifully engraved with bulls and *gaúchos,* protected by ornately chased and engraved sheaths. Real movie *gaúchos,* tended the meat and bore it on its stake from the pit to our tables, where we cut hunks from it with our knives. They told us with pride that the animals had been killed only that morning. Indeed, you could taste the fur and hoofs— and the meat was hard and dry; in fact, my mouth only healed from that *churrasco* in time for the second which followed later at Pelotas. Potato salad was served with the meat, but it was the meat itself which was the feast. You just went on and on eating as your hosts insisted upon cutting you *their* idea of the most delicious bit.

The governor's lady, beside whom I sat, was very heavy going conversationally, replying to almost everything I said with a long-drawn-out "e-e-eh" which I have only just learned is another form of "yes". I have heard it often enough before but always thought it an exclamation, comparable to the so commonly heard "ai"—which has an agonized ring to it, as indeed it should have, being an expression of pain.

After lunch we were shown how to prepare *mate* or, more accurately, *chimarrão*—a green tea, high in caffeine. (*Mate* is the powdered leaf, *chimarrão* the finished drink.) A *cuia*, or hollow gourd, is packed like a pipe with the fine green powder, then placed on its side so the *mate* lies along the bottom. A small amount of cold water from the *gaúcho*'s kettle is added and when that has been fully absorbed the *cuia* is filled with boiling water. The *chimarrão* is drunk directly from the *cuia* through a *bomba* or wooden straw with a silver mouth-piece and a large, finely perforated end-piece which allows the liquid to be drawn up minus "tea leaves". This equipment is usually simple but, like the *churrasco* knives, it is sometimes silver-encrusted and elaborately engraved.

I couldn't help being suspicious about the *gaúchos*. Surely they are dusted off and brought out for visitors—so dashing in their black hats with upturned brims, bright shirts and kerchiefs, soft, thin, baggy pants, and short riding boots, the uppers of which are folded concertina-fashion; *churrasco* knives in their belts and *cuias* in their hands. We were later to discover that *gaúchos* really do wear this clothing. When mounted they also use a leather apron over one thigh—a protection against the lariat—and in bad weather they don a *poncho*, a wonderful garment which is simply a rectangular blanket with a hole in the centre for the head to go through.

When A. departed with the governor to call on local dignitaries, I was whisked off in a car—with the governor's wife, a librarian, a teacher of mathematics, and one other—to be shown Pôrto Alegre. It was hot. I was placed in the back seat in the centre. I was not asked if I wanted a bathroom—which I did, or if I could see—which I couldn't. Once in the car the governor's wife made up for her long silence at lunch and talked non-stop—that formless, subjectless kind of conversation about cousins and who married whom and who had babies and whose house that is and what they paid for it. It was as if she had been dammed a very long time and now all the words rushed out, dragging me down with them, drowning me.

I was taken to the shore of the great lagoon, the entire circumference of which has been subdivided; here and there what might be called "sumptuous mansions" were clustered together incongruously in the middle of open and still uncultivated country. The good modern architecture which we saw in Belo Horizonte seemed not to exist here, and traditional Spanish or Portuguese styles were not in evidence either.

I had not expected to see A. until dinner, as he had a press conference after his calls, so I was somewhat surprised when he arrived a few minutes after the hour for which the conference had been called. In the rather surrealist manner of many things Brazilian, the official in charge had arranged for the room for the conference, right enough, but he had completely overlooked notifying the press. (The following day this order was to be reversed!)

At 7.30 we were received by the British consul, who might have been a model for Lowry's consul. It was a good party. I was amused to be approached by an Englishman with a rather professorial face who hurled questions at me: How do you start to write a poem? Do you make up words? Do you like your own work? Would you, in a field all by yourself, say your own lines aloud?

Fábrica Renner, one of Brazil's largest factories, which we visited the following morning, provides a crèche, cafeteria, and co-op food stores for its employees. It is what A. calls "a vertically integrated plant"—that is, it starts by processing raw wool and flax, and among its end products are men's and women's clothing. I must say that since I have seen linen thread being made by the seemingly endless process of wetting and stretching the dry stems of flax, I understand why linen is so expensive a material. Clothing is only one in a long list of end products this factory produces: leather, steel rod and pipe, cans, stoves, sewing machines, paints, varnishes, boots, shoes, and chinaware.

Renner himself was large, young, and expansive. Like the figures in the mural at the airport—like, I suppose, the typical Rio Grandense—inches taller than Brazilians in the north. I, in fact, could be a *gaúcha*. Only need to speak better Portuguese.

We also visited Varig's chief maintenance base for all South America. Before the war Varig was the Brazilian subsidiary of Lufthansa. Today, Brazilian-owned, it bears some of the efficiency of German organization, and flies the Buenos Aires–New York route as well as extensive domestic flights.

In the afternoon I was entertained by the Pan-American Round Table, which consisted of fifteen women, each representing a Pan-American country. Asked to speak to them about Canada, I did the best I could in halting Portuguese. Unlike most Brazilian women I have met, they were all working women—teachers of art, ballet, or mathematics; lawyers, painters, writers. They gave me an orchid as large as my head.

That night we went to the Governor's Palace—immense, built around a courtyard, and still in the process of construction. The governor and his wife don't live there—not because it is unfinished but because, as he said quite frankly, "If you live in the palace you have to entertain friends of the palace, and when your governorship is over you have no friends of your own. Whereas if you live in your own house you can entertain your own friends."

I had expected the provincialism of Belo Horizonte in Pôrto Alegre, but when I was ushered into the large salon where the women sat in their usual circle, I could have believed it was a court scene. Such skirts, such hairdos! Such gloves! Elaborate and extraordinary. Dior not in it.

Then the governor took us on a tour of the palace, through the empty and rather garish bedrooms and finally to the ceremonial rooms which were covered—ceilings and walls—with frescoes by the same Italian whose mural had greeted us at the airport. Their subject matter: a Rio Grandense legend dating from slave days, of a Negro boy who allowed his master's favourite horse to escape. When the master discovered his loss, he beat the boy and threw his body on an ant-hill to die. Shortly thereafter, in the middle of the night, he heard a knocking on his door and there to haunt him was the small black slave, mounted on the missing horse.

At that party we met the wife of the military aide assigned to A. during our stay in the state. An enormous young woman, taller than I, of German extraction. Brunhilde herself, with a round face, large liquid brown eyes, and an expression of great sweetness. Despite her enormous bosom and even more enormous hips, she was beautiful. She told me that she came from Pelotas, a small town which we shall be visiting, and that the same artist who had done the frescoes in the palace had decorated the cathedral in Pelotas, using her as a model for some of the angels..."But I was much thinner then!" She also told me that she had two children and a foundling. The bell had rung one night four years ago and there, on the step, was a three-week-old baby, so ill and starved that it was past crying. By the time she had nursed it back to health it was not only part of the family, but someone quite special among them. She smiled as if she were relating a miracle. I don't think a foundling could have picked a better door-step. In her home town a few days later, we learned that she had been Miss Pelotas 1949.

On Wednesday we drove eighty miles north to Caxias, through steep green ranges where the bellbirds sing. I use the Australian name. Here they are called *ferreiros* (blacksmiths), with good reason. Their song is exactly like the ring of metal. Hard to believe they are birds.

As we drove we caught glimpses of German settlements and Novo Hamburgo, which spills picturesquely over the foothills of the Serra do Mar into a carefully tilled valley—complete with Lutheran church!—might have been a town in the middle Rhine.

Caxias (pronounced Cash-ee-us) is of Italian origin and has a population of 40,000. It keeps going on grapes and a determination to establish industries, despite inadequate power and poor access to raw materials.

There we were met by the mayor and his wife and heaven knows how many public officials and taken to a social club for luncheon. I was presented with a large bunch of roses glistening with plastic and we ate through interminable courses and listened to interminable speeches.

After lunch, a quick tour of the city and a thorough tour of a metal-working plant—an almost unbelievable rabbit warren with Heath Robinson machinery which produces twenty thousand different metal objects. (How could there be twenty thousand different metal objects? Doubting my own notes, I checked with A. I was wrong, as I had expected, but *not* as I had expected: he says they make twenty-*two* thousand metal objects. Well!) We watched curtain hooks being born, and thumbtacks and tea sets and swords and spurs. And we walked miles and miles and miles—a great party of us, with someone always lost.

Next morning, accompanied by the military aide and his vast and gently smiling wife, we flew to Pelotas—there to be guests of the manager of a British meat-packing firm, Anglo Frigorífico, a subsidiary of Vestey's. We had been told that our host mightn't meet us as he was minus his teeth. But there he was, *sans* teeth and *avec* a rather frightened-looking wife, and the mayor.

Pelotas is a port city of 90,000, a hundred and thirty air miles south of Pôrto Alegre, situated on the Lagoa. It is as bare of vegetation as the heart of Rome. But there the comparison ends. It is a flat city and its pale arrowroot-coloured houses, dating from an earlier period, were blinding in the morning sun. Remarkably, the company guesthouse where we were to stay was right beside the abattoir. Luckily it was also on the river, and boats were tied up at a wharf immediately outside our door, which made it both interesting and noisy.

After A.'s round of official calls, we all met at the cathedral, of which the Pelotans are very proud. It was much like modern Catholic architecture the world over, except that it had Miss Pelotas 1949 on the ceiling as a number of angels. We were entertained by the priests in their reception room and drank—unconsecrated communion wine, I suppose. It was sweet and as hot as the day. Our British hosts were astonished by everything. They had lived there twenty years as if on the point of returning "home", and so had taken little interest in the local people or sights. The manager's wife, in fact, spoke hardly a word of Portuguese, and when she and the aide's wife and I were together, I had to interpret. They informed us that they had arranged a reception for us in the club, to meet the local English colony, but, they added apologetically, the *prefeito* had got wind of it and was insisting upon coming and bringing other Brazilians with him, "and there is nothing we can do about it". Later we learned that the governor had specifically asked the *prefeito* to look after us.

For luncheon we drove off into space over hot, red, dusty roads, across plateau country that grew greener and greener, to a *churrasco* offered by the owner of one of the district's largest rice and cattle *estâncias*. Already the language was changing; It was no longer a *fazenda*. Proximity to the border introduced a different accent and many Spanish words.

The house itself, surrounded by shade trees and set down—bung!—in the midst of that glorious green country, was neither old nor beautiful. Our host, a small, wiry man, introduced us to what I supposed was his wife—an immense woman who looked as if she had been made out of two overstuffed, flesh-coloured chesterfields. I was appalled and intrigued as I tried to figure out how many metres of material she would need for a simple frock. Miss Pelotas 1949 whispered in my ear, "It alarms me to see her. I feel I am looking at my own future." We were led into a back room swarming with women and children. A large table in the centre was covered with hors d'oeuvres which, in turn, were covered with a thick black blanket of flies. We had a warm drink and I endeavoured to make conversation in Portuguese with the people nearby and then, mercifully, we all trailed out—close to a hundred of us—to a clearing in a eucalypt wood, sweet-smelling, capacious. Sunlight dappled the long trestle tables, bright with coloured wrapping paper in place of tablecloths. Brazilian wrapping paper is yellow or cerise or jade-green as a rule—never brown.

Once again the women were separated from the men and seated together. Once again *gaúchos* carted the great sides of meat about from guest to guest, and once again we were told with pride that the sheep and cows had been killed for us that very morning. It makes sense, of course, in tropics where meat can go bad quickly, but it did nothing to increase my hunger. It was quite impossible to tell lamb from beef. Neither tasted of either, or both tasted of both—a new "on the hoof" taste that I wanted no part of.

After the *churrasco* we returned to the house for *sobremesa* (dessert)—on this occasion, those mouth-watering sweets made from freshly grated coconut, coconut milk, and eggs. A great Brazilian dish.

Then off to see the bulls, or *reprodutores*, as they are so specifically called. *Touro* is bull, *reprodutor* is breeding bull. Obviously designed for one purpose only. Their tiny feet looked as if crammed into high-heeled shoes too small for them. Colourful *gaúchos* led them from their barns and posed with them against a background of prairie so green that, had I seen it in a colour photo, I'd have put it down to some odd quality in the film.

Finally, a too-sweet *cafèzinho* before returning across miles of red dust roads to the house by the abattoir. We slept that afternoon, A. and I, stark naked on single beds in separate rooms. On waking I discovered that my uncurtained window was overlooked by the path to the front door.

That evening, during the reception at the social club, I learned a good deal about the company that was entertaining us. An English company with worldwide holdings, it originated in Brazil as a producer of *charque* (dried meat), and has since expanded to process refrigerated meat, frozen meat, and canned goods. The manager told me that the president, who lives in England, would sell at the drop of a hat if he could sell it all at once. When I asked why, he said, "Because of the ill will against the English in Brazil." And when I asked if the answer might be to gradually make it a Brazilian company, his answer showed me all too clearly the possible source of the ill will: "Not enough brains or energy in this country to run the show."

It's odd that such a high percentage of people from the U.K. have this attitude to Brazilians. Not only to be found among people from the U.K., of course. We have, in the Canadian office, a stenographer who in a recent conversation said that when she arrived she thought Brazilians "awful. Why, I thought they weren't fit to know. They were so ignorant they couldn't even speak English. Why...I thought they weren't even...white. But," she went on, "I find I was very narrow-minded. Why, now I'll even dance with a Brazilian." Later in the conversation, she forgot her broad-mindedness and said, "I'm surprised you aren't going home for your operation. You, and your family too, I bet, must be very frightened by the thought of a Brazilian hospital." Prejudice dies hard indeed.

Next day, Friday, we flew from Pelotas to Bagé—an hour away by plane and only forty miles from the Uruguayan frontier—a pampas city of 40,000 where a cattle buyer from the meat company met us. His wife joined us later—a pretty girl in a bad temper. Their house, bungalow-style, was beautifully situated in a large, colourful garden on the edge of rolling country. The air was filled with birdsong. Rufous ovenbirds darted low across our path. On arrival we stood about awkwardly in a rather ugly living-room and were joined by a Brazilian couple—neighbours and friends of our hosts—whom they afterwards apologized for, saying that there were so few English in the community that they had been forced to make friends with Brazilians.

Our host drove us to a nearby *estância,* through lovely, open, sunny country. *Gaúchos*, splendid on horseback, went about their business. And birds. Cardinals with red heads only; tiny, brilliant red birds called *sangue de boi* (ox blood); *emas* (emus) like rag mops; fields of plovers, egrets, and all kinds of waders—the most spectacular being the *colheireiro* (spoonbill), popularly known as the *ajajá ajajá*. It is a large, flamingo-pink bird with, as its name suggests, a wide, spoon-shaped bill.

When we arrived at the *estância*—spacious, beautifully kept, planted with many trees, and owned by an ancient, childless man— we discovered that preparations had been made for our arrival at ten. It was now twelve. The manager had gone home and the girl in charge had washed her hair—and us out of it, presumably. A large Canadian silkscreen of Canada geese greeted us inside (gift of Jean Désy, a previous Canadian ambassador), and while the Brazilian friend of our host tore off at a fabulous rate across the country to retrieve the manager, I sat on a swing in the garden in the sun, listening to the myriad small sounds of summer, for the moment without responsibility—not even the responsibility of having to talk.

Then the manager came. Ah, what a *gaúcho*! An enormous belt! An enormous knife! Thin, baggy pants, almost oriental; accordion-pleated boots; black hair, black eyes. Such teeth! A true movie-star *gaúcho*. With him as guide we clambered up ramps and looked at sheep, some as white and pretty as Mary's little lamb. More interesting to me, the grove of tall eucalypts in which there were vast nests—surely belonging to storks. But no, these were communal nests built by the *caturritas*—a species of green parakeet.

In the afternoon, when the men went off to an Agricultural Station, I asked if I might press some clothes. My hostess looked slightly chilled and asked if her girl could not do it for me. I replied that I was sure her girl had plenty to do without that. (They were having a buffet supper for forty that evening.) She then asked if I could manage a flat-iron. This was my first introduction to difficulties in this part of Brazil. Interesting and eye-opening. In a small back room I struggled with two flat-irons which were heated by a spirit lamp. It was a monstrously hot day and the flat-irons—if hot enough to iron—sent such heat through my hand that I could barely endure it. Cooler, they wouldn't iron. I finished just in time to have something to change into for tea, where I met the only two Englishwomen in the community—elderly, hard-bitten, and immensely likeable, despite astonishing nineteenth-century biases.

The first to arrive—large-bosomed, slim-hipped, untidy steel-wool hair, slip showing—had lively brown eyes, an attractive slow voice, and a curiously girlish quality. Her movements conjured her up as she must have been at eighteen, leaping off a horse or twirling a tennis racket and giving the boys a provocative glance. The second, older, in a halo of soft white hair and a lace blouse, looked frail. "Don't kiss me, I've got a cold," she said to the first who replied, "You've *always* got something." "No, I *haven't!*" protested the second. "You know very well I've not had a trace of asthma or bronchitis or anything for months—not since the operation. It was the baby upset me. He cried so much."

I later learned that some months ago this woman—wife of an Australian who had gone to Bagé as a boy, got a corner on ox-tongues, and made a fortune—had been operated on by the local doctor, a brilliant French surgeon "doomed to live out his life in this small town because of his unfortunate marriage". While performing some kind of abdominal operation, he had—without so much as a by-your-leave—performed at the same time a very new operation for asthma: that of grafting a fresh placenta onto the asthma sufferer. She claimed she knew nothing about it until she remarked some time afterwards how odd it was that she had no trace of asthma.

Much that the two women said was outside my frame of reference. Their principal subject, however, was Brazil, or more specifically Bagé, which they claimed to hate. The tongue magnate's wife said that she would leave it in a minute. I asked, "Could you?" And she replied, "Of course not. Our bread and butter is here." I said that I didn't mean financially and her friend said, "Don't be silly. Of course you couldn't. It would be like moving an old tree." But they both agreed that they hated it, that Brazilians hated them, and that their servants, whom they preferred to be without, loathed them. "Do you think they really do?" I asked. "My servants are often lazy, unwilling, thieving, but for all that I don't feel it's because of any particular animosity to me." "Ah," they chorused, "but yours aren't Rio Grandenses. Rio Grandenses are different."

Santa Catarina, on the sea coast and adjoining Rio Grande do Sul on the north, is a small state, on the Brazilian scale, but still the size of Portugal. Mainly rural, its principal primary products are wheat, manioc, oranges, sugar, tobacco, rice, *mate*, and corn, as well as the timber and coal to cook them with. We saw none of this as we did no more than visit the capital, Florianópolis. (What a floral metropolis of a name!)

The road from the airport to the city followed the sea and reminded me, in some ways, of the north shore of the St. Lawrence, east of Quebec City—villages straggling along a strip between mountains and water. But this was tropics—bananas and large-leaved plants and black people. And as we had arrived on a saint's day, there were decorations and processions and little boats in the sea gigged up with coloured bunting and pennants.

Florianópolis itself was like a series of Dufys. Old. Narrow-streeted. A great pink President's Palace. An old *praça* full of lovely shade trees covered with tree orchids. The little streets jammed with people just standing talking. The endless good-natured talk talk of Brazilians. No skyscrapers. No modern buildings.

An Englishman, local manager of a communications company, took us home with him to tea. Poor fellow, he was very defensive— about having a Brazilian wife who spoke no English, about living in a slum, about being manager in Florianópolis, about being hard up, about having no servants.

His house, half-way up a mountain, surrounded by *favela*-like shacks, was a wretched establishment, poorly furnished by his company; and he had done little to improve it. But it did have two advantages: an absolutely superb view and—because it was on a point of land—it caught one or other of the two prevailing winds. It also had disadvantages—including the considerable one of being practically inaccessible during the wet. (When we arrived the wet was well over, but the roads had been so washed out by rain that it was impossible to get a car to the house.)

His wife, too anxious to please, was like a little giggling girl. She produced a formidable tea—giant cakes, sandwiches which a deplorably dirty child from one of the neighbouring shacks had been engaged to serve. She too giggled, did everything wrong, giggled some more, while he squirmed in paroxysms of anxiety.

Until a year earlier, when they moved from Rio to Florianópolis, she had had servants and been surrounded by family. Now, deprived of both, living virtually alone in a house on a hill, doing her own work—something none but the poorest Brazilians do—she was isolated and lonely. The Brazilian women in the community spoke of her with compassion.

He told us he had fled England as a young man because he had three sisters, all more intelligent and better at sports than he.

Obviously he had sought a woman who would see him as a superman, and this he had found in his gentle, childlike wife.

He said they were so hungry for English-speaking people that they planned to spend every waking minute with us. And so they did. Poor fellow. He wanted to talk—talk, not listen. He wanted someone to tell things to—his theories and his likes and dislikes, even the likes and dislikes he had held at age seventeen! And we were able to listen, to give him some brief companionship. But whatever we had to offer was not what she needed, and my heart went out to her.

The following morning A. was scheduled to call on the governor—Jorge Lacerda—an ex-newspaper man of Greek origin, from Rio. There was to be a ceremony in the *praça* outside the palace, with guards of honour, bands, etc. I arrived at the *praça* early to get a good vantage point with my camera. Already a mob of people was waiting. One old woman asked me if I knew what was happening and I told her that the Canadian ambassador was going to call on the governor. She became very excited about that, claimed she had read something in the paper about it but couldn't remember what she had read, and wanted to know if he had come that very moment from Canada especially to call on the governor. Then she asked me if I was an Argentinian and when I said no, a Canadian, she was positively overwhelmed by the coincidence.

At this point Charles Butterworth, our consul in São Paulo, who was accompanying us, came thrusting through the crowd in a great hurry and announced that I was to be part of the show too and that the governor's wife, with a group of ladies, was waiting for me in the palace *now*. I rushed back to the hotel and managed—in the drenching heat and in two minutes flat—to change into something suitable to the occasion. I then discovered that we were all to be part of the public procession. A. was to inspect the guard of honour, with its captain, and then lead off; I was to follow behind with the English manager of the communications company; and Charles was to take up the rear. Thus we were to walk up the main street from the *praça* to the palace. Who choreographed this, I have no idea.

I didn't dare look at my old friend in the crowd—the whole thing was so absurd, I feared I might get the giggles—but I could see her out of the corner of my eye, and hoped it gave her added pleasure to see me. The crowd clapped as we passed—strangely unnerving. And then, as A. drew level with the Brazilian flag, I saw him turn to it and bow. I quickly asked my partner if we should do the same. He replied that, no, only ambassadors bowed. But as we drew inexorably nearer to it, I muttered that I too planned to bow—which I did, whereupon he gave a little short bob that was somehow hilariously funny and nearly the end of me. He had no more idea than I what was appropriate. (Afterwards, I asked A. about the flag. He said he didn't know what one should do, but as he could not get to his feet to acknowledge it, because he was already on his feet, and as he could not remove his hat, because his hat was already in his hand, and as he felt the flag should not just be ignored, he had decided on the spur of the moment to bow!)

We finally arrived at the palace—its interior painted with the traditional imitation marble—and ascended red-carpeted stairs to where the governor, straight out of the soda fountains of my Calgary childhood, and his black-eyed wife, waited with a sea of hangers-on. A. and I were received on opposite sides of the same room, A. surrounded by a circle of men all drinking champagne, I surrounded by a circle of women all drinking *guaraná* —Brazilian-style cola.

In the middle of it all, the press arrived for a conference and one single-minded radio man—even as A. stood cheek by jowl with the governor—began with, "What do you think of the governor?" "*Ele é muito simpático*," A. replied, as the governor stood by.

After further exchanges of courtesies we were taken for a drive to see the city. A lovely drive. All along the beautiful coast—tumbling, tangling vegetation, sweeping beaches, little islands, and great smooth round stones in the sea, rather like the Devil's Marbles in Australia. The perfect place to find a simple house and have a holiday.

In the afternoon we went to a lace factory. Interesting to see enormous black machines going clank-clank and turning out fragile white webs—lace by the yard for brides, long strips for trimming, eyelet embroidery. The contrast no greater, I suppose, than that of the spider and its web.

Dinner with the governor in the official residence—a large, new, not particularly beautiful house. We were told that, with the exception of one carpet, everything in it—crystal, sheets, pictures, silverware—had been made in the state of Santa Catarina. I regret to say I can believe it. But I cannot reconcile it with the governor—can't make sense of him at all. Before going into politics, he was editor of the literary section of a Rio paper. He is well read in English,

French, and German as well as Portuguese. He claims to have been responsible for the first Portuguese translations of the Duino Elegies. Said he commissioned them and ran them in his paper. From his conversation at dinner—which was far from easy, as he is a reluctant conversationalist—he appeared to be well informed and to have good taste in literature. He is a great admirer of Rilke and Lorca. After dinner he showed us his files of the paper and it looked interesting. He also showed us his collection of Skira art books. Yet about the house he pointed to ghastly ashtrays of kittens perched on the edges of their eating bowls, crude amateur paintings, and—as if proudly—announced that they were all made in the state. What could one reply?

He wasted no smallest opportunity to get publicity from our visit. The dinner was broadcast from beginning to end—along with the governor's speech and A.'s reply.

This is the first governor I have met with whom I have any interests in common and yet he was the first whom I found really veiled. Although he spoke good English, I spoke Portuguese to him, and he told me it was gracious of me to allow him to appear at his most articulate—but for some reason it sounded less like appreciation than criticism of my Portuguese. All in all, a very strange man.

December 6

Home again and in bed with a heavy cold. Not surprising, really, considering the crash trip, but very ill-timed in view of the fact that I am due in hospital in three days.

December 9

Saw the surgeon yesterday to ask if he could operate when I have this cold. He was doubtful but, for many reasons, suggested that I go to hospital as planned, and that I take intensive anti-cold treatment in the hope of reducing my fever and clearing my head.

So here I am, in a very nice bedroom/bathroom suite, with veranda overlooking the Sugar Loaf. Am having Vitamin C injections twice a day and infra-red treatments four times a day and hoping for the best.

December 27

Well, it is over—the operation, that is—and I am back in my own bed and grateful that, if I had to go through this, it was in such ideal conditions.

I felt remarkably like Gulliver in the land of the Lilliputians when I was wheeled into the operating room and put on the table, for I was immediately surrounded by a horde of small men in white (most Brazilians are short) who went at me with needles and elastic bands. I couldn't help being amused by the thought, during my last conscious moments. How remarkable the return to consciousness—one is a living organism and that is about all. So still. Do amoebas feel like this?

On the floor I was on, there were four nurses who rotated: one Brazilian, one German, one Latvian, and one Scottish. Working with them were four *ajudantes*—two Brazilians and two Portuguese—Sylvana, Aurora, Piedade, and Antonia. With the exception of Aurora, they had all worked in the hospital for more than fifteen years, and they were marvellous. The nurses said they were quite capable of running the floor, and I can believe it. But most wonderful was the love they gave with their service. They evidently knew that when ill, one becomes a child again, and so they gave the uncomplicated and simple affection a nanny gives her charge—along with praise for the simplest achievements—never coming or going without a caress of some sort. I swear it was better than all the medicine in the world. The same was true of the surgeon, who sat on my bed, held my hand, and generally made me feel human.

Also—and remarkably—when I came out of the operating room all vestiges of my cold were gone. Perhaps, like the doctor in Bagé, my surgeon is skilled in placental grafts.

The heat has begun in real earnest again—the steam-bath variety. I'm not minding it too much, largely because I am doing almost nothing. The child of one of the servants is staying here for the Christmas holidays and she is a perfect convalescence present for me. We sit together on the patio and draw, or take slow walks in the garden—two children, really, for my Portuguese is just about at her level. It is all like a wonderful dream. Very beautiful, very static—a painting, perhaps.

January 9

Nearly finished *The Brothers Karamazov*. For all that it is meant to be his masterpiece, I prefer *Crime and Punishment*. The kind of madness he portrays seems to be a direct forerunner of Kafka's surrealism.

I've managed to get coloured inks for my felt pens. Have been experimenting. A. says they are very limiting as they don't really mix. But so—if it comes to that—is an entire range of colour. It's a matter of learning how to work within these limits to create an illusion.

January 12

Very hot with that utterly motionless heat—like being immersed in hot water.

Employed a new upstairs maid, an *arrumadeira*—what a wonderful word. A room-adera. But that isn't what it means. *Arrumar* is "to put in order". I hope she is good. The house feels uneasy and will probably collapse when we go on our holidays next week. If only our highly paid head servant were more intelligent! He put all our gramophone records out in the midday sun the other day in case they had mildew. The results were ruinous. How can one anticipate such caring stupidity? Could I have thought of saying, "Graciano, never spread the gramophone records on the terrace in the sun"?

January 13

Nature note: I've only just discovered the "some enchanted evening" bird is the *tico-tico*—the little sparrow-like fellow with the striped black-and-white head who sings the opening notes of the above song in a tiny voice and who, poor chap, raises cowbirds. (And surely I have my genders mixed.)

It is very hot. Duque, despite the excellent brushcut I gave him with the hair scissors, finds it terrible. This is really no climate for a dog. Nor for us, come to that! Both of us look forward to getting off next week for Poços and cooler air.

"Bandeirantes beach, where a high, conical rock joins the sea to the sand...."

January 21

After one false start, one four o'clock rising, and a two-hour flight, we arrived in Poços de Caldas the day before yesterday in time for breakfast. This famous spa in the state of Minas Gerais, though small, has forty hotels. It is a Brazilian, as opposed to tourist, summer resort. We now know what Brazilians like.

Our hotel is old, not very comfortable, and overlooks a beautiful park in the centre of the town. Nearby streets are filled with small horses—two-toned pacers—with brilliant yellow, orange, and red dyed sheepskins over the saddles. Starting before 7.30 in the morning, Brazilians of all ages and sizes ride up and down the streets. The Brazilian equestrian is quite a sight: slacks (toreador chiefly), open-toed shoes, no bra, is fairly uniform for the women; the men in baseball caps. The little town is full, too, of every conceivable type of conveyance—small horse-pulled go-carts in which you can squeeze tight between your sweetie and the driver; smaller go-carts pulled by goats or sheep, in which tiny Brazilians in pink organdy, with bright jewels in their pierced ears, trot by with the same serene and blissful expressions on their faces that you see on the faces of the adults drawn by horses. Sometimes the goats and sheep go full out and their miniature drivers, whip in hand, rush screaming past. It is as if the Brazilians' dearest wish is to sit in a buggy and be drawn.

Sunday evening the park became a real circus. The fountain—a mere basin by day—shot a changing kaleidoscope of coloured waters into the black night. Loudspeakers filled the air with music and the entire populace stood in mute admiration of the wonders before it—breathless children before a birthday cake.

The hotel is full of families—the women with their tiny waists and large behinds in toreador pants; mothers and fathers immense in their folds of fat; their little children tended by white-starched *babás*. At night the scene changes and the grotesque women—the younger ones, at least—look pretty again in their dresses, black-eyed above their fabulous pearls.

It is easy to see why the older ones are fat, and difficult to understand why the younger ones aren't too. The meals are extraordinary beyond measure. Literally beyond measure. Our first experience was lunch. We floundered about pretty much, not knowing foods by their Brazilian names on the menu, and not understanding what the dishes were as described by our waiter. What we thought was an hors d'oeuvre plate turned out to be cold cuts—ham, roast beef, bologna, sausage, etc.—with a salad of cucumber, beets, tomatoes, lettuce, and potatoes. Having ordered it as an appetizer, we found it more than enough for lunch. Unbidden, it was followed by soup, then an immense dish of pork, garlic sausage, black beans, and vegetables, *then* by steak and fried potatoes, and *then* by dessert. Needless to say, we could not stay the courses. But the Brazilians around us—oh, I forgot a dish of spaghetti between the soup and pork!—ate it all, and not small helpings either—plates piled high.

Have spent the better part of our two days here prowling about and exploring. It feels half-way between a toy rodeo and a midway. The surrounding country is bare and hilly and not very beautiful, and as far as we can make out, most of the visitors are interested mainly in the waters. It is necessary to get a doctor's advice on which waters are suitable. It is also necessary to get a doctor's prescription to go into the only swimming-pool, which is some two kilometres distant. A. has already managed to get into the pool without a certificate, the man at the gate making an exception because it was Sunday. Very few people in the pool—a matter of money rather than health, I should think.

We were glad to discover last night that the special musical fountain is evidently a Sunday feature. Last night we had a band which streaked like neon lights up and down the dark avenues of my sleep. A man on a hill with a merry-go-round and other attractions brightens the black hours with a series of explosions. These, for some reason, are dear to the Brazilian's heart.

Went to the market yesterday and bought a bag full of the most wonderful mangoes and then joined a crowd on the street to watch a performing monkey. A dear little thing in a dress, doing back somersaults and straightening chairs as bidden, looking very worried much of the time but occasionally breaking into a real grin of pleasure.

At eight o'clock this morning a pair of lovers in the park had a small boy in tow, taking pictures of them embracing against the ornamentally cut hedge, embracing on a public bench, embracing with the hotel for backdrop—while tiny Brazilians were whipping their sheep and screaming joyfully as they tore across the cobbles.

Our hotel has, unfortunately, a series of handicaps: 1) a most perilous bed; 2) noise which is impossible to escape: music, loud-speakers, bands, screaming children never stop, from before one is awake until after one falls asleep; 3) a shower so slippery that I have had to change my habits and bathe instead—so un-Brazilian a custom that the hotel has no bath plugs and A. has had to whittle me one.

Poços itself has shortcomings too, from our point of view. First of all it is a town. In the beautiful park opposite one is not allowed to walk on the grass, let alone lie on it. There is nowhere—or we haven't found it yet—where we can swim, lie in the sun, and be lazy and untidy.

January 22

The rain continues. This morning, as we waited for it to abate enough to make a dash for the car, a man nearby said, *"Chuva!"*

> Me: *Muita chuva! Sempre tem chuva assim, aqui?*
> Man: *Tem chuvido todos os dias depois do dia quatorze. Americana?*
> Me: *Canadense.*
> Man (with a kind of moaning sigh): Much better!

Yesterday in the late afternoon we drove to a local lake. Not much more than a large pool with newly planted conifers on one bank. Their pattern is very pretty and geometrical—first the pattern of their planting, and then the new needles at the end of each branch, which make a linear design one would have to paint by light green horizontal lines over a dark green base. There was also another very spindly conifer, and onto the tallest and thinnest of these an immense bird landed and proceeded upon its most intimate toilet—searching under wing- and tail-feathers as the tree swooped earthward, bent almost double, sprang upward, and swayed again. The bird, I think, was a *bem-te-vi-do-campo* (a country I-see-you-well), but I had no binoculars, so can only guess.

Farther out, the country beyond the lake, though desolate and bleak, was a riot of wildflowers—one, remarkably like an Australian kangaroo paw, bright red and greenish yellow, I have solemnly painted as a specimen. I find I do it with the same facility I had as a child. Really think I could have been a botanical painter.

The continuing rain rather wet-blankets the spirit of this place. The young man with his camera outside his cardboard "flying machine" and no tourist face in the cockpit window looks pretty depressed. The wet, unridden riding horses await the unexpected burst of sun. The reins they use here are extremely decorative and pretty—rope woven of two colours, natural and brown, used sometimes with links of brass.

We spent a long time in the market today. Very attractive with the exception of the meat, which might well sicken the most determined carnivore. But the fruits and vegetables are lovely—stalls full of mangoes, *mamãos*, and *abacates* (avocados), great plaited strings of garlic and onions; stalls full of baskets of every shape and kind from the largest down to miniatures of each type. Toys—hand-made tops; a man who, when knocked, totters back and forth on the edge of a shelf "sawing", a whole collection of *tatús* (armadillos) very primitively made and one, armadillo-shaped, painted black with a human face. *"Um tipo de macaco,"* the man said, "A type of monkey." Monkey business, more like. There are great coils of tobacco like tarred rope and jars and bins full of beans of every colour—black, scarlet, white.

At that point, and eating one of the delicious mangoes, I broke the cap on a front tooth. Enquiries led us to a dentist able to see me at once. The waiting-room was nothing but the hallway at the top of a flight of stairs, equipped with some wooden barrel chairs—but I didn't wait. The dentist—tall, middle-aged, lean, and rather saturnine—ushered us both into his office. He went to work as gently as one could possibly wish, announced the tooth still firm, that I should have it recapped on returning to Rio, and that he, meanwhile, would do a temporary patch. This he did while conversing with A. about the bauxite in the region. When A. asked for a bill, he said, "My bill will be heavy. I want literature about your country." So we all shook hands, thanked each other, told each other how nice we were, and parted, well content. This is the sort of kindness that is overwhelming. He also, as I think no dentist has done since I was a child, showed me with the help of a hand mirror and a little tooth mirror what the patch looked like. I felt he should also have given me some quicksilver.

January 23

Bad weather continues. Yesterday torrential rains. We finally saw the doctor who issues certificates for swimming in the local pool—when and if the weather ever clears. As his nurse extracted three hundred *cruzeiros* from me before I had even seen him, I had visions of us being "taken". But no, indeed. He made out certificates for us both to go swimming and to take the waters, told us there were some Canadian engineers here if we would like to meet them, and bade us a warm goodbye. No examination, no nothing. It *is* a racket, of course, as we expected, and the doctors must make a killing, as no one can enter the baths without a certificate designating the type of bath to be taken, the temperature, and the length of the immersion. As for the pool, your certificate merely states that you won't contaminate it. As further protection there is a kind of foot-rot dip—too wide to jump—between the dressing-rooms and the pool.

A. is reading Brazilian history in Portuguese, translating aloud into English as he goes.

February 4

We have moved from the "de luxe" hotel to one that is much quieter, less pretentious, and altogether better. Also the diluvial rains have stopped, and we have had various sorties into the country and down off the tableland on which we perch.

Our most adventurous outing was the first day of sun, when we set off for Caldos, some thirty-seven kilometres distant. It was a beautiful day and the mud road had miraculously dried to a hard ceramic surface. The countryside was hilly and planted with corn, and the air heavy with a hot sweet smell—a mixture of molasses and manure which we thought might be sugar-cane. Almost before we knew it we were entered upon a long, slightly inclined stretch of deeply rutted road from which there was no escape, and there we came to an ignominious halt—our low-slung car simply hanging on the centre of the road, our back wheels helpless. A. thought we'd be all right if we filled the ruts with rocks. And this we proceeded to do.

Immediately opposite us was a small shanty with some peach trees which a skinny black man was busy spraying, a skinny black boy at his heels, like a dog. On seeing our predicament the small boy quickly deserted and, collecting a pint-sized sister, came to watch. Finally Mamma—a very pretty Negress, her head in a bandana, a tiny child at her skirts and another in her arms—joined them and watched delightedly. She would laugh and show her lovely teeth in a wide and charming mouth, and rock her baby and say, "*Vai tirar carro!*" ("Go pull the car out!"), and kiss her baby and laugh again. Various trucks came by which, by dint of having four-wheel drive, managed to get through. A few solitaries on horseback or foot passed without so much as a "*Bom dia.*" We began to see the Mineiran as a Vermonter. And then our luck turned and a great truck with three men in it stopped; they carted stones of enormous size, and in two ticks had us on our way.

For some reason we imagined that if we continued on to Caldos we could come home by another and better route. We hit two more bad patches but, through a bit of preliminary scouting and roadwork, managed them well enough. We crossed a small fat river in which naked boys were swimming, then ascended the cobbled streets of Caldos. It had such a strange air. The women rode astride in flowered house-dresses under which they wore trousers; and they knew their crowning glory and wore it in long braids or twists over their shoulders. I wonder why they haven't thought of the side-saddle.

On one of our excursions from Poços we saw a small, blue-black bird apparently jumping for joy. He was sitting on a fence-post and on the count of five up he went, about a foot in the air, singing. He was not catching anything, as far as we could tell, nor was he showing off for a mate. He was just jumping for joy on a fence-post in the middle of Brazil—for longer than we had the patience to watch. We learned later, from the head of an experimental farm—in countryside that was probably the most beautiful hereabouts, a great expansive valley like a lap where they grow forty different kinds of wine and table grapes, coffee, and figs—that the bird is a *tisiu*. When I asked, "Why does he jump?" the man laughed and said, "Ask the *tisiu*." But why *does* he jump? This is the third kind of bird we have seen jump in Brazil. In all my amateur birding, I have never seen anything like it.

Watched a local birdcatcher at work. From the branch of a tree he suspended a cage containing a pair of *canários da terra*—enchanting little yellow birds, the male with a flame-coloured skull-cap. Attached to their cage was a small box with a spring top. Almost immediately, two wild *canários* appeared. One, in a rage, flew at the cage and attacked. The other hopped onto the spring-top box and the lid closed over him. There was something wrong with the spring, however, and the trapped bird escaped and both flew away. We thought that was the end of that, but the local boy assured us they would return, and return they did—their fury over the invaders stronger than fear or longer than memory.

The weather is absurdly perverse. We can't even take photographs. I spent the better part of yesterday morning waiting for enough light to take the horses with their decorative saddle-cloths, but as I could never get a high enough reading to give any depth of field, I finally gave up.

February 7

We've been to one Brazilian movie; and last night went to a football game. Very pretty. One team in white, one in green and white, on green grass with a white ball. It's a good game to watch and I enjoyed it, sitting on the bleachers. Those moments when, at the height of speed, they slow right down, really sends my blood pressure up. Ballet dancers do the same thing. However this was football; the fireworks sounded like pistol shots and the crowd was roaring.

February 16

We left Poços de Caldas somewhat reluctantly on the eleventh. Our destination was São Lourenço, another spa. A. had enquired about the road and had been told that it was under construction but driveable. We had misgivings as we set out, for the weather was still not settled and we knew from experience the effects of rain. However, the rain held off and we drove over a difficult, rough road through mountainous country with crops of corn, grapes, rice, and coffee. At first we even hoped to average twenty miles an hour and arrive in good time for dinner. But that was pure dream.

Just beyond Itajubá we hit a stretch of what must be the worst road I have ever seen. Our alternatives were to go back an unconscionable distance over a road we had barely managed, or to continue. We continued. There were deep wheel ruts in what looked like a moraine. But we kept going—the car lurching and leaping for a hundred yards or so. Then, a few car lengths from firm ground, we came down with a tremendous *whomp* and the oil warning-light flashed on the dashboard. In the same instant A. stepped on the gas, and we seemed to rise like a horse over a jump—extending ourselves as we went—to land on the other side of the fill.

By some miracle, although in the middle of nowhere, and day ending, we came to a stop exactly opposite a truck that was pulled off the road. In it were four men and a boy and almost before we were out of the car, they were under it. To our amazement, one of them— as if by a kind of conjuring—wore a mechanic's uniform with a red ESSO over his breast pocket. He announced no damage done. We had merely lost a screw plug for the oil pan and with it, of course, the oil. The nearest town was a half-hour drive distant. They would go for oil and a replacement plug if we waited. Waited, indeed! What else could we do?

None too certain that we would see them again, we ate our dinner—cheese and crackers from a picnic basket. By the time we had finished it was dark and we began to think we might be spending the night there. We looked at the one car rug despairingly. And then, in the distance, we saw a faint glow which, as we watched, turned into two headlights and then into "our" truck. Within minutes of arrival the men had supplied the missing screw, replaced the lost oil, helped stow our picnic things in the trunk. We gave them what we had of chocolate and cigarettes and anything else we could find and, roadworthy again, avoided the rain wash-outs in the new fills by following faithfully in the truck's wake. Led to safety in the next town, we said appreciative goodbyes and attempted to pay the men for their time and trouble. Money for oil they would accept. For the rest—*nada, nada.* It was nothing.

It was now seven. There were still hours of driving over uncertain roads in the dark if we were to reach São Lourenço that night. But we decided to try it. Luckily the road improved, the sky was full of stars, and along the roadside, much as in New Guinea, shrubs had been planted in meticulous straight rows—one on either side—and were picked up, prettily, by our headlights.

Arrived in São Lourenço about ten—a hilly town full of hotels and noise. Went straight to the largest hotel. At first we were told it was full, but when the desk clerk realized we were foreigners we were ushered into an incredible room full of heavy, expensive furniture and antimacassars and a wide, firm double bed—the presidential suite. I slept like the dead but A., who had done eleven hours of driving, spent most of the night with more and more deeply rutted roads unfolding before him.

Next morning when we went to pay the bill, we were greeted by the manager, who told us there was no charge. It was a pleasure to have us as guests and he hoped we would come again. Small wonder we are overwhelmed by Brazilian kindness and generosity!

We continued on to Caxambú—the third of the trio of famous spas—which we reached in time for lunch. Quite different in feeling from its sisters—smaller, more attractive. The streets lined with hibiscus trees in flower, their trunks painted white, so that each little tree looked like an old-fashioned nosegay with a twist of white paper around its stem. The central park has tennis courts, a roller rink, old-fashioned squeaky swings, and an outdoor swimming-pool. We found a room, with difficulty, in a rather doubtful hotel; had a doubtful lunch, a wonderful swim; bought some very nice basketwork, took photos, looked at the church, and then made tracks for the best hotel for dinner.

The following morning we set our noses for Rio, driving through fabulous mountain country—the height of land 5,000 feet. Lunched beside a freezing mountain stream and home by dinner-time.

Retrospectively, I find that the most interesting parts of the trip were two outings into a valley where there were a number of fine *fazendas*. The bougainvillea (*buganvília*—what a much simpler spelling) was in full bloom, the villagers' houses all painted white, orderly and vivid. Most of the land belonged to the owners of the *fazendas* but the workers were allowed time to cultivate their own individual plots, and with the price of coffee high they could sizeably increase their incomes. There was a school and a church and mass was performed one Sunday in four. One Sunday we watched a football game in a natural amphitheatre adjoining the village. Both teams were uniformed, but one hadn't managed boots yet and had to play barefoot. They played a kind of each-man-to-himself game—no team play that one could detect. All the locals were out to watch, the girls dressed in their best and carrying parasols. As we conversed with them they, of course, wanted to know where we were from. When we said "Canada" their faces took on the look of the deaf. They clearly had no idea what we were talking about. For orientation, A. offered them "*América do norte, o oceano Atlântico, o oceano Pacífico*", the North Pole. No reaction. The deaf look persisted. Finally, in desperation, he said, "Well, you know where the Estados Unidos is...." They shook their heads with the same bewildered incomprehension that Columbus might have had from Spanish villagers on his return from America; they obviously had never heard of the United States.

A fascinating variety of buildings on the trip. Of the villagers' small houses, very few had windows or doors—merely openings into which shutters could be fitted from the inside. They were built with wattle and thatch, wattle and tile, or wattle and brick. Immediate surroundings were always bare of grass. Fences mainly of split bamboo, but in one area they were giant cactuses, strangely disciplined in their growth, seemingly only putting up one tall prickly "paling" per plant. Transportation was by truck; oxen—sometimes as many as ten; mule-team—six to eight mules; burros; and horse-drawn carts. Most of the cattle were *zebú* or part *zebú*—honey-coloured tropical animals with big humps, and ears on upside down. One day we were held up by a herd of them and I saw the youngest calf I have ever seen, tottering along behind its mother. I called to one of the cowboys, his voluminous cape covering him and the top of his horse, *"Muito jovem!"* ("Very young!") to which he charmingly replied, *"Muito bonito!"* ("Very pretty!") Such an unexpected answer.

Birds were legion. I'd give a great deal for a good bird book. We saw one flight of thirty to forty long-tailed black birds with faces like point-nosed fish. (What are point-nosed fish?) There was a blue hummingbird with a tail, our own little emerald, tailless humming-bird, and a third—brown and fast as a snake, almost impossible to see. And an enchanting little black bird with a snow-white head. This is rather common in Brazil—birds with heads that seem to belong to altogether different bodies. There was a very fine woodpecker who tucked his tail into a post as if it were spiked; he wore yellow, black, and white and made the most God-awful racket as he landed— rather like a kookaburra. And there were masses of wildflowers—at this season, mostly lilac-coloured and mauve and purple. Even the convolvulus—in other places white, pink, or blue—here was lilac through to purple.

We achieved a kind of absurd, unwanted fame while in Poços. As foreigners we were oddities and noticeable anyway, but by crazy coincidence, at the local theatre one night, they showed a six-month-old film clip of the day A. officiated at the delivery of the diesel locomotives at Campinas and I unveiled some of them. And there we were—exposed. Sweet anonymity gone.

"We have moved from the deluxe hotel in Poços to one that is much quieter, less pretentious, and altogether better."

February 23

Quite overlooked our highly dramatic night when we had what seemed like the whole of the Rio police force here.

It began with an anonymous telephone call warning Graciano, the *mordomo*, that the Pernambucinhos—a vicious gang of killers—were planning to raid our house that night. Graciano reported the call to me, and made his usual request for a gun. After deliberation, I reported the call to A. who, in turn, reported it to Itamarity. The Pernambucinhos are not to be trifled with.

A Brazilian couple we had known in Australia were dining with us that night and as we sat on the patio having a drink before dinner, and told them of the chain of events, he promptly rose to his feet and said, "If the police are coming, I must lock my car."

Soon the police arrived—in cars with walkie-talkies. The driveway filled with them. All walkie-talkies were used at once—orders issued and counter-issued. The din was indescribable. No self-respecting Pernambucinho would have ventured near us. The police at last departed and quiet reigned once more, but panic was in the air, for the following evening one of the cleaners came running in to give the alarm that there was an interloper on a bench in the garden. Our two guards were called and we all went rushing to the scene, only to encounter an awakened and enraged Ricardo, the gardener, who had fallen quietly asleep as the evening cooled.

Later that night, just after dinner, A. and I were on the side veranda when a paralysed-looked *copeiro* and cleaner arrived to ask if they could see me in the *sala pequena*. There they pointed, trembling, to a single shoe lying on the carpet and asked if it had been there when we left the dining-room. Obvious to them that a *ladrão* had entered the house, losing a shoe en route. This shoe I had seen five minutes before in the mouth of our dog, Duque, who—with a fine Brazilian sense of drama—had dropped it where it would cause the most commotion.

I shouldn't laugh. The whole business of robbers and gangs is no joke. The crime rate, not surprisingly in a world where the rich are so rich and the poor so poor, is very high. Our house, what's more, is no great distance from two of the city's largest *favelas*. Our head servant and our driver have both asked for revolvers, which A. will not allow. Nor will he carry one himself. If I am intrepid, it is simply because A. is so cool. Helena, who lives nearby, has advised me to put my jewellery in the vault. "But I don't have anything worth stealing," I protested, to which she replied, "Your diamond earrings!" Were I to tell her they are paste, she would probably not believe me. Our near neighbours, an American clergyman and family, have been raided three times within the last six months—twice in broad daylight. The last time, the robbers beat up their little boy.

February 24

I suppose what I really want to write about is drawing—or painting or whatever it is I am doing. The three artists who afford me most pleasure at the moment are Klee, Dufy, and Matisse, not necessarily in that order. Dufy and I are drawn by the same subject matter. How much better put, had I said: I am drawn to the same subject matter as Dufy! Interesting the shift in meaning—the first sentence making me sound as if I thought myself Dufy's equal, the second removing the inference.

March 6

The heat has continued relentlessly ever since we returned from Minas three weeks ago.

Went last night, despite it, to the opening of a play, *O Santo e a Porca* (*The Saint and the Pig*), by Ariano Suassuna. His *Auto da Compadecida* (*An Act of Compassion*), which we have read, is a witty, anti-clerical play about a wily peasant and the problems that arise from his managing to have a cat blessed and a dog buried in holy ground. Strongly pro-Catholic, Suassuna nevertheless whacks the materialism of the Church. Interesting to see his attitudes to the Virgin Mary, whom he portrays as infinitely merciful, and to Christ, whom his peasant views with suspicion. "Are you a Protestant?" the peasant asks, when they meet.

There was something quite comic about Girl Guides in tropical uniforms lining the route into the theatre and handing out programmes. And flowers, apparently, are sent to the theatre. Dozens of *cestas* in the lobby and on the stairs. None presented to the performers at play's end.

We had the almost impossible task of trying to understand a highly idiomatic play spoken—much harder than reading it. The company was fast-paced and acted in a curiously mannered way, prancing and posturing. The central figure was a miser who kept his money in a wooden pig. (Does the piggy bank stem from cultures such as that of New Guinea, where you count your wealth in pigs?) There were three couples, all endeavouring to marry each other but hampered by much intrigue and misunderstanding. It smacked a bit of Molière and the acting was rather in the manner in which I've seen Molière done. But I'm afraid we missed most of the subtleties and a great deal of the humour.

It is the second Brazilian play we've seen. The first was by Nelson Rodrigues. I had previously read two of his plays—*Anjo Negro* (*Black Angel*) and *O Vestido de Noiva* (*The Wedding Dress*). Rodrigues is a highly poetic and very sombre writer and his plays are outside the mainstream of Brazilian theatre. In *Anjo Negro*—his best, in my opinion—his theme is colour. His principal character is a Negro, psychotic about his skin colour. Immense and powerful, he rapes and subsequently keeps a beautiful white girl. She repeatedly bears him black sons which she kills. It is a terrifying play. Relentless like a great black sea. It reminds me a little of some of Lorca, but it is slower, heavier. The current play, *Perdoa-me por Me Traíres* (which I think means *Forgive Me My Trespasses*) is highly contentious. It was removed from the Teatro Municipal, and is running in a small theatre which has a large sign outside announcing the number of people who think it should be closed and the number who don't. We were told, when we suggested going, that we would see things on the stage such as we had never dreamed. What we did see was a girl having an abortion. Strangely, not shocking. The scene was so stylized and mimed with such beautiful movements that it created an unreality while in no way detracting from the impact. It was, in fact, one of the highlights of the play, matched only by a scene in a brothel where an impotent senator attempted to work himself up by violent speeches.

I paint like a fool, without direction, knowledge, or control.

March 8

The exhibition of Eskimo carvings opened today at the Museum of Modern Art. It is a small and disappointing show, in my opinion, and makes me despair of us. Despite the fact that the collection was poorly chosen, the museum handled it well, and thanks to A. there were six blow-ups of excellent photographs which helped. Also it was better displayed than in São Paulo. Dona Mathilde at the museum here grouped together all the human figures, which were almost identical in size and colour. As a result they became a series of stills animated by one's own movements. It was as if the same little grey man moved from a standing to a sitting position, extended himself on the ice, plunged his spear through a hole in the ice, and so on. Many of the animals and birds in this collection are flattened on their undersides as if dropped from some great height. In the case of the walrus, he might be emerging from a hole in the ice, but the birds...? Perhaps the warmth of their breasts is melting it.

Our supper party afterwards went well. All of Rio's best art critics and many of its best artists were asked and arrived. Henrique Mindlin, who has seen my work before and therefore knows where it is kept, took some critics to see it. Surprisingly, they were enthusiastic. To be taken with a grain of salt, of course.

The upshot of all this is that I am going to start classes at the Museum of Modern Art after our trip to Bahía later this month. My teacher will be Carvão.

The heat broke dramatically the night before last with a tropical downpour which had A., me, and the *mordomo* out of our beds to put our fingers in the dyke. Rather, it was the other way about. Our little stream had become a raging river and the lock gates were shut. A. in his bathing trunks, in a tumble of water and rocks, struggled to raise the gate by the light of a couple of feeble flashlights. The power was out, of course, moon and stars hidden, and, black like everything else but our two tiny beams, the gusting wind and diluvial rain. All yesterday it rained solidly—with the usual inevitable lack of services. Telephone and electricity non-existent. But today dawned like a young girl—cool and beautiful—and so our planned outing by yacht from the Iate Clube was perfectly in order.

On arrival we were introduced to Ludwig Bemelmans. The *verdadeiro* Bemelmans—small, dumpy, bald. Such a surprise! I had read, but forgotten, that he was here to do a piece on Brazil for *Holiday*. He said he doesn't know how he has survived as a writer when he considers how enormous the number of questions he doesn't ask. He didn't ask what the weather would be like in Rio in March—and having been built for the Alps, he hates heat. He said he once decided to go to Bermuda, asked no questions, drove to Key West, and on the ferry asked for a ticket to Bermuda. That was how he first went to Cuba.

Nothing, he said, would have persuaded him to come to Rio in the heat, had he known. But being here, he began to enquire where he could find some relief from it. He was directed to the Hotel

Corcovado. It is run by a German who rises at five, scrubs everything within sight, places six pots of geraniums at five-foot intervals along the terrace—they each have four flowers—washes and cooks and keeps a clean hotel. In it Bemelmans has met an English scientist who, in the nearby *mato*, has found an extraordinary number of moths and creatures previously undiscovered. This find is so phenomenal that *Life* (which he deplores, along with *Time* and *Fortune*) sent one of its top editors here to work on the story. The *Life* editor had no sooner arrived than a moth flew straight into his ear, and he hasn't been heard from since. Arrangements are being made to ship the poor fellow to an institute for tropical medicine. Bemelmans, who considers the whole Luce lot evil, reads divine retribution in the incident.

I may be giving the impression that Bemelmans spoke a great deal. Actually he is a mute and solitary man who sought his own company whenever possible. But he also said that he had given Chateaubriand an idea that would probably drive the latter crazy. Regarding his violent opposition to Brasília, the new capital which, under Kubitschek, is being pushed madly because, its detractors claim, "Mediocrity wants a monument," Bemelmans advises that to oppose it now is useless. It is already too late. The only remaining course is to make of lunacy (if such it is) a major lunacy by planning for a world's fair there within ten years. This will either bankrupt the city completely or get it off to a triumphant start.

He is, I think, a most gentle writer—although to be dead sure I would have to reread him. Not so gentle with the rich or with officials, as I remember. Yet what he knows of people, if today is typical, is through observation. His visual curiosity seemed insatiable.

In order to entertain him, our host had borrowed a yacht. Large enough to accommodate thirty or so, manned by a crew of three, it churned off into that fabulous blue bay and finally anchored near an island where we swam—Bemelmans swimming off by himself. Then a wonderful lunch and on to Paquetá, an island where there are no cars—only bicycles and carriages. We drove around, clop clop; drank sugar-cane syrup from an itinerant sugar-cane squeezer and discovered that it tastes a bit green and rather sweet. Then back aboard the lugger and, an hour and a half later, our voyage was done. The sea had stiffened (do only winds do that?) and Rio, with the sun setting behind it, was divine.

Driving home we found the sea had stiffened indeed. Fabulous waves were breaking on Copacabana—over the *avenida* itself—with crowds out to watch. In Ipanema and Leblon it was even worse—the entire sand beach had disappeared. A flight of steps from the sidewalk to the beach now ends dramatically in mid-air.

The frogs are going bongk bongk and the black tropical night is tangible and close…building slowly, heavily, to another heat wave.

March 28

Back last night from Bahía, one of the key states of Brazil's early colonial history. Slightly larger than France, it lies north of Minas Gerais and extends five hundred miles inland from the coast. The climate ranges from hot and steamy on the coastal plain—just how hot and steamy I shall describe later—to hot, nearly desert-dry in the interior. It's mainly agricultural—sugar, cocoa, coconut, beans, tobacco—but in recent years oil discoveries have made it also the only significant producer of petroleum in the country.

We flew the eight hundred miles from Rio to Salvador, the capital—commonly called Bahía by Brazilians outside the state. It overlooks the Bahía de Todos os Santos (Bay of All Saints). With its upper and lower towns it reminded me of Quebec, a tropical Quebec. Founded in 1549, it is Brazil's oldest city, and its first capital. It was also first landfall for Portugal's royal family when the crown, in 1807, fled to the Americas in fear of Napoleon. And the port where tens of thousands of African slaves were landed to work the early sugar plantations, bringing with them the religion which was to become *candomblé*.

Our drive in from the airport was by the sea road. Groves of tall, wild palms tossed their dish-mop tops on our left, and inland, on our right, incongruous pines grew from dunes as white as snow. The beaches golden, glistening. And the great blue Dufy sea and sky. Houses on the outskirts of this ancient city were modern and brightly painted.

At the square near our hotel, some none-too-tidy troops were lined up and played "O Canada" and the Brazilian national anthem. The hotel was large and modern. Much use of glass and coloured contemporary tile. Interior walls covered with murals by Genaro de Carvalho—the young artist whose tapestries we had seen exhibited in Rio.

It was apparent early in the game that our programme was not only skeletal, it was also uncertain. The head bone was not connected to the neck bone.

In the afternoon we called on the governor and his wife in their summer house—an old, recently remodelled *fazenda*. No carpets on the floors in all that heat, but beautiful wide floorboards, dark and light wood alternating. Openwork wrought-iron doors between rooms, capacious verandas. A house designed for air. There was very little furniture and what there was was modern and of bold solid colours—red, yellow, purple, green. And orchids like great strange moths.

They showed us their gardens, which bordered on the zoological gardens, and we looked down on an island where monkeys were scampering about in their brightly painted jungle gym, like children at a play centre. We were also shown a restaurant, garden, and playground which the governor had built nearby for "the people". All very beautiful and fine but I can't help wondering why he would build it right on top of his own summer house. Do Brazilians enjoy noise? I sometimes think they do.

At six we went to a reception at the university. We were received in the rectory—a new building and very nice indeed. In style it is modern, but the use of old Portuguese tiles in the interior, coupled with the nature of its design, makes it kin to the colonial buildings which are its neighbours. At the reception in the board room we sat at a T-shaped table entirely banked with orchids. A member of the faculty delivered an impassioned speech. A. replied with less passion. Then we all went off to the common room for champagne. Pleasant enough but we saw next to nothing of the university.

The following day we put our "fighting clothes", as they called them, in order to go by launch to the oil country across the bay. To reach the lower town—which is the port, business section, and market—you can choose an elevator or one of three steep, narrow streets. Some of the oldest and most beautiful buildings in the city are here, the quayside is choked with boats, their tall sails like the wing-feathers of giant gulls, and the sea, if possible, is even *more* Dufy.

The light danced and glanced and sparkled as we embarked in a Petrobrás launch with an immaculate skipper into the Ricketts-blue bay. Bahía from offshore is a white city with centuries-old buildings, double-towered Portuguese churches, and ancient forts set against the dense brilliance of tropical grass and wild palms leggy as colts.

Luckily the oil wells in the sea are still not visible from Salvador, for they change the blue bay into something desolate and empty. It would not look empty without them. Why do they empty it? Turn it into science fiction? Somehow make it monstrous?

At São Francisco de Conde, a 400-year-old village, we disembarked by iron ladder, and for the first of many times that day I thanked my gods that I was younger than average for an ambassador's wife.

More Petrobrás people met us, including a dreamy-looking young man said to play sixteen instruments. No time to ask him to play even one, no time to stop and look at the beautiful buildings, for the target of this trip was Mataripe, the Petrobrás oil town, and the car was waiting to take us there.

We drove through sugar country—green and lyrical. But the people live in strip housing. Unforgivable and horrible in all that space. They work the cane fields for absentee owners and the poverty is ghastly. We had been told we should find poverty in the cocoa country but no one had warned us about this.

Odd and rather bleak to drive through almost uninhabited land and come across 300-year-old churches standing by themselves, unused. Clearly some of the early slaves had been Moslems, for we passed a mosque with twin onion-shaped towers. And occasionally an abandoned *casa grande*.

Came finally to the oil country, the derricks making a metal jungle of the landscape. The paraffin-based oil was thick and black as tar. It was almost too hot to think.

Lunched at Mataripe, the refinery town, and there in the midst of all the raw ugliness of the local club were two quite lovely paintings by Carvalho—abstractions of birds in sunlight, birds in moonlight. They had been commissioned by our host, a pleasant, unpretentious man. Lunch was endless: one enormous platter of cold mashed potatoes, *farofa* (manioc flour), spaghetti, *feijão* (black beans)—we didn't lack for starches!—meat, salad, fish.

After lunch and a tour of the refinery, we reboarded the launch. The harbour was busy—crude oil going out, pipes and supplies coming in. The principal craft on this part of the coast are *saveiros* —large, wide, seagoing vessels with dhow-like sails. Scudding through the waves, fully loaded and under canvas with a bare eight inches of freeboard, they look as if they are sinking.

Arrived back in Bahía an hour earlier than scheduled, so of course there was no car. But the girl who had accompanied us, by a kind of sleight of hand, produced kitchen chairs through an overhead window of a nearby building and lined them up in a row on the sidewalk, and there we sat, hot but comfortable, the life of Bahía going on around us and paying little heed. Through the same window she even produced a carafe of water and some glasses, and so we passed the time happily enough until the car arrived to take us to the cathedral and the São Francisco monastery and church.

The two squares onto which these buildings face are paved with the same black and white stones used in Rio, but the Bahíans have added sun-bleached cockle shells, and so created a three-colour design, the white stones appearing grey by contrast. The date of the monastery is 1708; its elegant exterior elaborately carved. The church of the same name, tiled outside with unornamented, semi-opalescent *azulejos* (glazed tiles), has the soft, pale glimmer of a fish. Inside—almost unbelievably—every inch is carved and covered with gold leaf. "A hideous beauty," some French painter wrote of it. I agree. It is heavy, demanding. Like gilded worms and snakes, the golden convolutions catch your eye from all directions at once. I would have thought it hard to find the quiet in which to pray, yet the church was full. Mostly women. Some kneeling at the side altars in front of their golden god, some sitting on the steps of the altars gossiping and awaiting the five o'clock mass.

The cathedral, built by the Jesuits in 1657, is an almost perfect building, quite different from São Francisco. Part of its perfection lies in its proportions: the proportion of ceiling to altar—both rectangles, the one larger and darkish, the other smaller and shining gold. Not the convoluted, carved gold of São Francisco, but the true light of God's eye. There is an infinite mystery about this interior which may be mathematical. Here the whole is unquestionably greater than the sum of its parts—the way the gold, at its most blinding, is concentrated in the chancel, the use of plain, unornamented areas, the quiet, all combine to focus the eye and with it the mind, perhaps even the heart. Totally unlike São Francisco, which seems intent upon distracting.

The cathedral was shut when we arrived but we managed to find the sacristan—a repulsive old man. I wonder why they almost always are? He told us a robber had slept in the church the other night and not stolen a pin. There was probably no pin to steal. It must be good for people to spend time in such an atmosphere, whether they have a God or not. Yet the sacristan...?

Next day, while A. went about his business, the governor's wife undertook to look after me. She is attractive, youngish, totally natural. She took me for a drive through the old parts of the town and to the Church of the Senhor do Bomfim. This church, though more recent than the others (1754), has a special significance for Brazilians. "You haven't been to Salvador if you haven't seen the Bomfim." The guidebook says: "This famous church belonged originally to the Negroes, and it had an image that was supposed to work miracles. Once a year, thousands of pilgrims, mostly sick, go to the Miracle Room to pray for a cure. Later when many of them are well again, they return with a present.... This church also has a wonderful *festa* once a year when rich and poor go there to clean it. They bring scrub brushes, mops, and pails. Everybody works with high fervour to wash the church for the Lord."

The church is smallish, modest, with interior carvings of white and gold, the white predominating. A woman was decorating the altar when we arrived and she and the governor's wife kissed and chatted while I went off to the Miracle Rooms. In one, a multitude of small silver images—arms, legs, heads, entire bodies—are mounted in glass cases and hung on the walls. In the other, the entire ceiling is hung with white wax models—nearly life-size—of the affected parts. White wax legs, feet, hands, heads, etc. form a ceiling above you—each garishly marked with red where the ulcer or cancer was. It is fascinatingly awful. The walls, too, are covered with photographs and drawings of afflicted people. There was one extraordinary waxen image of four heads joined together, one below the other!

At an antique shop in the lower town I yearned, rather, after beautiful old furniture *estilo* Chippendale, Hepplewhite, and Queen Anne, made from Brazilian woods by Brazilian craftsmen, which could not survive a winter in a dry Canadian house. Was fascinated by the religious artefacts—altar candlesticks, and carved and painted saints always—unaccountably—with their hands broken off; and the sometimes more sinister objects associated with *macumba*, or *candomblé* as it is called in the north. The most exotic and elegant of these are gold or silver *balangadás*, made in the form of large oval keyrings, from which hang a variety of amulets: pomegranates, bunches of grapes, fish, parrots, drums, keys, *figas*—fetish objects from eastern and western magic—executed with great mastery. Imagining a day when I should have to do the polishing myself, much as they fascinated me, I was not tempted. But I nearly bought (and now wish I had!) an old, black, wooden *candomblé* figure about a foot high, hands over ears. I wonder if their magic is dissipated by the time they reach antique shops?

Then to the market. And what a market! We spent our time at the stalls that sell hammocks, pottery, beads, musical instruments, and indescribable articles used in magic. I bought a white bridal hammock and a *berimbau*—a musical instrument peculiar to this region which looks like a large bow (as in bow and arrow) with half a coconut shell attached to its string (in this case a wire). Difficult to play. You hold the bow with your left hand and apply varying pressure to the wire with a large coin, while with your right you hit the wire with a drumstick, which movement shakes the small stones in a little wicker container hooked onto a finger. It's a kind of one-man-band instrument that whines and rattles and bangs!

In the afternoon the governor's wife sent me her car and driver, and her husband's private secretary as companion. The secretary had been with the governor since his days as Minister of Education in the federal government and clearly thought very highly of him. She talked of his efforts "to do things for the people". He supported small industries and established centres with water and sewing machines where the poor could wash and mend their clothes or make new ones. He is also responsible for the construction of a theatre, which his wife calls his "Brasília", to replace one destroyed by fire a hundred years ago. Designed by a Brazilian, its equipment German-made, it is to be the most modern theatre in South America. The stage not only revolves but moves up and down and forward and back. Both stage and auditorium can be reduced to half-size without acoustical loss. Backstage, elaborate dressing-rooms, bathrooms, rehearsal space for ballet, voice, and drama. It will seat 1,600—in theory. I wonder if it ever will. Bahía doesn't look like the kind of place where "Mr. and Mrs." are longing to go to the theatre, and I would have thought it needs other things more urgently. But perhaps not.

The secretary also said the governor is a very modest man, and to meet, he seems modest. He is small, attractive, half Negro, I should think. This latter accounts, perhaps, for his wife's reference on our first meeting to the number of coloured people in Bahía. "We have no feeling against colour here—more or less!" She added that in her grandmother's day there were so few white males that girls "were brought up to think in terms of marrying coloured men." When we watched the troops march past she said, "You see, they're nearly all coloured." It hadn't occurred to *me* that they were.

When I spoke admiringly of the governor to a member of the Anglo community on my return to Rio, he said, "Did you hear about the movie director who was in Bahía looking for a Negro to play a part in a film and chose an American Negro? All Bahía was insulted, saying that in Bahía he could have chosen anyone from the governor down."

Well, so much for all this. But no. There is more. I've read that Brazilians prefer to entertain in cafés or clubs because most families have one black member living at home. Shortly afterwards, when I went to Helena's, an enchanting coffee-coloured child answered the door. On Helena's arrival her first question was, "Have you seen my *mulata* grandchild?" I cannot help wondering if this self-consciousness is for my benefit. If so, how ill they read me.

While in Bahía we naturally were taken to the district from which Carmen Miranda came. Its perilously steep main street, flanked by graceful colonial public buildings and brightly coloured stores, was a jigsaw of donkey-carts, dogs, pedestrians, cars. Suddenly a donkey-cart minus driver hurtled down the cobblestone hill, releasing all the energy dormant on the street. Donkeys brayed and bolted, dogs fought, people yelled. Total pandemonium.

Next day, an hour's plane flight to Itabuna, in the cocoa country. Even at nine in the morning it was stifling. Our first stop, a Swiss cocoa mill where we gazed glazedly at the crushing and grinding, the extraction of cocoa butter—but perhaps I should say "I", for A., no matter the heat, is as alert as a baby; interested, questioning, and, afterwards, able to remember it all.

Then on to the social club—"as chic as anything you could find in the city". Such a dreary establishment: rings on the tables, dirt under them. The waiter could offer us nothing chilled—no ice, no mineral water—only a little tepid gin, which we declined.

As in all small communities, we had to see every square inch, walking about in a little parade in the sweltering heat which, now that noon approached, reached stupefying intensity. We saw a school for girls financed and run by the daughter of a cocoa king; the new Catholic cathedral, which looked like a factory; the local newspaper office—one room full of presses and a tiny cubicle for the editor into which we all crowded while he asked us how we spelled our names. By then we hardly knew!

At the Cocoa Association guest-house we were able, at last, to quench our almost unquenchable thirst with *água de côco* or coconut milk—ambrosial after so long a drought. The old hands mixed it with whisky. This was followed by the inevitable Brazilian "ambassadorial" luncheon—or do they always eat like that?—dozens of platters of food, ending on this occasion with cocoa jelly for dessert and a demitasse of cocoa, very thick and sweet. Just what we craved.

To provide cocoa trees with the shade essential for their growth, they are planted under taller rubber trees. At this season, the unripe cocoa pods look like small paper lanterns tied to the trunks and boughs—Scott's-emulsion green against the black bark. Three trees in Brazil that I know of grow their fruit right out of the trunk: the *jaca* or durian, the *jabuticaba*, this name is untranslatable, and the *cacau*. We wandered about very, very slowly in the dappled light, sucking the sticky white-coated cocoa beans and picking up the speckled seeds of the rubber trees, which look like killdeers' eggs—flattened, softened—by the heat, perhaps, which by then was softening even our brains.

After another reviving draught of *água de côco* we boarded a bright yellow rail-service car and set forth for Ilhéus, Bahía's cocoa port, through coconut plantations with their great plumed crowns, the two-tiered cocoa–rubber plantations, some pineapple. A variously patterned, green, and good-looking land. And the people not too badly off as long as we stayed with the cocoa. Once out of it, the poverty was appalling, the people lethargic, depleted. Heartbreaking.

Occasionally we had glimpses of the jewel-sea flashing and shining, and here and there, two men and a small sail—their *jangada* or balsa-wood fishing raft so low in the water that it was invisible.

The flowing ribbons of country on either side of us were broken by occasional houses and then, suddenly, there were ribbons of houses. It was clear that we were nearing Ilhéus. Were there, in fact. Before we had time to gather our wits, the rail car rattled to a triumphant stop at the station, where what looked like the entire population of the port had gathered for the show. The local military band was playing a barely recognizable "O Canada" and A. forced his way out of the car, almost disappearing into the bass horn. "O Canada" reached an extraordinary climax. It was followed by the Brazilian national anthem, which, like the Russian, goes on for a very long time. The

Brazilians in the car, patriots all, sprang promptly to their feet—that is, they stood from feet to waist, but due to the car's low roof their bodies were forced to describe right angles—and thus immobilized, they remained like set squares until the very last note of the very last verse had melted in the gelatinous air.

This glorious arrival would have been the final straw for me—the heat, the indescribably enthusiastic brasses, the contortions demanded by national ardour—had it not been for the fact that pressed to the long windows of the car, only the thickness of the glass away, were the noses of the curious Ilhéusians. I couldn't give myself up to hilarity.

All national anthems concluded, I forced my way through a tangle of instruments and hot bodies to A.'s side, unassisted by the normally courteous Brazilian men, who had sighted friends in the crowd and leapt ahead to hurl themselves into feverish *abraços*.

A., the centre of a dense knot of newsmen, was being interviewed for radio. High comedy. The interviewer talked into his hand mike. No word of what he said could be heard above the noise of the crowd. He then handed the mike to A. who, apparently operating on the theory that as he couldn't hear himself speak, nobody else could either, talked happily and freely in Portuguese. The mike was grabbed from him again for the interviewer to make his remarks and then, with great courtesy and many smiles, returned to A. who says he has an uneasy feeling that he began saying the same thing for the second time. Luckily, someone yelled "*cultura*" in his ear and A. pounced upon it greedily and spoke of the *grande cultura de Ilhéus*, which gave him the opportunity to break away from the mike to congratulate and thank the conductor of the band. And so we were delivered from the hands of the media into those of the municipal officials, and thus to an apartment two circular stair flights above the Bank of Bahía, where we gave ourselves up to long overdue laughter and took off our wringing wet clothes.

Dinner at the local hotel consisted of fifteen men and me drinking whisky and *água tônica* in an ugly bar and eating an endless meal at which two speeches were made. Then we were packed into a car and, in pitch darkness, taken on a scenic tour of the town. "One of the best views of our city is from here," we were told as the car came to a stop to give us time to consider it. Then up another hill to survey what, by day, was "the finest view of the port"—all of us stuck together by sweat in a small car, imagining a seascape.

How grateful we were to be finally back in our apartment, once again peeling off our damp clothing, laughing, making ready for bed, for we were to be up by five in order to catch a plane back to Salvador. "It will be so hot by five, you'll have to get up," they comforted us. But it was so hot *then* we could hardly endure bed at all, and the less covered up we were, the larger the skin surface we offered the mosquitoes.

Someone in Bahía described Ilhéus as a fever-ridden town and although there is no yellow fever now, it has all the feeling of what a fever-ridden town might be. Such an extreme of salty, humid heat gives an absurd unreality to every movement, every thought—and now, as I write, every memory. It is as if we dissolved and re-formed that day, starting in the cocoa mill; dissolved and re-formed over and over again, never quite returning to the original shape, until, nearly liquid, we became part of the sticky jelly of midnight.

By five o'clock, it is true, we could no longer endure our beds. Yet the morning was lovely in its way as we sauntered down to the beach where we were to pick up a launch for the airport across the water. No wind disturbed the surface of the sea, which perfectly reflected a pale dawn sky. Sugar-cane, chickens, and who knows what? were already arriving for the market in dug-out canoes. The early morning light touched the world with magic—turned white feathers gold and imbued us, two punctual North Americans, with that disregard for time so much a part of the Brazilian nature. No plane could make us hurry. When the launch landed us on the wet sand, we positively dawdled our way to the airstrip. We might, both of us, have become Ilhéusians, so unurgent were we.

By nine we deplaned at Salvador, and on the drive back to the city stopped to take photos of the highly coloured contemporary houses rising, apparently, out of snow. Why are the beaches golden and the dunes snow-white?

And then, a real stroke of luck! Is luck a matter of perfect timing? In this case, yes, for we were right there on the seacoast road as a troop of fishermen began hauling in their net. Laid in a great long arc, by men in *jangadas*, it has weights on the bottom and floats on the top, so that it stands up in the sea like a fence. When the time comes to pull it in, the entire fishing community—men, women, and children—divides into two teams, one at each end of the net—each team with a beach boss—the one at the end nearest us being a sizeable Negro with tremendous shoulders, wearing a straw hat and equipped with a spiked stick. As the serious pulling begins, a rhythm is quickly established and the ancient songs to Iamanjá, Queen of the Sea, rise above the sound of the surf. The netters beseech her, implore her to give them a good catch. Their voices are high, the men, surely, singing falsetto. As the net draws closer to the shore, the pulling quickens, as does the rhythm of the song. Now the beach bosses go wild, exhorting the pullers to greater and greater efforts— running, jumping, yelling. The excitement and the tension mount.

When the net finally slides into the shallows, spilling its catch, the beach bosses run into the water, spear a fish, race with it up the beach, and throw the great silver arcing creature onto the golden sand; race back again, spear another. We were told there is a practical reason for this—heavy fish break the net. But clearly it is part of the denouement—the climax, really. The long arc of the lightened net now comes in smoothly and fast—a metallic "breaker" rolling in on the sand. All tension has evaporated. The fishermen are indifferent to their catch—there is no divvying up, no pushing or scrambling for it. Like beads scattering when their string breaks, they disperse up the beach, wander aimlessly off. This was only explained later when we learned that these are fishers, not fish-eaters, and that the catch would be sorted and sold and the money divided among them at a future date.

I would love to go back. Six days is not enough. Given the chance, I would move to Salvador and live for a time in that two-tiered town— ancient/modern, Portuguese/African, Catholic/*candomblé* —with its blinding blue days and its velvet nights—and take in the thousand and one details of architecture, vegetation, and dress which so teased me when we were there. Well, one day, perhaps.... Who knows?

April 3

Life goes on much as before in Rio: Graciano comes, pleased as punch, with a small spider he has found in his hair—its back a perfect skull—bone-white, fascinating; and we dine with the most café-society of all café-society couples. Why am I surprised that they should also be darlings? Their apartment is immense—marble floor after marble floor stretches before one. A poignant Modigliani. Superb food on old and beautiful hand-painted china. And once again, incredible women! Never have I seen such clothes.

April 9

Spent Easter on an island near Angra dos Reis (Anchorage of the Kings), two hours distant from Rio, with our friend the newspaper editor and his wife. Brilliant sunshine and hot. We were met at the town wharf by a *mulato* boy in an ancient cabin cruiser who took us to the island dock, about twenty minutes away across the blinding sea.

Our host is famous for, among other things, having worked forty years with Chateaubriand. That alone is considered a feat. A revolutionary in the São Paulo Revolution, he was exiled for two years during the Vargas regime. He is now in his sixties and his wife—his first—is about my age. She is blonde with blue eyes and a very white skin and it was she, I think, who at a ladies' luncheon I gave for some visiting Canadians—to the outrageous question, "What do you do about your colour problem?", replied, "We marry it. My grandmother was black." They have one daughter, already married, and two boys of eight and twelve. He is infatuated with Brazil—and with himself, I rather fear. But he has great charm and warmth. He looks like a Brazilian Indian. In Rio he told us he had all the comforts on his island but no luxuries. In Brazil, it is difficult to know what that might mean.

We walked from the dock along a path by the sea. To our right, on a dry mud flat enclosed by a low stone wall, some boys were playing *futebol*. We passed through tunnels of bamboo, coconut palms, mango groves, and so to the bare ground I now associate with peasant houses in the tropics, and finally, up a concrete path to an unpretentious one-storey tile-roofed building, flanked on three sides by unscreened verandas.

The living/dining-room was full of bric-à-brac and a portrait of our host looking like Mussolini. (In his city house, one room is full of portraits and busts of him—looking like Beethoven, looking like Byron, etc.)

Our host said, "Here, each does what he wants. We'll have a *cafèzinho* and go swimming." We walked to the sea down a wide concrete path through another tunnel of bamboo. Near the beach there was a cross mounted on a rock, and a small chapel. The sea was dotted with bathers, the water warm, but it was not particularly good for swimming. "Don't go too far in that direction because of the current. Don't go too far in that or the oysters will cut your feet." Then all of us to the pool for a finish—the two children, the *mulato* who had driven us across the bay in the boat, two very quiet white-skinned girls, and two *mulato* youths. The pool is moss-green from the algae and bathwater-hot from sitting in the sun like an alligator all day without moving. I lowered myself into the scalding salt water and came up splotched with green slime.

It being Good Friday, lunch was codfish. One of the girls who had been swimming with us, now looking slatternly in a striped uniform and dirty apron, served it. Immediately after lunch our hostess, with her children and hordes of servants and servants' husbands or wives and their children, went to the chapel to attend Good Friday observances. Our host said, "Here, each does what he likes. Come and see my pigs." We watched an enormous sow, covered with toothbrush bristles, give suck to eleven small porkers. She had only ten teats. We looked at the chickens and ducks. The place depressed me absurdly. It seemed dirty and—grey. Discarded bamboo "collars" lay scattered over the ground. Discarded banana leaves the same. We saw banana trees, avocado trees, mango trees, cashew trees, *goiaba* (guava) trees. But it was all grey. The mosquitoes and sand fleas loved the 6-12 in which we covered ourselves. We walked to the far end of the property, passed various small houses for the employees. It was very hot. But giant snails walk the island in long, roseate shells.

By the time we got back it was dark and dinner-time. And immediately afterwards, bed. Our room was the end of the line and the electricity barely reached it. We felt our way to bed, lay down on the straw mattresses—almost universal in Brazil, and very comfortable and cool—and gave ourselves to the mosquitoes and sand fleas.

Breakfast, an informal affair of fruit and ham and cheese and rolls and *café au lait*.

"Each does what he likes." We went to the other island. Our host wore—as he had when he greeted us, and continued to wear—a too-large cream-coloured sports shirt buttoned at the neck and hanging loose over too-long blue jeans. On the way to the wharf he showed us a sago palm—a low, finely fronded palm with a crown of sago beans of flaming red—and in the boat-house, two cabin cruisers and three dug-out canoes, the latter made on the property from logs grown there. While we waited for the boys to get the boats ready, we watched the crabs on the nearby *futebol* field. The largest are an inch and a half in length—or is it breadth, with a crab? They are like silent orators, constantly gesturing with a bright orange or yellow claw as large as their body. The other claw is infinitesimal, barely visible. They hold the large one up to see which way the wind is blowing. If they don't like it they retire into their holes. Or they emerge and wave at their friends. It's hallucinating. They begin to seem life-size, human.

In the stone wall that encloses the crabs, some small bees have built a wax spout through which they come and go to their stone home.

The boats ready, we accompanied the two swimming children to the shore of the neighbouring island—a long swim—and walked to its crest where the married daughter is building a house. We found a large bunch of cooking bananas, ripe on their tree, each fruit as thick as my forearm.

Conversations produced some astonishing gossip: that café society, as distinct from other rich Brazilians, feels responsibility for nothing but appearance and parties—clothes, jewels, hairdressers, beauty treatments, love affairs—and that many traditional Brazilian families—the old rich—will not accept their invitations. A well-known hostess, we were told, was an unscrupulous woman who had had for lover, among a hundred others, Mussolini; an ageing novelist with the mask of a twice-lifted face, hair-raisingly (!) youthful-appearing, was once a Fascist; and an attractive Latin-American diplomat had once been Wallis Simpson's lover.

More interesting to us, their talk about colour. They say there are no throwbacks—that white is the dominant and that Brazilians grow whiter all the time. They say that Brazilians have no colour prejudice, even as they say they have found the way to solve the colour problem: intermarriage will produce a white race. When you suggest that their whole argument could indicate they *are* prejudiced, you feel uncharitable, knowing that they are so much *less* prejudiced than we, and why are we wanting to find them prejudiced anyway? Does it salve us, in some way?

They were fascinating on Brazilian character, claiming that the Brazilian cannot say no, and that this is one of the reasons he is superior to other people. He will say "next week" or "I'll do my best" or any number of things to give the other fellow hope—the more so, the less hope there is. That the key to the Brazilian character lies in the phrase *"dar um jeitinho"*—which means, roughly, "to find a way". Actually, it means more than that. The word *"jeito"* is knack, style, manner, way. With the diminutive ending *"inho"* it takes on a different quality—personal, intimate.

Our host continued proudly, "If a Canadian came to me and asked me to arrange for him to bring a car into the country, and I said the law didn't allow it, that would end the matter for the Canadian. He would accept that as final. Not the Brazilian. The Brazilian always has hope. He believes a way can be found. He believes that his friends are capable of finding a way. He doesn't just accept the answer. He says, 'But you can *dar um jeitinho* for me.' And his friends, however hopeless the case, will never say no." This sweetness, as he calls it, he claims they get from their African blood. Likewise their gentleness. He says their revolutions are largely bloodless, and there is some truth in that. He cited an incident in the São Paulo Revolution. He and his comrades were aiming a cannon capable of blowing them all to oblivion at a large group of Vargas's men, when one of the revolutionaries said, "It seems a pity to kill them. They're probably nice men." And so they lived.

April 13

Rio. Hot, loose winds blowing in large gusts. Sunny this morning, temperature about 85°, humidity high. Swimming-pool temperature about 80°. Very pleasant.

Evening. And torrential rains. We've battened down the hatches and will now sprout, I've no doubt. The noise is deafening.

May 1

Labour Day. To the Museu de Arte Moderna to see the drawings done by Portinari in Israel. An excellent show. Many sketches and some finished drawings, a dozen or so small paintings and two large ones. I was amazed by the different effects he was able to get with different media. His pencil drawings were so warm that I felt, for the first time, interested in pencil. He has much to say about human beings and he says it with great sensitivity. Two of his small paintings I would have loved to own—one had a cadmium yellow sun in a pale chrome yellow sky, which sounds high-keyed, but is not. All the paintings in this group are low-keyed with small areas of brilliant colour. For instance, the cows in one painting were done in such a way as to suggest a muscle chart—strange lines, and the lines unexpectedly of lapis lazuli or amethyst. His drawings of little girls caught all their jumpiness and untidiness and energy. Sometimes they looked like bats or birds—winged. And bedouins on bicycles like large arcane bats or birds.

Returned late Sunday from Paraná, the state immediately south of São Paulo. Curitiba, its capital, just over four hundred air miles from Rio, is a rapidly growing city of modern—no—modernistic skyscrapers and government buildings. To my eye, most of them ugly.

Shortly after our arrival there, while A. set off on his official calls, I was picked up by the wife of the *chefe de cerimônia* to call on the governor's wife. The governor's wife, however, was out of town, so it had been arranged that the daughter receive me. The house seemed well nigh impenetrable but we were finally admitted by an agitated *copeiro* who ran ahead of us turning on lights. We cooled our heels in a baroque *sala* from where we had a good view of one even more baroque—gold furniture, cerulean blue carpet, carrot-coloured curtains, immense chandelier, and a life-size portrait of the governor's wife to which I was presented, rather as if it were she herself. Practically felt I had paid the call. At last a small, rather dowdy woman arrived who obviously hadn't a clue why we were there. When it was explained that we had come to call on the governor's daughter, we were told she was in bed with the grippe. We were given a *cafèzinho* and spoke at some length to the— housekeeper, I think. Then we left. Went on to tea with the wife of a local general, a nice woman in a furnished army house which was hideous. It was a largish female tea at which I had to speak Portuguese only, but I now know enough to be able to move about in a crowd.

Next morning we visited a *mate* factory and sampled a *chimarrão*. I could become addicted. It has all the advantages of a cigarette holder—something to chew on—plus the comforts of a drink. Paraná produces most of the *mate* in Brazil and exports it in leaf and powder form.

In the afternoon I was taken to an air force base to see some houses built from Canadian designs. (It is cold in Curitiba at this season and the site where the houses were might have been Calgary looking towards the Rockies.) Identical houses painted different colours and not separated one from the other by hedges or walls. The women were very pleased with this, thought it gave the children such a lovely playground. What really baffled them was why the *copa* was beyond the kitchen instead of between the kitchen and the dining-room. I said that it saved steps for the Canadian housewife, who rarely has any help. This fascinated them—it was, of course, the very last explanation they would have thought of, as the middle class in Brazil always has help. A merry party at which we cheerfully drank cherry brandy at three in the afternoon.

Next port of call was the Clube Hípico—a very popular riding club for the rich. Members supply their own horses and are trained—horse and rider—to enter international shows. Despite my cavalry riding lessons as a child, I find this elaborate—more like chess than horsemanship.

One whole wall of the clubhouse was Paraná pine, cut in cross-section at the point where the ring of branches joins the trunk. The trunk itself is light in colour and the knots, where the branches join, pinkish. The effect is that of petals—a kind of lazy daisy. A beautiful wood in grain and colour. It is also handsome as a tree. When small it looks much like any other pine, but as it grows it takes on a distinct personality. Its branches now encircle the trunk like the spokes of a wheel, the "wheels" becoming more widely separated from each other every year. When fully grown, all its lower "wheels" have dropped off (deciduous branches?) and its tall, bare trunk is topped by a splendid umbrella-shaped crown. I hate to think its end is paper.

Dinner at the palace—a large, ugly, contemporary, boxlike building on stilts. Much glass. We were met by a smartly uniformed band playing "O Canada" magnificently, and equally smart guards lining the approach to the entrance. Inside, a vast marble floor, flanked by walls of great height, led to a beautiful wide spiral staircase. The upstairs rooms were enormous—with glittering chandeliers—unexpectedly light and furnished sparsely with a mixture of traditional Brazilian and modern. Chairs traditional—carved or painted; and carpets of two kinds—tufted, split-level, like modern Swedish, or woven in cross-stitch with a smallish geometrical pattern. Very nice indeed! They told me they were made in Curitiba but I suspect they may have given me the answer that suited the occasion.

Governor Moises Lupion, our host, is a plumpish man of mixed Spanish and German descent and soft-spoken manner. To us he couldn't have been more gracious, but he and his administration have been the centre of a heated controversy over land policy which, some months ago, became so acute as to result in an outbreak of violence. We were told that salaries of many state employees were months in arrears. In light of this, the munificence and grandeur of the palace seemed a bit incongruous.

Next morning we flew 110 miles north-west, by single-engine Cessna, to a pulp and paper mill at Monte Alegre (Mount Happiness)—a name out of allegory.

It was a crisp, clear, sparkling day and the trip was bumpy. I arrived feeling green and A. with a sudden streaming cold. Two rather uncivil men met us—the owner and the manager of the paper company. The reason for their behaviour became clear when we learned that whoever was in charge of our travel arrangements had changed our time of arrival without consulting or notifying anyone. They had been waiting all morning at the airport and the delay had put out their entire programme. A bad start.

As it was late, they took us at once to the company guest-house where A. was able to lie down. I had a drink and felt a bit better. For one thing, I found myself liking the owner, Samuel Klabin, a first-generation Brazilian of Russian extraction. He looks a tough guy—an American tough guy, at that. He has the terrific energy and curiosity that so often go with successful men, but in his case the latter covers a wider field than usual because his family has been equally successful in the arts. His mother's brother was Segall. As a result, there are good paintings in the guest-house.

In the afternoon he took us around his mill, of which he was obviously very proud. We were lucky enough to see a "break" on the paper machine and the excitement and drama that followed, for it was a case of all hands to the cylinders to get the paper threaded again. The movements of the men were ballet-like against the big, roaring machine that seemed as relentless as a locomotive. There was something so puny about the length of paper no wider than a toilet sheet that the men finally fed through the great monster—and then the moment of consummation when the monster took over and, as if by magic, stretched that narrow strip across the whole width of its rollers and spilled it out in a great wide sheet at the end. Klabin loved it. His face showed his pleasure as clearly as a child's. He told A. of his plans for the future, his dreams; and when A. said, "And after that, what then?" he looked frightened and old, as if for the first time in his life he was uncertain, without direction, his world ending. But that evening at dinner—fabulous food!—we saw a light-hearted Klabin, all set to play.

We were scheduled to fly next morning to Iguaçú Falls, on the borders where Argentina, Brazil, and Paraguay meet. It is a famous waterfall, more impressive than Niagara, we are told. But it meant flying three hours there, spending the day in a small boat, and flying three hours back, and with A. feeling as miserable as he was, we reluctantly cancelled the trip. Our host was kind enough to let us stay on where we were. It was warm and sunny in his big garden. I managed to borrow some drawing paper from a local artist and fondly imagined I might spend the day lazily drawing. But of course, that was absurd. In the morning we were whisked off to see the town. At the school we learned that the director—a state employee—had not been paid for five months and was only able to carry on courtesy of the paper company. A spotless establishment. Teachers and pupils dressed in white. In the kindergarten the walls had been decorated by a young Brazilian artist who had simply copied paintings done by children. Very effective.

We visited the company store, cinema, hotel, social club, well-baby clinic, and hospital. This last, which appeared superior from the outside, was like the Dark Ages inside. Overcrowded, dirty, with ghastly-looking food and neglected-looking patients. The doctor in charge, a decent young man, said it was almost impossible to get nurses or staff.

A great deal of money and good taste had gone into the town planning, but I discovered that simply walking around a company town got my back up.

Next day, flew a further 110 miles north-west to Maringá, one of the newest of new towns—population 40,000 and only eleven years old. Built on coffee.

The story as told to us: a German ex-Foreign Minister and a group of his friends came to Brazil with machinery (Hitler not allowing them to bring money), acquired forested lands in the then undeveloped north of Paraná, and, after clearing it and devoting a few years to experimental planting, discovered they were sitting on the richest coffee country in Brazil. They now live very well indeed, in fabulous *fazendas* with European governesses and tutors for their children.

Maringá is a red town—every way but politically. The soil, known as *terra roxa*, is a deep rust-red and it stains everything—houses, people, vegetation, even darkness. It was amazing to look out over that flat land from our hotel room at night and see a kind of underpainting of red beneath the blackness.

An exciting country, undoubtedly, but made for pioneers. When people say to them, "How do you stand the dust?" they reply, "Dust never hurt anyone, and anyway it washes out easily with a million-*cruzeiro* cheque." They are rolling in money, energetic, eager. They have a riding club where their young canter to the commands of a French riding master. They hired a São Paulo architect to design their country club—an attractive building with elegant double swimming-pools set in a newly laid out tropical garden. Their bishop has made plans and a model for a cathedral which is to rise—a giant pink cone ruched with chapels—from the flat, red land, neo-gothic, and soaring to the height of a thirty-five-storey building. You could surely reach God from its peak.

But all this is based on a fantastic gamble. The area is so far south that it is subject to frost, which can be deadly to coffee plants. Twice in the last eight years the frost has struck. The whole region lives in fear of winter. Even the survey of the land is determined by this fear. The terrain is an irregular succession of low, broad ridges separated by shallow valleys. So that each planter may get an even deal, each *fazenda* runs from the crown of a ridge to the trough of a valley—from warmer upland to cooler lowland—for the temperature gradient may be as much as three degrees, and those three degrees may mean the difference between fortune and bankruptcy.

Neighbouring Londrina, a twenty-year-old city, is paved, so the dust is kept more at bay than in Maringá. Perhaps it is that very lack of red stain that makes the place appear devitalized, dull. Londrinans are proud of it, however, and the day we arrived they were inaugurating a new air terminal building. Six jets had come from Pôrto Alegre for the occasion and the air was shrill with their screams. Our poor plane barely seemed to have space to land. Enormous crowds. We all shook hands and waited about for the movie cameras.

Spent the better part of the day touring what seemed to me an unattractive city and ate a gigantic luncheon in an incredibly noisy restaurant. Calves-foot jelly for dessert!

When we returned to the airport to leave for Rio, the morning crowds were still there—tired now and with nothing to do, but not wanting to go home. The floor was red from dust, and the windows bore the noseprints and fingerprints of all the swarming celebrants.

"I've been trying to draw, to recreate the wonderful shapes of the leaves...."

May 5

Yesterday Ricardo killed a venomous snake. According to the staff, it was killed while in the act of hypnotizing a rat. They report that the rat got dizzy and fell. The snake book says hypnotic powers are not among this snake's skills, which include, however, growth to nine feet and striking without provocation. I saw him well dead—a pretty fellow as thick through as my wrist, with husk-coloured diamonds on a grey-brown base. Ricardo warns that they always travel in pairs. Name: *surucucu.*

The image of Maringá is still very vivid in my head. Somebody should paint it. A young man—a remarkably young man—has made a park out of virgin forest. It contrasts strongly with Maringá itself—Maringá horizontal, hot, red; the park vertical, cool, green. We were introduced to a stand of giant bamboo and the *pau d'alho* (garlic tree)—the bark of which smells exactly like garlic. The young man himself was most pleased with what I would call a larch—an exotic in Brazil, perhaps. We were more interested in the peacock-tails, elephant-ears, and the wide variety of philodendrons. The plant known as *mysteriosa deliciosa* in Australia, where its fruit is considered a delicacy, is here called *banana de macaco* (monkey's banana) and even the poor spurn it. It is a cut-leafed philodendron—large-leafed, dramatic.

May 12

So difficult to keep a journal unless you have time when you need it. I have been totally swamped preparing a speech for the Academia Brasileira de Letras (Brazilian Academy of Letters), which is modelled in all particulars on the French Academy. Austrégesilo Athayde, its president, wrote saying the Academy wants to honour the wife of the Argentine ambassador, Courtney Espil, a historian; the wife of the British ambassador who, as a novelist, writes as Stella Zilliacus; and me. He told us that we would be received by the academicians in the Pequeno Trianon, that to each of us would be assigned an academician who would introduce us, and that we should have to address the assembly.

Like an imbecile I put off writing my speech until about a week before and then I nearly went mad. I had not been able to take any of it very seriously. I felt that, had we not been wives of ambassadors, this would never have happened—and, of course, it wouldn't have.

But what bothered me even more (and I have the additional bother about being received as a writer when I am no longer writing) was that no Brazilian woman writers had been so received. Perhaps we shall be the thin edge of the wedge.

The others prepared their speeches immediately, asked about mine. What was I writing that was taking me so long? I didn't know. I milled around, read every Brazilian book I could lay my hands on, read Machado de Assis's inaugural presidential address to the Academy, read its history, the biographies of the academicians, and wandered around in an anguished dream, trying to make whole cloth out of all the bits. Eventually, due, I can only think, to the direct assistance of the Holy Ghost, I wrote two small nature poems in Portuguese and then the whole speech began to move—an account of the places we have visited in Brazil, as described by their poets. With the help of A.'s editorial skills and a translator who was able to provide me with Portuguese words I could pronounce, I finally had something that was usable: my discovery of their Brazil. It was to end with me addressing the academicians directly, with a quote from Gonçalves Dias: "*Meninos, eu vi.*" ("Little boys, I've seen it myself.")

There was then the additional problem of clothes. The weather is still hot but it is no longer fashionable to wear cottons! So a dress and a hat had, miraculously, to be produced at twenty-four hours' notice and that involved fittings up to and including the actual day of the event. Nerve-racking! Dressed, but unsure what I looked like in my new finery, I drove to town to meet A.

At the Academy we were greeted by the president, Athayde, and wife, various ancient academicians with and without wives—and all light-hearted as schoolboys on a holiday. I was delighted to see that they really were *meninos*. Upstairs in a dining-room, a table was set with so few places that only the women sat and one man—ageing Macedo Soares, ex-Minister of Foreign Affairs. Mysterious glasses of heaven knows what were placed randomly on the table—*guaraná*, Coca Cola, a fruit juice which is rather sweet and thick known as *canja manga*, some little glasses of what turned out to be port—and cups of rapidly cooling tea. The wife of the foreign minister, a real cake-eater, enormously stout, solemnly ate her way through various plates of sweet cakes. The men ran in and out of the pantry, helping themselves to this and that in a most informal manner, while A. and the two other husbands sat about unhappily.

We were finally escorted downstairs to the entrance hall and there the three of us found ourselves receiving everyone who arrived—everyone we had ever met, in fact—the diplomatic community, all our friends, plus people one would never have expected to be there. Once the doors were shut and the academicians had taken their places, we were ushered by three academicians into a well-proportioned oval room utterly jammed with people. On one of its long sides the president of the Academy and honoured guests, the foreign minister one of them, sat on a raised platform. In front of them, on a lower platform, in comfortable chairs, the academicians. The two short sides of the room were packed solid with guests. We were escorted to chairs in the front row.

The president, sitting, announced that the session had begun and that Dr. Cardim would make a speech of welcome. It was long and flowery. We were called The Three Graces. All courtesies possible and impossible were expressed. He spoke from a little rostrum in the centre of the academicians. Then Calman, the Most Reverend Rector of the university, spoke in high-flown, elaborate English to introduce the wife of the Argentine ambassador. He spoke mostly about her husband (!) and what a wonderful hostess she was—all of which confirmed my worst fears. It was a splendid if over-florid eulogy of a married couple.

Then Rodrigo Otávio Filho introduced me. I liked him. He spoke quite simply, without flourish. He had taken the trouble to read my last book and think about it and come to some conclusions about it. He was, of course, overly generous in his praise—what Brazilian isn't?—claiming I was one of the best, if not *the* best, Canadian poet! But I liked his simplicity and the fact that he spoke of me in my capacity as a writer. Next, Peregrine Junior greeted the wife of the British ambassador. He spoke well, humorously. But little Rodrigo—my boy—had gone to more trouble to do a critical assessment.

The moment finally came when Courtney had to rise and reply. I was nervous for her. It was appallingly hot, the sun pouring through windows closed against the noises of traffic. I was wet through by this time. She, speaking in Portuguese, as would I, was pretty jumpy about it. She began calmly enough and read a rather long speech, most of which I couldn't understand. I was interested to hear her accent, which was markedly Spanish—and why not? Although American, she is married to a Spanish-speaking husband.

My turn. I was grateful for the little rostrum. It meant I didn't have to hold my text and that meant I wouldn't see my hands shaking. That is one of the worst aspects of public speaking for me—my hands shake so I can barely read what I've written and that gets me more nervous and my hands shake even more. However, I couldn't see my hands and I kept my text on the desk. I realized I had to throw my voice in order to be heard, so I threw it. Athayde, whom we know well, was sitting exactly opposite and whenever I looked at him he smiled so lovingly that it gave me heart. I got a laugh in the first paragraph, which assured me they could hear me and understand my accent. My "*meninos*" climax worked like a charm.

Stella's turn. She spoke prettily, in English, but made the mistake, I think, of being too general in her remarks. She ended with a paragraph in Portuguese, excellently pronounced.

During her speech I allowed myself to turn and look at A., who gave me the *ótimo* sign, and I suddenly realized that my speech must have been good. He looked so extraordinarily pleased.

That night in bed I couldn't stop saying it over and over, mispronouncing words and getting panicky and then realizing it was past, that I didn't have to worry any more. But the relentless record player that wouldn't turn off went on and on. At four I took a sleeping pill. At seven I was awake again—those Portuguese sentences streaming through my head.

A considerable press next day—front-page stories. Photographs and excerpts from speeches and some very garbled reports. Quite funny. President Kubitschek complained he hadn't been invited. I received flowers and phone calls and telegrams. It might have been my birthday.

May 14

Went yesterday, out of the blue, to Brasília. We have a Canadian Convair here giving demonstration flights, and President Kubitschek suddenly decided that he would like to go to Brasília in it. We were to be at the airport at eight in the morning. So, accordingly, we breakfasted at 6.30, arrived at the airport by eight, and awaited the president until nine, when he finally arrived and we took off into that gorgeous sky. We were told we would be back by four at the latest, as the president had to kick off at the Brazil–England football game. We were surprised, as indeed were members of the crew, to find so many people going just for the ride—with such quantities of food.

Among the joyriders were two new ambassadors whom we had not met before; the Portuguese ambassador and his wife; and a planeful of Brazilians—one, an ancient priest in his soutane and beret, clutching a large bunch of lilies carefully wrapped in cellophane. We were no sooner airborne than we discovered the president was sitting under an air vent that leaked—not air but water—and we had to move him. Not the best introduction to the Convair!

Arrived in Brasília to a brilliant day—blinding sun and the red earth of Brasília orange in the light. Deplaned into that great heat and waited endlessly with no idea as to why. Various people had referred to Nossa Senhora de Fâtima during the day, but it was some time after our arrival that it dawned on us we were waiting for her. Finally an air force plane arrived from Belo Horizonte and Fâtima, life-size and looking as if made of plaster—actually she was made from Brazilian wood carved in Portugal—was removed from the body of the plane and placed erect on a large float decorated with bunches of everlasting flowers and streamers of crêpe paper. A group of children began to sing, voices were raised in *"Viva Nossa Senhora de Fâtima, viva!"* and there were flags and people dressed in their best and the wonderful, warm, friendly, good-natured quality of a Brazilian crowd.

At last we were ushered into cars and driven to the president's Palace of the Dawn, passing, as we went, the sites for diplomatic residences, the beehive and pudding bowl which are the congressional buildings, and, incomplete against the sky, wall-less sixteen-storey buildings with concrete floors and steel uprights—unreal and light as some kind of dream image.

The palace proved perilous and devoid of any human warmth. We sat in it for a very long time, waiting for all that food from the plane to be cooked in its kitchens. "We" by now consisted of an immense number of women who had appeared, seemingly from nowhere. Gradually we learned that Nossa Senhora de Fâtima was being officially placed in the small chapel built as a *promessa* by the president's wife and financed by her charitable organization, the Pioneiras Sócias. Accordingly, many of her Pioneiras had been flown to Brasília, and were taking advantage of the occasion to officially open—by the simple act of having everyone sign a very long document—a Pioneiras headquarters in the new capital-to-be.

We waited in the heat—it was an incredibly hot day—the president dressed entirely in black, like a strange Latin Hamlet, sitting on a chesterfield in that enormous glass room, jiggling his leg (a very Brazilian male habit) and flirting with the younger and prettier Pioneiras.

Eventually we had lunch—"American-style". Great billies of food were dragged out—*vatapá, feijão,* rice, *lingüiça,* chicken, salad, pizza, baked bananas, *mandioca,* sweet potatoes. And quite suddenly, without warning, our mouths still full, we were off. Where? No one seemed to know. By the time we got outside all the cars had swept off, so we boarded a bus which roared through the red dust and caught up with what proved to be a procession, with Nossa Senhora de Fátima on her float being pulled through this half-built city, past workers' houses decorated with streamers and petitions: Nossa Senhora de Fátima bless our home. Then to an ignominious halt in the dust and another interminable wait. Why? What? Where? The car that was pulling Our Lady had broken down!

Our destination proved to be the chapel—a small building shaped like a friar's hat, which whimsy fails to move me. Chips of broken beer bottles glinted in the plaster of its door and interior walls. Outside, a very frail platform had been erected and microphones set up. Nossa Senhora de Fátima was carried in a standing position up the steps and set down on the platform, on which were assembled brothers in brown, archbishops in pie-crust cerise hats, the old Portuguese priest from the plane—now changed into his lace cassock onto which his fountain pen had leaked in three large stains— and the president. Behind us, the musicians: a small pipe organ manned by a priest; another with a violin—like a Chagall painting— who all the time he was not playing was frantically fingering as if he might forget the order of the notes; and a group of singers— women in their best red dresses carrying babies in pink organdy. The musicians struck up unexpectedly now and again with great vigour, as if pitting themselves against the other attractions but, seemingly, without reference to anything else on the programme. The speeches—sonorous, endless—began with the aid of microphones and finally became dumb-show speeches as the mikes broke down.

Meanwhile it was hot. The platform looked precarious. There was no shade. Two small schoolgirls recited a verse duologue about Nossa Senhora, and were kissed by the president. The local tart, hair down her back, transparent blouse showing dirty underwear, cotton lace skirt threaded with ribbons and topped by a red gauze overskirt, scrambled onto the platform and asked to be shown the president.

Finally, three small children dressed in Portuguese peasant costume frolicked on a nearby patch of grass and re-enacted the original vision of the Virgin, who appeared at a great height—white and miraculous above the treetops—and made gestures with her arms of the old-fashioned dancing school "look at the mouse running from my shoulder to my wrist" variety.

At last it ended. Very hot, very late, very thirsty, we once more embarked, this time for the airport where, gratefully, we sank into our seats in the Convair and headed for Rio. But who kicked off for the president at the Brazil–England football game, we never heard.

A wonderful day. Everything apparently spontaneous or lately improvised. Everyone good-natured, pleased, overjoyed even. Endless surprising rabbits out of a hat for us, who had merely set out for Brasília on a demonstration flight of a Canadian-built plane.

Canada was never like this.

May 24

The day before yesterday, a party of us set off for Lages, the "Light's" hydro plant between here and São Paulo. Our plan was to see something of the plant, spend the night at their guest-house, then continue on to Volta Redonda, the steel plant, about an hour's drive distant.

We drove onto the "Light" property at the site of a projected new dam and saw the—to me—always melancholy sight of a community which, with its houses, church, and memories, is soon to be flooded. Toured the three levels of the powerhouse—exciters, generators, and turbines—and watched a descending cable-car land at the bottom of the mountain—rather like a small car ferry coming in on slow, gentle waves. And then, in the dark, we rode up the face of the mountain ourselves. We were told the trip was more impressive by daylight. But I don't know—there was a mystery about it in the dark. Impossible to know what was mountain and what was night. There were moments when all darkness gave the illusion of being mountain which dematerialized for us as we swung softly through it. And there were moments when there seemed to be no mountain at all—no solid anywhere except where we sat in our swaying cradle—our ascent through black space a kind of nudging at the membrane of the imagination.

The company guest-house, a charming old *fazenda* with a deep veranda on three sides, had been not much improved by a tasteless

decorator. In the garden—illuminated by the lights from the house—
we were shown a *pau brasil* —the red-wooded tree after which Brazil
was named and which has now practically disappeared. A pretty tree
with delicate acacia-like leaves. In the morning, before breakfast,
I picked a pomegranate and ate its red crystals—crystals which so
startlingly break to bitter-sweet juice in your mouth and leave you
with nothing but tasteless woody pits. The tree is small and lacy, with
slender whiplike branches at the ends of which hang the heavy fruits.
The *bicos de papagaios* (poinsettias) were in flower, salmon-coloured
and red, and the garden was filled with the smell of sweet grass that
had followed us everywhere on our holiday in Minas. A daisy tree—
a bush more than a tree, I suppose—which grew taller than I was
covered with blossoms much the size of a Canadian meadow daisy.

After breakfast, to Volta Redonda, an attractive valley town which,
before the steel plant was constructed fifteen years ago, was no more
than a village.

We were met at the hotel by the general and his wife. He is
president of the company; was once governor of the state of Rio;
once in the army; once a revolutionary. Interesting how many ex-
revolutionaries are now "establishment". He is a square-shaped man
in his fifties with a younger wife. We have entertained them occasionally and I had found her handsome and closed. She spoke only
Portuguese (fair enough) and never smiled (unfair). As hostess, she
spoke English and was very smily. An example of the theory that the
world is divided into hosts and guests?

We were taken on a well-organized tour of the great mill and I
was excited by it. We saw, first, the immense red-hot ingots in the
rolling mill, the machinery that handled them as if they were neither
heavy nor hot, and the rollers that extended and flattened them—still
clear red—at phenomenal speeds, into thin plates. We saw the blast
furnaces and the molten and starry pig-iron pouring into immense
ladles. A painless inferno, and I am cock-a-hoop with the wonder and
beauty of it all.

Back to luncheon at the president's *fazenda*, which was chock-
full of people, whisky, and the Portuguese language. Delicious food.
Champagne. My Portuguese improved with each course.

Much involved recently with the Minister of Trade for the U.K.
and his wife. He charming, she a frozen-faced English woman,

daughter of the late king's physician. One of the most remarkable events in their honour was a party given by Chateaubriand, Brazilian ambassador to the U.K., in the offices of his O Cruzeiro building. As many cameras as people. Speeches made in execrable English and execrable Portuguese over loudspeaker systems that only sometimes worked. On an easel at one end of the room, a painting by Portinari—yellows, lime greens, and oranges, of two children standing on their heads—with Portinari himself, tiny—an old child in a white suit—standing beside it. And beside *him*, a painting by Churchill which Chateau is reported to have bought from Churchill's butler. Three French models from the Jacques Heim show, wearing the new, pale grey make-up which gives the appearance of cadavers dressed up, were clustered around a mike. Strange human orchid-faces growing out of a metal stalk.

And that reminds me of an experience I had at Volta Redonda. We were standing outside the mill, the men talking and I not listening, when I saw, moving on its course through the grass, a metal—what shall I call it? Animal? It was not, of course, like an animal animal, having neither head nor legs nor feet nor the usual animal characteristics. It was about a foot long and moving as metal moves, with that kind of atomic weight. It was some little time before my mind rejected the concept. And I felt a certain *saudade* for the metal animal when I realized it was merely some man-made mechanical object, moving on a track. Strangely, during the period of thinking of it as a metal animal, there was nothing foreign in the idea. I accepted it as naturally as I would have accepted a rabbit or a bird.

The experience was akin to the time when, in a room with one other person, I gradually became aware of a third being with us. Nothing changed with the awareness of that third person, who sat in a chair on the other side of the room and was as closely with us as I was, myself. It was only when the third person left that the full realization of its having been there broke upon me. Although in no sense unnatural or unknown, it had no sex and no form. It was an entity as natural to me and as much a part of me as was the man who was with me at the time. And with its going there was a kind of absence, an emptiness in a trinity that had had a totality. A sense of loss. I felt a similar loss when the metal animal became a metal object.

Have been having a new front tooth made and am greatly amused by my dentist. He told me how, during the Eucharist Congress, an elderly and prominent Catholic who lives in the same building had as his guest a Canadian archbishop who performed the mass in the apartment every morning at seven. An archbishop's mass is fairly elaborate and additional assistance is needed. Dr. Vianna, my dentist, who had been an acolyte in his youth, was pressed into service. Totally in the dark as to what he had to do, he phoned an old schoolfriend who had recently been associated with these rather complicated services. The friend was only too willing to help him and they set up an altar in the friend's bar. Vianna said that at four in the morning, when they had really hit their stride, his friend's wife appeared, having been summoned by a terrified maid who said something awful was going on, "The master is on his knees and Dr. Vianna is making funny signs over him." When the wife appeared, he said, he was tolling the bell and everything was going swimmingly.

A very Brazilian story—high-spirited, childlike, and—curiously— not irreverent.

June 1

To Niterói, across the harbour, for the first time. Crossed by pedestrian ferry—lovers leaning on the rail, enfolded within each other.

By some mistake, we had a fine tour of Niterói by taxi. It was rather like a drive through Trinidad or Barbados. I wonder if the British leave a kind of stamp on the air. Finally arrived where we were trying to get to—the Cricky Clooby (Cricket Club).

About church saints: we bought a small one in Bahía. It was quite elegant but had no hands and we wondered about having hands made for it. Apparently those little statues are offerings taken to church as supplications. If the saint didn't produce what was prayed for, the supplicant broke off its hands in a rage. Or other people seeing it in church would break off a hand, promising that it would be given back when their prayer was answered. A fine way to treat one's divine interceptors. This whole matter of *promessas* is very strange. One woman I know promised that if her child recovered from an illness she would wear odd shoes for the rest of her life. And she does.

My art teacher very nearly drove me over the edge the other day and is a good teacher for that reason, I think. He will tell me nothing.

His name is Serpa, and he is a small, hunchbacked gnome of a young man who teaches in a kindergarten. I had seen and liked his work and asked if he would give me lessons. He agreed provided I came to the kindergarten at recess. And so the two of us sit on tiny red chairs at a tiny red table and talk, while the liberated children in the courtyard scream the sky down. Our conversations go like this:

> "What paints should I buy?"
> "You must select your own palette."
> "What paper is good for gouache?"
> "Find out what is good for *you*."

He told me last week that some of my paintings, had Dufy done them, he would have admired. But that I have to find my own means of expression, make an original contribution.

> "How?"
> "How should I know?"

However, he did make a couple of suggestions—that I throw away my pen and dream a bit more. He said the combination of paint and pen as I have been using them leads me straight to Dufy.

It was like an amputation renouncing that pen.

June 9

In the doldrums. Nothing right. The day is beautiful but I have no polished surfaces to reflect it.

June 14

Went to our third presidential reception within a week—this one for the Crown Prince of Japan. Rather dreaded it. Two was already one too many. It was held at Itamarity, in the garden surrounding the ornamental pool on which swans float. For backdrop, rows of imperial palms, immensely tall and straight and dating back to early colonial days. The buildings too are colonial. Elegant proportions. All around the pool, tables had been set—three hundred of them—with scarlet tablecloths and candles. A kind of grandstand had been erected for the guests of honour, its canopy the same red. The perfect colour against the green of the grass and the grey of the stone. Hundreds of chrysanthemum heads had been thrown into the lake. We sat at one of the little tables in the candle-lit dark, just looking. Someone said it reminded her of Versailles. She could already hear the ring of the axe!

My painting, with which I am almost totally preoccupied, progresses again. Such a struggle. Painted the scene at Itamarity the following morning. Couldn't get out of bed fast enough. Serpa very encouraging at my last lesson. Claimed I had made great strides and he thought two of the things I had done beautiful. Well, so far, for me, nothing I have done is beautiful.

Fearfully busy week and next week will be too. Begins with a meeting of Commonwealth wives, various receptions, and we give two dinners. At last Klaus, our cook, has produced a really good meal. We shall just go on and on serving it.

Went the other night to the New York Philharmonic directed by Mitropoulos. Marvellous orchestra, poor programme. They began by playing the Brazilian national anthem with such brio that the audience clapped and cheered. I wish we had been able to go the second night when they had a better programme. Music here is a society event. Everyone dresses. Interesting contrast to the Berliner Ballet for which no one dressed. (How do they know when not to?)

It was with a considerable jolt that we discovered there was no orchestra for the ballet. Luckily we were close to the front, otherwise I think we would have heard nothing of the recorded music that trickled feebly out of the loudspeakers. Dancing good. The first ballet—*La Dame aux Camélias*—was rather alarming as they had a character who might be called Her Haemorrhage—dressed in a red tutu, with a red eye-mask which gave her a faceless look—whom Camille saw whenever she looked in the mirror. This was done sufficiently well to be absolutely horrifying. Then *Don Juan*, a *pas de deux*—the choreography rather too literal (much lying down!) Interestingly, Don Juan was seen almost entirely through the eyes of the woman he was making love to. A mere shade of a man, as sometimes the male in the *pas de deux* is—and perhaps that is what Don Juan is too, although I had not thought of that before. The last number, *Cain*, was full of a dark symbolism I was unable to disentangle and there was not much original choreography. But the most serious problem was the lack of music. And if one thinks of ballet as dance, one only has to see it without music to realize how much of it is music.

During the week A. attended a state funeral. His description warrants a despatch, I think, but he will certainly not write it. An ex-president was killed in a plane crash. After much uncertainty and conflicting reports we learned there were to be five days of official mourning, so we cancelled a dinner we had planned for that night. At 8.45, just as I was thinking of treating myself to an early bed, one of our guests arrived, not having received our message. We brought him in for a drink and then took him off to Copacabana for dinner. Our second.

Next morning A. struggled into his morning suit with black waistcoat, which latter he had to rent for the occasion, and so make a mourning suit of it, and went off to the funeral. On his return he said, "Brazilians may be disorganized in life, but you should see them in death."

When he arrived at the entrance to the Senate building he literally had to fight his way in, and succeeded only in reaching a kind of circular foyer, totally packed with sweltering morning-suited men in black waistcoats. From there he could see the doorway into the Senate Chamber where the service was taking place. After some time, there was an impression of movement in the Chamber, and the president of the republic and various ministers appeared, struggling to carry the coffin through the dense mass of solid bodies. When they reached the foyer, the president in the lead, they actually had to use the coffin as a kind of battering-ram to force their way out into the street. And at the cemetery it was much the same. No police to control a swarm of the idly curious, urchins and dogs crowded around the open grave as if they were chief mourners. A. never got to that service either!

The Senate building, incidentally, has a curious history. Originally the Brazilian pavilion at the St. Louis World's Fair in 1904, it won first prize, and was thereupon dismantled stone by stone, shipped to Rio, and reconstructed in its present site.

June 28

And still I write nothing in my journal. Am too absorbed in painting when I have a free minute. Now that I'm working in oils it is much more time-consuming and all the preparations are slow—although even oils can't slow me up completely, so on fire am I.

Went the other day to the Museum of Modern Art to see a show entitled "Four Thousand Centuries of Glass". The pre-Christian glass was so beautiful. Blues, greens, yellows one can hardly believe, and lovely designs. All the objects smallish—partly, I suppose, because the people were. I found it a pleasure up to the fifteenth century. I hated the German and Dutch glass—heavy, bourgeois articles, ornate and ugly. And the very modern I didn't like either. Everything looked like a Henry Moore figure—not that I have anything against a Henry Moore figure, except when it takes the form of a drinking glass. I wonder if that Moore figure is in the air and everyone is picking it up or if it is a matter of copycat.

The show, for me, was the collection of little beakers and beads and bowls as beautiful as anything I have ever seen. But how compare beauties?

On Sunday by yacht, with a collection of friends, to the Ilha do Governador to visit a Bahían couple who have built a house on the beach across the bay from Rio. Quite exquisite: exotic foliage in the garden, all the paths shells—either small, twisted conch shells loose like gravel, or bivalves with crimped edges set into cement. The house—old tiles and jacaranda furniture. He is a collector of glass paper-weights and has, I believe, a famous collection—the finest in the world, if not the largest. The mate of one, with a snake and plant in its centre, sold recently in London for two thousand pounds. I loved seeing so many together, some so realistic, others geometrical, some like coral caves. He also collects glass door-handles and I must say I was sorry to see so many sitting on shelves instead of being the means of opening doors.

Incredible luncheon. *Vatapá*, the special Bahían dish of shrimps and glue and chiles. And then a sweet of egg yolks and sugar formed into two immense bunches of grapes. A work of art.

The Israelis gave a dinner for the Ecuadorean who is painting portraits of the Rio beauties. I was lucky enough to sit beside Portinari—a tiny man, plumpish and plain, who reminded me of the baby *gambá* that we had in the house. And when he said, "E", the Brazilian expression of accord, it sounded just like the Geiger-counter noise the *gambá* made. He was rather a menace as a dinner partner, as the softness of his voice, coupled with his shortness of stature, gave me a crick in my neck listening. Add to that his use of imagery and metaphor, and my difficulties with Portuguese, and the results were hilarious.

A large fish was served, covered with scales made from overlapping slices of radish. *"Uma sereia"* ("a mermaid"). Did he say it? I wanted him to say it. He must have said it. At any rate, I replied as if he had. Later, when he was talking about his son—or so I thought—I asked his age. "He is dead," he said, and before I had time to condole with him, "he died before I was born." So. That gave me cause to think. I had missed a transition somewhere. He was talking about William Blake.

July 1

The house agog with preparations for our National Day reception. Perfect weather made it possible to spread out in all directions and so we erected the garden lights to show up the big *jaca* trees, shed a soft glow on the stream, and illuminate the spiky plants and the lovely curve of the nearby tile bench. Also placed a hundred little night-lights around the swimming-pool to reflect in the water. All day flowers arrived—*cestas*, cut flowers, roses, tropical wild beasts.

The surprise of the evening was John Grierson, who arrived, was rude to the wife of one of Brazil's leading diplomats, and then left. I am told he gave a talk at the Cultura Inglêsa which was much disliked. He criticized the *favelas*—and as a free agent I think he was entitled to. *We* have to avoid criticism but he doesn't. One Brazilian friend said, "What did he have to do that for? We all know we have *favelas*." But knowing is not enough.

July 10

The day after the party I took to my bed "*gripada*" and there I stayed until our formal dinner on Thursday—an incredible party which changed about every ten minutes beforehand, until there were only four of the originals left. Everyone has flu. The food, I think, was good, although I couldn't taste it, and despite the changes in the guest list everything went well. I was none the worse for getting up, but I was not cured either, so when A. set off on his official visit to Pernambuco and Ceará he left me behind. Sickening, as the north fascinates me and I had so looked forward to this trip.

My time in bed with A. away has had a strange unreality to it— time, all of a piece, without intervals. Reading Henry James. The days have poured like honey from the pot, filled with the magic of the winter light.

Our household is full of its own drama. In the kitchen José, a new *ajudante* (assistant), coal black, who wears a chef's hat a foot high. In the laundry a new laundress—likewise black—from Bahía, who wears a white bandanna on her head and speaks slowly and softly and dreamily and makes all her laundry spanking white—perhaps just in contrast to herself. Our Fâtima, the Portuguese upstairs maid, in the "plenitude", as Athayde would say, of her love. Orphaned very young, she was taken in by a family in Portugal and trained by them. A little over a year ago she came to an aunt in Brazil. Within three months, one of the sons of the family in Portugal had written proposing marriage. She agreed. About six months ago he came to Pernambuco, where he is studying engineering, and he has given her orders that she is not to go out on her day off—not just not go out with anyone, but not go out at all. And she has obeyed. Now he has arrived in Rio. Until this point Fâtima had not discussed it with me but I knew through Graciano, teller of tales. The other day she finally broke down and told me the story.

I asked her if she had known he was interested in her before she left. She said she hadn't. When I asked if she had liked him particularly, she said she hadn't thought about him, that she had called him *senhor*, that he and his brothers were simply the sons of the house. I asked her if she loved him now. She said she didn't know. She said he claimed the reason he wanted to marry her was because she was honest. Can it be so? The thought of her being taken to her nuptial bed for her honesty.... She feels a certain alarm over the disparity of their riches and says her aunt does not approve of her marrying a rich man.

A strange experience a few weeks ago while I was at the Pioneiras. Suddenly saw one of the very beautiful Brazilian girls with quite new eyes. Saw her as a work of art. From that moment on my whole point of view has changed—become Brazilian. Previously, I had thought one is born with one's face, one's responsibility is to keep it clean and looking as attractive as possible, but that was it and there you were, age altering it, death destroying it. But a Brazilian doesn't think of her face like that at all. For her it is simply the paper on which she makes her poem—changing it when she finds a way of improving it. She stands, in relation to it, as an artist—creating, by whatever means she can, a work of art. And she *is* an artist. The girl the other day had made her hair wide at the sides and formed her eyebrows into wide black wings and the whole impression, while artificial, was artificial in the way a work of art is. I couldn't help thinking that, to Brazilians, we who wear our real faces must seem both lazy and without talent. I think if I lived here long enough I too could become inspired to make a face—except that I really haven't the temperament. I *am* too lazy.

The Brazilian woman is quite different from the Canadian. Not only in the matter of her face. She is quite different in her attitude to abortion. Abortions are not legal here, but they are performed by good doctors in nursing homes which exist for this purpose alone. They cost anything from five hundred to seven thousand *cruzeiros*. A friend of mine told me, the other day, that she has had four. When I expressed surprise, she said, "That's nothing. I have a friend who has had twelve." According to her, it never occurs to a wealthy Brazilian to have a baby she hasn't planned, and getting rid of it is almost as easy as having a manicure. Accepted for married women, for single women abortion is still not approved of socially. For them the problem is one of secrecy. As I understand it, medical ethics don't enter into it and the matter of taking a life seems incidental. This may, of course, represent the point of view of a special group—just as my point of view may not represent that of most Canadian women.

July 11

Daugival, one of the cleaners, bought himself an expensive piano accordion some time ago. Every free minute it demands his time. As I sit in the sun this morning looking out into the *mato* and trying to paint the pink house where Daugival has his room, I am filled with a kind of wonder by his music. It is almost as if the instrument has gone mad. Never was there such a muddle of notes, and a tumbling out. He is not tentatively trying individual notes, rather he is striving for chords, for whole orchestrations, and all at a speed as if he will die tomorrow. More interesting still, he began playing that way and so he continues. I have never heard him play a scale or a melody that was in any way even remotely recognizable. His is a kind of virtuoso performance of musical gibberish and it tumbles, cascades, falls like a crazy plant out of his bedroom window—fast, faster, faster—and, as suddenly, stops.

July 12

Have painted a kind of triptych. At last—after how long?—I know what paper I like for gouache. What a difference it makes to have the right paper, the right tooth. The triptych looks a bit like an illustration for an Icelandic saga—brilliant colour, and me as model, in three different poses.

July 27

A. returned from the north a day early, to my joy—suitcases loaded with tortoise-shell bracelets and hammocks. But he has spent a week in bed with some infection. I, still only half well, have been tottering out to dinners without him. Since then, much absorbed by the sudden decision on the part of our government to send two observers—one from the Commons, one from the Senate—to the Interparliamentary Conference which is meeting here.

August 3

Our observers have kept us occupied and now, although the conference is over, Senator Dessureault is staying with us as his wife, Elise, is in hospital. It is Sunday and he has just gone off to mass and on to see her.

This afternoon we go to the races. It is the big race of the year. I would sooner birdwatch. It must be spring as the birds are returning and that wonderful whistler is again in the *mato*.

Received the B.C. Centennial Anthology the other day. When it comes to books, we're a long way from Canada. Liked Ethel Wilson's "Hurry, Hurry!" and "Haply the Soul of My Grandmother", and the reproduction of a painting by Bruno Bobak.

Am reading Joyce Cary's *Mr. Johnson*. It is so like life in Rio I can hardly believe it.

August 7

Elise, back from hospital to convalesce with us, promptly became very ill and had to return. Since then it has been touch and go. She is a bit better tonight and I am just home from seeing her and now plan to tumble into bed.

August 9

How choppy my notes. I run to the hospital and back. Elise is still very ill indeed. Today, in fact, seemed worse.

Yesterday I painted with Helena in the morning. We went to the charming square off Cosme Velho. Rough cobblestones, three sides of the square treed; the fourth, old houses built with extravagant use of Portuguese tile.

The weather continues to be perfect. Sunny and not too hot.

August 14

It is a two-steps-forward, one-step-back period. Elise is still in hospital—she gets better and then worse again. He is a very worried man—and a darling. Confusion with cars is incredible. A. back in bed again. I still have a cold. And yet, in between times, wonderful moments.

Must write about the palms. Each palm at this season, regardless of its type, has grown a pair of antlers—one on either side of its trunk, and high up. Lacy and lovely. I'm surprised I didn't notice it last year…all the trees turning into stags. One large palm has pale green "beads" on one antler, red "beads" on the other. Another has one ochre-coloured antler and one that is very pale green. The travellers' palm, however, which grows like a huge fan, squeezes an immense crested bird's head of purple and white out from between its ribs.

Before it is erased from my mind completely, should at least comment on having met John Foster Dulles, U.S. Secretary of State. The fact that our lives are in his hands ought to give him emphasis, yet my lack of sympathy for him and his ways, and the lateness of the hour of the meeting, tend to obliterate him. Itamarity gave a dinner and reception. For us it began at 10.30—the official dinner, in theory, being over by then. We are told the dinner was lavish beyond measure—certainly all the women who attended brought boughs of orchids away from the table with them. Later we were also told that the quantities of caviar and vodka, served for a first course, had been given to Itamarity by the Russian delegates to the Interparliamentary Conference.

American ambassador Ellis Briggs's story of the visit was riotously funny. He said all went superbly well while Itamarity was responsible but the whole thing broke down the minute the Catete (the presidential palace) took over. Dulles was rushed away from an American Club luncheon to be at the airport at two to meet the president—who finally arrived at three! On arrival in Brasília, Briggs was informed that Dulles and the president were going off on a helicopter ride. For where, no one said. The helicopter took off. Briggs—who was responsible for Dulles—with the other members of the official party, was left on the ground to wonder and opine. After some scurrying about, they acquired a jeep and tried to follow the helicopter—an endeavour which, as darkness fell, grew difficult, then impossible. When Dulles arrived at the scheduled tree-planting ceremony, the chief of the Botanical Gardens had been waiting, tree in hand, for hours, and it was so dark that Dulles was unable to read his speech.

Yesterday to São Bento with Helena. A great, heavy church, its twin towers surmounted by giant stone cannon-balls. Yet its three massive black-lace entrance gates miraculously make the whole structure light. The interior is completely carved and gilded and the rich red underpainting of bole shines through. Despite the fact that the church is in daily use, grey dust lies thickly on the cherubim and foliage. Dulls their glitter.

We drew one small side chapel and while we were there the monks came in and chanted, the slow undulations of their voices a counterpoint to the intricate convolutions of baroque carving. Twenty small boys from the São Bento College came in to say a quick prayer and stayed on to watch us. They were full of compliments and humour. One looked at the figure in my drawing and asked who it was. "An old woman who has now gone," I said. And he, devastated by his own wit and mock wonder, "But she has *stayed* in the picture."

Became really excited working with the new crayons, which are heaven. Wide range of brilliant and subtle colours which can be layered on the paper—light on dark even. Also you can scrape through the layers with a knife blade or pin. On returning home I did the chapel wall again from memory—much higher keyed, more emotional, less literal. If only there were more time.

August 17

It is undoubtedly spring. The *pau mulato* is shedding its orange bark and standing up slim and salad green on the lawn; the swallows are flying in and out the arches again; the "some-enchanted-evening bird" sang very early this enchanted morning; and the *sabiá* that sings "pot-pourri pot-pourri" over and over and over is singing it over and over and over. When sufficiently far away, it sounds rather like the whippoorwill. Peggy Mitchell, whose book on birds of Brazil is my best authority, describes one *sabiá* as singing a rotating phrase. This must be he. Listening, I get the impression of seeing the black and the white horse at the merry-go-round come round and round again.

Friday I returned home to find myself the proud possessor of an *arara*, the large Amazonian parrot we call a macaw. He is a remarkable and comical bird and he smells slightly of pepper. His underparts are a glorious orange-yellow, his upper back light ultramarine, and the top of his head pale olive green. His face of rather wrinkled flesh is made up like a clown's with narrow lines of tiny black feathers. His beak is black and his tongue likewise. It looks like a hard black candy moving about in his mouth.

He has a variety of calls and last night when he was put to bed he gave off a series of high whistles. I asked Graciano if Arara didn't like his bedroom and Graciano, with the utter confidence of one who knows, said, "He *likes* it very much. It's just that he's not accustomed to it yet."

We have improvised a stand for him until such time as one can be bought, and yesterday Graciano took him off it and placed him loose on the grass for a change. Just like the baby tortoises who, when hatched, know only one direction, so did Arara. He turned and with deadly accuracy waddled back to his stand and gazed up at it longingly. Graciano again carried him back to the grass. Exactly the same thing happened, except that this time he wasted no time gazing at his perch, but began at once, feet over beak, to climb the completely smooth pole.

Today, while at lunch on the veranda, A. said, "Is that bird meant to be doing that?" He was slowly waddling up the wrought-iron handrail to the steps and coming to join us, having eaten his way through his leg chain.

He is a real addition to the household—decorative and funny. I wouldn't have thought a bird could have so human a face—I suppose it's that flesh-coloured skin. I am told you can teach them to talk but their memory is not as retentive as a parrot's. Neither is mine.

Have spent a good deal of today working with my crayons and knife. Find what I do both unexpected and strange. Foreign to me yet familiar. Tomorrow I shall probably look at it with a cold eye but for the moment I'm under its spell. Crayons seem the perfect medium for me: brilliant colour that doesn't have to dry. So far I have worked fairly small. Working large presents much more serious problems. The question of paper is easy—about *that*, I just know—fairly thick, and the smoother the better.

Elise comes out of hospital again tomorrow. Do hope she is all right this time. It's been hard for them both.

August 26

How neglected my poor journal—not for want of things to write, but for want of time. The days wind by on their spool—golden day after golden day—with no time to enjoy them fully. The *pinheiro* (kapok tree) is in its powderpuff stage. An enormous tree, full of birds; every inch of its bark shaggy with parasites. In bloom, it is covered with purple orchid-like flowers which drop into the swimming-pool and look like little squids. Just pre-powderpuff, small, green, cucumber-shaped seed pods replace the flowers. As their skins brown, split along pre-ordained seams, and drop, their tightly packed, white kapok centres remain attached to the bough. Now, little by little, they are shaking out masses and masses of white swansdown parachutes—very like the milkweed—and much of the garden and the entire surface of the pool are covered with what looks like under-the-bed dust.

I have begun the *Diary of Helena Morely*, translated by Elizabeth Bishop. It is what it says—a diary, kept by Helena Morely "between the ages of twelve and fifteen, in the far-off town of Diamantina, in 1893–1895". Quite enchanting.

Am most enormously amused by Arara. He is naughty—can bite through anything to escape and waddle like a duck across the grass to peck at the trees. He emits high whistles and throaty purrs and an absolutely imbecile laugh that sends my blood cold.

He escaped the other morning in the middle of my Portuguese lesson. I went flying to his rescue—or rather, the garden's—the *professora* close on my heels, likewise Duque. Duque is, of course, jealous beyond measure of a competitor and was more than eager to give the bird a good nip when he saw him within reach. With me giving my attention to holding Duque at bay, Arara took advantage of the situation to attack the *professora*. He went for her feet with his great beak, and when she ran backwards he gave his imbecile cackle and attacked again.

I was sitting in the garden the other day, drawing, Arara behind me on his perch, when I first heard his repertoire. The whistle, the laugh, the purr. And then, most wonderfully: "*Arara, como vai? Como vai, Arara?*" ("Arara, how are you?") Duque, who hates him implacably, came running, blood in his eye, ready to kill an enemy who now demonstrates that he can talk like the humans whose love Duque so cherishes.

Needing advice on how to house and feed him, we contacted the Zoological Gardens, and two *arara* advisers arrived. They gave me his diet: peanuts, sunflower seeds, rice with honey, corn on the cob, *mamão*, and bananas. How could he be anything but sweet on such meat? They then described the stand they would build for him, complete with *guarda chuva* to keep off the rain and protect him from the sun. This was a week ago. Still no stand. Meanwhile, from his temporary perch made from part of an old clothesline support, a grid from the refrigerator, and half a broom-handle—the first and last mentioned he is demolishing with all speed—he throws his dishes to the ground in a kind of mock fury. If we give him food on cardboard plates, he shreds them into tiny bits.

His head, when he goes gentle, is small and sleek like a silk handkerchief about to be passed through a ring. But when he is cross—how fine a blue-green pine-cone.

How he pleases me, this bird with his Groucho-Marx-in-a-bathing-cap face.

August 31

Friday, at a minute's notice and in the middle of a heat wave, I flew with a group of Heads of Mission's wives, at the invitation of the president's wife, to Brasília. We left Santos Dumont airport at eight in the morning (theoretically)—eighteen of us plus the president's wife, a couple from the Catete, and the president's wife's sister. A flight of two and a half hours.

Brasília, from the air, is to look like an airplane—with apartment buildings in the fuselage axis and residential districts in the wings. Now it is nothing but a shanty town and a few red gashes in a dreary landscape. Landed, one is in the centre of a large plain—dry and brown—like Alberta or Canberra but with none of the redeeming features of either. No mountains or high hills to break the endlessness. Also there are few trees taller than I, and the river, which is to produce the large blue lake of the plans, is a very small and unpretentious stream.

We went directly to the president's residence—the Palace of the Dawn—a Niemeyer design, built in eleven months by a thousand men working two shifts a day. A long, glass rectangle, seeming to float on white scalloped columns as if on white-capped waves. In the hot, red surroundings, this creates a fresh and spanking effect, doubled in reflecting pools where two rather pseudo Henry Moore-ish terracotta females sit and tear their hair. To the left, the president's chapel, a crisp curl of white paper.

The main entrance to the palace is a vast glass door which slides open. Immediately inside is a hall of mirrors, gold tile, and marble. A most bewildering hall. You never know what is mirror, what is glass, and what is—after all—just space. I found myself unnerved by it, especially having nearly fallen off a red-carpeted ramp walled, so I thought, by glass—which proved to be just air. Having built his house of glass, Niemeyer has now had to hang curtains in order to create walls, to provide the president with some degree of privacy, and in such large areas fabric isn't tidy or attractive.

We were taken on a tour: two de Cavalcanti murals, sugar-cube chairs. The presidential library, decorated by Niemeyer's daughter, has jacaranda panelling and modern furniture in shades of grey. Austere. No place to curl up with a book. The presidential bathrooms—both with sunken baths—square porcelain holes in the floor—are for sober bathers only. But perhaps we are seeing it too soon. The family hasn't moved in yet.

Luncheon at the hotel—another Niemeyer building. The corridors which lead to the bedrooms on all three floors are faced by an outside wall pierced, from end to end, with a repetitive pattern of drinking glasses laid on their sides, bottoms flush with the outside surface. Visually very light and attractive, but one of the most effective heat traps ever invented. By noon in summer, if you want to go to your room, you have to hazard a virtual furnace.

We washed, lunched, and then went on a tour of the town, and as this time we were not part of a religious procession, we had a better chance to look about us. Stopped at the friar's-hat chapel, and then on to the Free Town, a wide, red, mud street with shacks on either side, where the life is.

One day, undoubtedly, it will be a fabulous city, but I am glad we shan't be among the first to move there.

I keep waiting for the swallows to fly into the house again looking for a "bijou" nesting site. Must check on the date last year when they woke us with their shrill conversations as they perched on open doors, merrily circled the bathrooms as we took showers, and flew off as accurately as bats through the archways of our veranda. This year they are skimming the pool but so far have not thought about making a mud nest over the lavatory.

Went to the zoo the other day in order to see the kinds of perches and *ambientes* that *araras* like. O what birds! Ours is *Caninde, Ara ararauna. Linnaeus 1758.* There was a blue one—incredibly beautiful. Lapis lazuli, highly polished. And the red, which I had thought I didn't like, was divine. He had a beak of old ivory.

September 15

Just back from a weekend on an island off Itacuruça, with the Norwegian ambassador and wife. A heavenly sandy beach and a garden full of the most beautiful tropical plants and trees. You can walk miles along the shore—which we did—picking up shells. We finally climbed over some rocks to a tiny cove where local fishermen were hauling in their net. We helped haul and throw the multicoloured fish—some little fellows like copper engravings, others with bands of metallic mauve—into a basket. It rained from start to finish but it didn't seem to matter. I collected a number of shells and did a drawing.

Drew with Helena last week in the Parque da Cidade, which was her old home. She grew up there and had not seen it for fifteen or twenty years despite living so close by. It is a beautiful park—what other word can I use? She says it was much more so when it was half wild but she is remembering it through the eyes of a child. All her memories came tumbling out—there, they had played a Brazilian cops and robbers. She was excited again, reliving it all. Now let us go and see the palm trees—so slender and elegant. Alas, there were only two left, and growing now out of a dump.

Last week I was given a *cuia*—or the fruit from which *cuias* are made. To make a *cuia* or cup—much used here to scoop food from sacks at the market and as an all-purpose vessel—you halve the fruit, remove its pulp, and then paint and carve the shell. As instructed, I scraped off all the green rind and, no more than an eighth of an inch down, came to what can only be called bone. I couldn't bring myself to deface it with carvings or paint.

This weekend I saw a *cuia* tree—a low, wide-growing tree hung with green fruits, not quite globular, with small raised platforms from which the stems emerge. There was also a vine covered with reddish-brown and yellow mimosa-shaped flowers called *sapatinhos* (little shoes).

-1958-

I am drying various palm antlers on the railing of the terrace. They fill me with wonder—one all dimpled green balls, one white as ivory, others like knotted and tarred string.

Went to an art show by Felipe Orlando—Cuban. Strangely luminous work. I am on the verge of buying one of them. Wakened, the day after seeing his work, determined to persuade him to give me lessons, but, alas, he returns to Cuba almost at once. However, as a result of asking him, I learned of Frank (pronounced Frankee) Schaeffer, who might be persuaded. Went to see him today. What a studio! How I would like one room in my life like that. Wooden saints and woven belts and primitive ceramics—colour to knock your eye out. I don't know if he is my teacher but perhaps he can help me with oils. He is attractive and his paintings are large and bold and full of colour but he is a much more literal person than I am. However, I can start and see.

Have bought, with considerable feelings of guilt, three strings of pearls and an emerald-coloured tourmaline (small). Strange how oddly debased I feel when I spend money on my own adornment. A. wants me to let him buy them, but I won't. If he gives them to me I will be reluctant to sell them when the need for them is past—for actually, *I* don't want them. It is some ambassador's-wife role I seem to be playing at the moment that finds them necessary.

The surrealism of life here—pearls, tourmalines, tropics—seems able to absorb assault and battery without too much strain. Between 3.30 and 5.00 a.m. Saturday the house was attacked by *ladrãos*. I was wakened by a salvo of shots but thought them firecrackers. (In the past, I've heard firecrackers and thought them shots.) When I saw a crack of light under my bedroom door I wakened A. Then we heard sounds of movement in the garden. We peered over the balcony railing to see a flashlight stabbing the darkness below. Duque was barking fiercely somewhere downstairs. We pushed the bedroom call button on the assumption that a stranger in the house would not answer but a *mordomo* might. Cautiously A. then opened the bedroom door, and found himself eyeball to muzzle with a revolver backed by a black face topped by a steel helmet. An agitated *mordomo* was waving his arms in the rear. "Go back!" he hissed. "Go back!" A. went back.

By the time we sorted out the events leading up to this denouement it seemed that the scenario had gone something like this:

Because of revised Itamarity rules, our two police guards, who were supposed to be patrolling the street in front of the property, had gone up to the tile bench by the waterfall for a quiet smoke. From there they had spotted a shadowy figure lurking in the lower garden. They challenged. No answer. They fired. The intruder scuttled away in the dark and escaped through the upper gate to the street.

Half an hour or so later our guardians decided it might be a good idea to reconnoitre the house. So they divided forces and marched on their objective, one up each arm of the driveway. Police Guard No. 1 rounded the corner of the house to find another intruder attacking the main entrance door, and fired. The attacker fell to the ground, then scrambled to his feet and disappeared into the *mato* up the mountain. Meanwhile Police Guard No. 2 on the other flank had discovered a third intruder trying to smash the door to the swimming-pool gallery. More shots. Another escape. Not surprisingly, the racket had wakened the *mordomo*, who decided to commandeer a guard and search the house. Result: the confrontation at my bedroom door.

In the morning light, a check of the premises revealed substantial bloodstains on the stone sill of our front entrance.

September 18

I feel I am Mrs. Midas, with this difference: everything I look at turns to beauty. On a rational basis I find it difficult to believe that *everything* is beautiful, and yet, to my eye, it is. The leaves, the beach, the sea. The streets with their lazy people and their racket. The antique shops full of saints, old prayer rugs, candlesticks.

Yesterday I bought an Orlando. A highly poetic abstraction entitled *Fase Solar*. I'd have preferred one the Norwegians bought which is luminous as fish scales and soap bubbles.

September 23

Were wakened last night by raised voices in animated argument on the terrace below our bedrooms. Following the *ladrão* attack Itamarity again decided to change the rules governing our protection. Henceforth, guards on the night shift—with permission—would patrol immediately around the house. By absurd chance we drew a Mutt and Jeff team—with Jeff deaf. Mutt, to be heard, has to shout up at his comrade and Jeff, as is normal, shouts back. A Brazilian lullaby, so to speak!

Observation: Arara's eye dilates and expands independent of light. I cannot determine what causes it to behave in that way. The pupil of the human eye adjusts to light only, as I remember it. What is his adjusting to? He *is* funny. I gave him a bath the other day with a garden spray. He dropped his jaw in astonishment and then emitted a great, blood-curdling scream. Clearly not his idea of a good time, as I had been led to believe by *arara* lovers. His new feathers appear, tightly furled, in cylindrical plastic containers.

Have begun lessons with Frank Schaeffer. He is trying to train my eye to see related forms. Enjoyed my time with him. He played the Concerti Grossi of Corelli and next week he has promised to play some recently recorded ancient baroque music from Minas, which includes work by Mesquita.

Life very pleasant indeed. Have just read James Reaney's *A Suit of Nettles*, which surprised me beyond measure—amused me and moved me. That *enfant terrible* has matured. Last time I saw him he seemed nothing more than a giggling boy. No boy could have written this remarkable, rich poem.

The frogs are pounding. So are the *favela* drums. All the noises of summer.

Drove to Novo Friburgo in the state of Rio—a small town about nine hundred metres up. Settled in 1814 by the Swiss. And Swiss it is. Very mountainous, with pines, sheep, and cactus-type plants in bulbous bloom. At night a million fireflies invaded our room and glowed and glowed. In the morning, dead, they were like rather gothic beetles, bearing two yellow plates in their otherwise brown armour. We left temperatures of around a hundred in Rio, but Novo Friburgo is cool at night. The inn is Swiss-run—German Swiss—and all the German population of Rio was staying there, I should think—round heads, square heads, all. An incredibly good record-player provided oom-pah-pah music from a speaker that looked like a Japanese lantern.

The town itself is full of immense schools on hilltops reached by nearly perpendicular roads paved with little stones. Large parks also, and everything very clean. Attractive, but strangely un-Brazilian.

Glad to find I can like something that isn't Brazilian. Had rather begun to fear I couldn't, so in love am I.

The new British, as we get to know them, seem nice. She is youthful-looking, blonde, pretty, and serious-minded and he is handsome, intellectual, and a pleasure to talk to. Much more my cup of tea than their predecessors. *He* always used to greet me with, "Written any more little pomes lately?"

Much preoccupied painting and thinking about painting. Schaeffer is nearly killing me, making me think. If it is something I have to do—all right—I'll grit my teeth and think. But is painting really so cerebral? Spent some time the other day really trying to do what he told me to do but in my own way. Already he has helped me in the straight physical handling of oils and that is something. But he *is* so analytical.

Rio is bearable again—much cooler, praise God. And I, at last, have got a successful pair of shoes out of Dornelles. Praise God, likewise. I cannot buy shoes here. Brazilian feet are smaller than mine. In the past, although Dornelles has carefully traced my foot, when I have gone to pick up the shoes, they have always been too small. "Why, when you had the tracing?" I have asked, to which he has always replied with a wild waving of his hands which I take to mean, "Yes, but after you have gone and I have *only* the tracing, I cannot believe it." But he doesn't say that. He is far too polite.

The support for Arara has still not arrived. For almost two months I've had that bird pinned to part of the clothesline. He is growing very beautiful—puts forth more and more feathers, as smooth as ivory— daffodil, hyacinth blue, and scylla-coloured ivory. A lovely creature. But—when he speaks and laughs—do I recognize myself?

October 12

Saw a show by one of Schaeffer's students and hated it. Felt it was formula painting. Came to the conclusion he is trying to teach me to paint like that, so decided to leave him. Burst my brains puzzling over his concept of linear composition and the inter-relationship of masses. Decided to stay with him at least until I have presented him with my doubts. Accordingly, at this week's lesson, we talked for an hour. At least he doesn't pretend to know everything.

-1958-

I think I have never been happier than living as I now do, almost entirely through my eye. The Orlando is framed. A beautiful and very personal painting but in this immense house I can find no corner small enough for it.

Am told that the Holy Ghost hears through the horn of the unicorn. I must write and tell the man who has the piece of unicorn horn.

Hot again. A. has spent all day on a report and I have worked on a large canvas which is not yet finished. I am delighted with the quick-drying white Schaeffer has introduced me to. I really think I might become a painter.

> If the Sun and Moon should doubt
> They'd immediately go out.

"The houses on the outskirts of São Paulo are mainly two-storeyed, white and austere."

October 26

It is to be announced tomorrow—thank goodness, for we have been sitting on it for weeks!—that Sidney Smith, our Secretary of State for External Affairs, is coming to pay an official visit, the first such visit by a Canadian foreign minister to a South American country. And all the Canadian ambassadors to South American countries are coming at the same time for a two-day policy conference— another first.

We have been struggling frantically for some time to push servants, dressmakers, plumbers, etc., into activity. With no goad, it was difficult. Now I hope it will be easier as there is an immense amount to be done.

They will arrive in November—just in time for my birthday. In the first five days of their visit, we entertain five times: first a luncheon for the Commonwealth Heads of Mission and their wives; the following evening, a dinner for fifty in honour of the Brazilian foreign minister, with our minister as host; then a reception for five hundred; and, finally, a sixty-guest buffet supper to entertain the Latin American ambassadors to Brazil and our ambassadors to South America.

None of these worries me too much. What does worry me—oh, vanity!—is clothing, all of which has to be made. So I run to endless fittings.

But if I think *I* have details to attend to, they are trifling compared to the embassy's preparation of the official programme.

In between appointments I have painted. Also tried to translate, for my Portuguese professor, Emily Dickinson's:

> I never saw a Moor,
> I never saw the Sea;
> Yet know I how the Heather looks,
> And what a Wave must be.

> I never spoke with God,
> Nor visited in Heaven;
> Yet certain am I of the Spot
> As if the Chart were given.

My attempt, for the record, with all its liberties:

Nunca vi um matagal
E nunca vi o mar;
Com tudo, conheço a urze,
A onda—como fôr.

Não falei eu com Deus,
Nem visitei o Céu;
Com tudo sei aonde é
Como se fosse meu.

Just back from Iran's National Day party. Small tables in the garden and very pleasant. Called on the new German wife the other day—young, pretty, intelligent; last post Mexico. Her house full of Mexican saints—more beautiful than Brazilian ones, to my eye. More primitive.

November 15

It is now Saturday evening and the minister arrives on Monday. I shall have one last fling at my journal before I shut my typewriter away.

Ever since we have heard of his coming—how long ago? six weeks?—we have been battling time and Brazilians to get everything in order. And more latterly we have been battling our own department in Ottawa. Most of the things we have been requesting for a year, we naturally requested again: a larger hot water tank, new pipes in the attic to provide enough water and pressure so we can wash in all bathrooms simultaneously; the annual paint job—necessary to combat the mildew, which stains everything. To all of these the government said no.

On the other hand, Ottawa was quite happy to have us, and preferably at once, dig a thousand-dollar hole in the garden—this being some elaborate plan to stop moisture entering the house. Presumably the theory is that if moisture has a hole of its own to go to, it is not likely to trespass. We might also—oh happy us!—pave the driveway. But paint, no. Change the pipes, no. Endless long-distance calls have ensued. Result: we are now painted and piped but it was left so late that it is only possible to begin the cleaning today. Well, so much for that!

Further, Ottawa could not make up its mind how the minister was to travel or, indeed, who was to travel with him. Until yesterday we were having new names added to an already terrifyingly long list. Also, all of Brazilian Traction top brass is coming along for the fun. Oh, it will be a three-ring circus, all right.

We have taken on extra servants and are having the largest parties catered, but the thought of the visit so frightened our good *copeiro*, Augusto, that he gave notice and I have been up to my neck in interviews. Somewhat reluctantly I have hired Victor, the only one whose references were acceptable at all. "An honest boy but lazy." All the others drank, stole, or fought.

There have been various other complications. On Thursday, when A. was up to his neck in last-minute detail, the president invited him to fly the following morning—yesterday—to Uberlândia in Minas Gerais, to witness the inauguration of a new highway to Brasília— and return today. Jean Coté, First Secretary, and his wife have been out of their minds—understandably—because their baby is running a high fever. Two friends of a cousin of mine arrived from Canada. And I had a bout of food poisoning and was in bed for two miserable days. But the final straw is a heat wave.

At one point I panicked—wakened in the night and couldn't sleep because of all the things that still had to be done. I was not afraid of the minister, heaven knows, but of the organization and planning, the tug and pull and strain of dozens of different people and events, with us the analgesic, the oil, the man in the middle.

It is funny, of course. And funnier still as it grows nearer and most of the metre-long lists are completed and the stage set. How people struggle to be king. They all think it is "their" visit. I wish it were.

November 16

Minister's Visit Eve. And the heat waxes. My personal shower floods me with a hot and saline fluid. Our incredible new *copeiro* does everything wrong and when I correct him he defends himself with a speech, at concert pitch. When he solemnly gave me my teacup on a plate for the umpteenth time and I pointed it out to him once again, he claimed that the plates and the saucers are so close together in the cupboard that it is easy to take one from the wrong pile.

Everything is done that can be done but because my "on" switch keeps me going, I am trying to scrape the graphite paint off Arara's perch (it's arrived at last!) as he is eating it and will, I fear, die of lead poisoning. It's a horrible job for hot weather.

A. and I have moved from our elegant bedrooms to a room at the end of the house so that the minister and his wife can use ours. This, in itself, was almost as good as a fire.

The embassy's brief for the visit—copies to go to all concerned—runs to 110 pages and covers everything from who gets into what car, at what place, at what time, on what day, to texts of speeches and appropriate answers to awkward policy questions from the press. It is as detailed and intricate as a written chess game.

November 29

Well, it's over and we are still alive. Remarkable. They arrived Monday the 17th at eleven p.m. A great mob out to meet them at the airport. He all smiles. She bland as milk—a mild woman with a good carriage, grey hair, and a small white hat. We returned home—the minister and wife, his parliamentary assistant, and his secretary—escorted by screaming motorcyclists, to a drink and sandwiches and bed.

Next morning, the minister and A. left for a series of official calls. Mrs. Smith rested, and I supervised last-minute details of the Commonwealth luncheon, *chez nous*. It poured rain.

More calls for the men in the afternoon and an unscheduled one for the minister's wife—and, willy-nilly, me—on the wife of the Brazilian foreign minister, who had returned, unexpectedly, from Italy. We were ushered into a dusky drawing-room where one table was covered with a hundred ashtrays, all close together, as if they were a collection—which, perhaps, they were. Had what can only be described as a sticky conversation—interpreted conversations surely only work when there are weighty matters to be exchanged. "I hear it has been very hot." "Yes, it has." "The heat is early this year." "So I am told." Neither woman seemed to know where to go from there and the interpreter sat mute and motionless, waiting, and so, "Italy," I said, in the hope of getting things moving a bit. Which it did.

That evening we attended the official dinner at Itamarity. Fiendishly hot. The men in white tie and decorations. I drank nothing in the hope of keeping my blood below boiling-point, but even so, I dripped. Not that I was unique. The men, of course, drip into their boiled shirts. The women, more naked, gleam. I sat between two Latin American ambassadors and tried to turn my not very good

Portuguese into even worse Spanish. The minister's wife had, as dinner companions, one of "my" ambassadors and the Brazilian foreign minister, Negrão de Lima, who has all of twenty words in English.

Next day, when the minister and A. lunched with the president, Mrs. Smith and I were entertained by Helena. What a party she had arranged! Specially printed cards: *"Homenagem a Sra Smith"*, a drawing of the Canadian and Brazilian flags crossed, and then the menu in French. Present were dozens of Brazilian women I had never seen before. Some unfortunate and inexplicable row was going on between Helena and Itamarity. They hadn't informed her of something she should have known. But I never did understand what it was all about.

That night a reception given by Toni and Mini Gallotti—he the senior resident executive of Brazilian Traction. Sumptuous! Exotic floral arrangements throughout the house, a wonderful band, and four Negro dancers who were superb. A truly Arabian Nights supper. The whole, worthy of crowned heads. Met the novelist Jorge Amado, who had come down from Bahía—rotund, urbane, charming.

I could have danced all night, but we left at the minister's pleasure—and our hostess's displeasure, I am afraid—and then sat about on our patio until far into the night, in a post mortem on the day's performance with this ebullient man and his silent wife.

Next morning Mrs. Smith wanted to rest. This gave me time to concentrate on the details of the dinner the minister was to give in the residence that evening. Weather still infuriatingly hot. It now looked as if forty-eight people—the latest count—would have to be fitted into two tables in the dining-room; and that was impossible. Also, as there was still no final guest list, no one knew how many would sit at an overflow table in the covered patio.

At one, a large luncheon given by the de Mello Francos in the José Nabucos' garden. Beautiful but blistering hot. De Mello Franco is Brazil's ambassador to Canada and protocol ordains he be here for a Canadian ministerial visit. Because of the intense heat we became more and more uneasy at the thought of our dinner indoors. Decided to place the three tables together, as one, on the long terrace overlooking the swimming-pool and garden. Outdoors, however hot, would at least be tolerable. But would the weather hold, or would it produce a sudden deluge—as it so often does—and drown us where we sat? A. and I spent much of luncheon on the phone (lucky it was a buffet) arranging the new plan, and making frequent checks with the weather bureau. Prediction: "Hot, clear, holding."

On returning to the residence at three, I found Itamarity's protocol officer busy working out a second seating plan, a calligrapher writing place-cards, and, as in any Brazilian establishment, any number of people doing—or not doing—any number of things. On the terrace, the three tables were now set up as one. Fifty chairs, extra flat silver, and candelabras had arrived—borrowed in an attempt to provide some uniformity for a one-table layout. Changes in the flower arrangements still to be made. Headaches all round. Everybody dripping.

By four, when Mrs. Smith and I left for her call on the president's wife, most of the problems had been resolved, and the glittering table on the terrace was set for sixty. If the final count was fewer, then settings could be removed.

The palace call was friendly but formal. No time wasted there. But home in the rush hour was an hour's drive and meanwhile the heat was increasing. More ominous still, there were rumblings of thunder. Was there anyone at home responsible enough and aware enough to get everything inside before the storm broke? Little point in my stopping to phone. I couldn't be sure of finding a phone in the first place, let alone one that worked. So I watched the storm build overhead as darkness fell, and talked aimlessly to Mrs. Smith, who seemed oblivious of all about her, as we crawled home—bumper to bumper—at the speed of a funeral cortège.

We arrived just as the dam in the sky broke. A drenching storm, accompanied by winds that made the trees scream as if they were being uprooted. All the lights in the house were out. A dozen *copeiros* met us with candelabras. Dramatic, cinematic, if one had the time to admire. Praise be, the reception rooms were a jumble of tables, chairs, china, silver—higgledy-piggledy, everywhere. But water was pouring into the dining-room and small *sala* from the side verandas. A., at the office, warned by the weather office that the deluge was imminent, had phoned the house and ordered everything inside, just before the phones had gone out, along with the lights.

We settled the minister and his party in their rooms with flashlights and candles. Then A. and I and everyone else fought the flood. Little by little, with mops and brooms, we forced the waters back. What had looked like a disordered second-hand shop was set in order—tables once again reassembled indoors. Placemats, crystal, silver, flowers returned to their former settings. The protocol officer, patiently and by candlelight, began the arrangement of the entire seating plan for the third time.

We were told that high-tension wires were down across the road to the city and I comforted myself that our guests would be as late as we. At 8.15—the dinner was scheduled for 8.30—I left the white-clad *copeiros*, who were putting the finishing touches to the tables, and went upstairs to shower by flashlight, scrambled into my clothes somehow (minus ear-rings which I couldn't find), and lighted myself downstairs by one small dripping candle, to greet the guests who had already arrived, punctual as no Brazilians had ever been before, and neat as gannets after a dive.

All things considered, the dinner went well. The lights even came on again as we were having drinks. I can't remember the food, but the flowers were unspeakably beautiful and the speeches flowery.

At midnight, we left for a charity ball at the British embassy. I must say that one of the things that kept me sane during our crisis—misery does like company—was the thought of the British with a ball for a thousand, and myriads of small tables on their terrace, having to cope with the same difficulties.

Next day, Friday, I was to show Mrs. Smith the sights of Rio, take her shopping if she wished, and give her lunch at a restaurant downtown with the embassy wives. She preferred to rest.

I spent the day phoneless. Meanwhile no one had come to hook up the public-address system to handle the cars for our reception that night. No one had come to do the flowers. And I still had no confirmed guest list for Saturday's buffet supper. However, as is always the case, everything *did* finally get done, everything looked splendid, everything went well.

Saturday, after a ladies' luncheon at the country club, Mrs. Smith rested and I got on with arrangements for the buffet supper, at which we were to entertain the Latin American ambassadors accredited to Brazil and their wives and Canada's ambassadors to South American countries and their wives. About fifty in all.

Next day, Sunday and my birthday, was a day of rest. The minister and his wife went off with friends, but their staff remained *chez nous* and in the evening we went out to dinner. Quite suddenly I developed a severe sore throat and thought the next day's trip—São Paulo by way of Brasília—would be impossible, but when in the morning the throat had not turned into a head cold, I put on my hat and left with the rest of them in an air-force plane at nine. The minister's party included two Brazilian couples, two Canadian couples, ourselves, and two embassy officers.

It was furnace-hot in Brasília, where we trailed around the palace. A new and large mural in the dining-room—although completely abstract—smacked of the prows of ships, and added to the nautical air the palace has for me. Also an immense new statue by Maria Martins—rather like a character from *The Wizard of Oz* or a giant Tinkertoy. Its scale was perfect for the landscape against which it is viewed, but what might have been bizarre seemed to me merely antic. We were offered an enormous luncheon in the blazing hot hotel—successfully solar-heated by that beer glass outside wall. Red dust, fine as face powder, clung to us in a sheer film, so that we were subtly homogenized with the landscape. Then a tour of Brasília in the president's helicopter—hovering in a roaring dragonfly and looking where the president pointed his immaculately tailored black arm with its length of white shirt cuff, roseate with dust. How proud and pleased he is with his dream.

Arrived in São Paulo, where we were met by the city's mayor and went straight to the hotel. Flowers to greet us, and the welcome, familiar smell of the Jaraguá Hotel.

Next morning, a call on the mayor's wife having been averted, I went in the rain and freezing cold to have the best hairdo of my life. Took our consul's wife to lunch and made an appointment with d'Horta, an artist whose scalpel drawings fill my heart with joy. He was—wonder of wonders—having a show and he collected me and off we went. A splendid oasis in the official week. Returned to the hotel in time to join the cavalcade to the school run by the Canadian Fathers of the Holy Cross, where the minister made a speech worthy of a bishop. Then a quick change and on to the consul's reception— an immense party under canvas among the bushes and flowerbeds of his front garden.

An early start next day in an endless procession of cars, to the Brazilian Traction power plant at Cubatão. Our hosts: Henry Borden, president of the company, and his wife. Down the escarpment in the incline-railway car in pouring rain; half-way back up again for lunch and a thousand congratulatory speeches. How they do all congratulate one another!

The minister and his wife were having two private days with the Bordens, long-time friends, so I gratefully spent those two days in bed nursing the cold that had developed on the chilly plane ride home. Rose from the dead the second evening to attend the Bordens' cocktail party and then on to a nightclub where we saw *The Merry Widow*, much lauded by the press. A terrible show, I thought—all cheesecake, or *carne* (meat), as they call it here. To bed at three.

This morning at ten, a champagne send-off and gift-giving, before we left—with the escort of screaming motorcycle police—for the airport to say our farewells. Thus ended the first visit of a Canadian Secretary of State for External Affairs to Brazil.

It is generally agreed that the visit was successful. Looking on from the sidelines, critical but interested, I am not really in a position to judge, for I saw only the social side of it and I even have a one-eyed view of that. But whatever the degree of success, all members of the embassy staff contributed to it. Brazilians and Canadians, husbands and wives—we were in it together.

The minister, with whom I have been on greeting terms for some years, so that his smile and his "hello" were not new to me, appears on further acquaintance to be rather vain, a bit mawkish, and given to flattery. I suspect he was more of a success here than he would have been in countries where extroversion and flattery count for less. Cheerful, noisy, and rather effeminate, he cannot bear not having the attention of all around him. His wife said of him that he sleeps much less than other people, "but he can't bear to be awake alone. I always struggle to keep my eyes open for him. As long as I'm looking at him, I don't have to speak, or even listen, just as long as he sees me looking at him."

I found myself liking her better than him, but I also found her baffling. In all the time here she never asked a question or showed any interest in her surroundings. She had no wish to do anything between official engagements—not even to walk around the garden. She retired to her room, by herself, resting. She can have learned nothing about Brazil. As we drove from house to engagement, engagement to house, I never saw her look out of the car window. She had no books with her, or knitting or embroidery. I asked her how she liked political life and she replied that she didn't mind it, that she wasn't hurt by it as long as it didn't hurt him. She was always punctual and always looked rested and bright, but she never volunteered any statement on her own—either question or opinion—and nothing seemed to fluster her.

At the university, when he received an honorary degree and made one of his best speeches—I suppose the atmosphere made him feel at home—he said that three things in his life had been better than he expected—Niagara Falls, his wife, and Brazil. I looked at her as he spoke and she was totally composed. Afterwards, I said something about having taken a pretty compliment in her stride and she said, "Well, I *was* surprised today. I didn't think he was going to say that again *today*." I felt she had heard it a thousand times—said not for her benefit, but for his. At Brasília, in the scorching heat, we stood for a time in a small cooling wind and the hot ashes from his pipe flew into her face and distressed her. When she remonstrated gently, he replied, watching my reaction to his wit, "Your fault, Mummy, you were standing there." She winced as another hot ash hit her and he repeated, "You're still standing there, Mummy. Your fault."

There were two episodes peripheral to the visit—one comic, one macabre. The first occurred this evening. Duque, our Welsh terrier— a scandal of a dog—had been relegated to the basement for the visit. Charming though he is, he has been known to take pieces out of gentlemen's trousers. This morning, as soon as the official party left, he was allowed up again.

After dinner, A. and I were sitting about limply on the patio, going over the past days, staring into space, when—like jam coming to that sudden, uncontrollable, rolling boil—a coagulation of dogs appeared in the archway of the far patio, poured through the dining-room, the large *sala*, the little *sala*, headed towards us. In the lead, a wretched mongrel bitch, tail between her legs, with the neighbouring pack of Romeos hard upon her, Duque ignominiously in the rear.

It could have happened, I suppose, minus Duque—at any point in the visit. Day or night. How little we know what we are being spared.

The second concerned our old *copeiro,* named Augusto, who had worked for us for some time. A Portuguese, a very good boy, rather given to drama. It was he who, one evening, came to me as we sat outside and asked if he could see me alone. When I went into the *sala* with him, he told me that a flying saucer was landing in the garden. Now there is probably no one alive who would like to see a flying saucer more than I, but confronted by so immediate a visitation, I found myself as skeptical as A. himself. And "Are you sure?" I heard myself asking Augusto in A.'s tone and his very words. Yes, he was sure and he urged me to follow him onto the terrace where, indeed, there was a most wonderful sight: a fire balloon of quite enormous size was slowly descending onto the grass. It was easy to understand his confusion. At night it is hard to judge distance, and so size, and certainly this was a very large fire balloon.

Well, it was this same Augusto who, in the midst of our preparations for the minister's arrival, told me one morning that he was giving notice. This was a serious blow. Staff who know you and whom you know are worth double their weight in newcomers, however highly trained. Augusto was totally reliable about everything but flying saucers and we weren't expecting more of those. I pleaded with him to stay. Just until after the visit. I offered him more money, more time off. Anything, in fact, if he would see us through the next two weeks. Nothing made any difference. He was sorry to let us down at such a time. Very sorry. He wouldn't do it without a serious reason. Earnest, urgent, solemn-eyed, he spoke as if he had an appointment with destiny. In fact, he had. During the visit we learned that Augusto had been run over by a *bonde* (streetcar) and killed. Had he felt his death at hand? Had he even gone forward to meet it?

"The private chapel of the house had been deconsecrated...."

January 2

Early in December we went again to Angra dos Reis on the Itacuruça coast.

The island where we stayed—within spitting distance of the little port and its large naval college, old monastery, and colonial churches—is symmetrical, shaped like a half orange, flat side down, sitting in an ultramarine sea. An incredible towered house occupies the exact centre of the orange. Stone from England, wood from Finland, were imported for its construction. The result is Victorian gothic as conceived by a Brazilian carpenter and set in a profusion of mango trees, cashews, and palms. It was built originally for one of Brazil's presidents as a wedding present from the governor of the state of Rio.

Interesting to compare it with the country house up the coast where we stayed at Easter. Life here is equally informal, but brisk. Here the servants work. Food excellent. Our host, an energetic man, did handy-man jobs about the place, dressed in jeans and shirt and a kind of bargee's cap. His *senhora* screamed in that curious Brazilian voice. I am baffled by it. Thought perhaps it was lack of discipline in childhood—and perhaps it is. Or is it part and parcel of the Brazilian's love of noise? For they *do* love noise. Certainly the most popular music is the samba or march, each with a strongly marked beat, and the most popular instrument, the drums. Melody, sweetness, don't really seem to interest them. But no, that is not true: one only has to think of Villa-Lobos, the early baroque church music from Minas, or Dorival.

Fabulously hot on the island. Prickly hot because of the salt air. A. and I slept nude, door open for a draft, barely caring. To swim was to float limply in hot saline fluid. But the great bay, of which Angra is only a tiny indentation, is beyond belief—high mountains and sand beaches and tropical foliage and blue, blue, blue.

Fascinating to watch the three generations in the house. All members of the family seemed permitted to give orders to the grandchildren. I would guess all children and grandchildren are dependent upon grandpapa for holidays and financial help. I was enchanted by two of the grandchildren: the three-year-old who was so co-ordinated that she could cut her own fingernails—both hands—and who was a strangely independent child, rather quiet except on rare occasions when she was lighted by a thousand lights and kept us all in the air at once, like a juggler. The tiny—just two—amused me too. He was unable to resist the water; he walked in fully clothed. A typical Brazilian male in miniature, he kicked a football with the earnestness and skill of an adult.

A more than strenuous December with too much heat and too many parties, but things should slow up now. I hope so, as tempers are taut everywhere.

The actual year's end, however, we enjoyed. Went to the British embassy to a buffet supper and dance, and afterwards to a party on Avenida Atlântica from which we saw the enormous curve of Copacabana beach alight with a million candles in honour of Iamanjá, Queen of the Sea.

On New Year's Eve all the *macumbeiros* swarm to the beaches around Rio, the women in white skirts with ankle-length trousers beneath them (I am told this is the old slave dress), white flowers, white candles. Little cup-shaped holes are scooped in the sand to protect the candle flames from the wind, white flowers are stuck in it as if growing, and the men and women—in their white clothes—dance. At midnight they all wade into the sea, offering Iamanjá drinks, cosmetics, flowers—whatever she might want. An abundance of gifts is thrown onto the waves.

From our height in the platinum apartment block, we could see the whole beach with its flickering lights and white bodies moving against the dark rhythmic waves of the sea. It was as if children were having some strange dream. It reminded me a little of Ottawa during the Marian Congress, when the lower town with its dreary, wooden, unpainted houses was full of a thousand children—small virgins in pink or blue or white gauze, golden crowns above their shining eyes. Or of *Les Grandes Meaulnes*. Such innocent ceremony.

Then we drove to Ipanema—I in evening dress and borrowed bedroom slippers—and walked among the groups of people on the beach. They varied considerably. Some had small altars set up, adorned with "photos" of Iamanjá, around which the celebrants danced and rang bells. All groups danced—if dance it is—and the men all smoked black cigars. A priest poured—what? *cachaça?*—into a *cuia* and drank. One man drank his lighted. Occasionally a figure would fall to the ground in a kind of writhing fit (a saint was said to be entering the body) but there was always a deadly practical, no-nonsense member of the group who would get him onto his feet again. Nearby, on the sand, lay babies covered with cloths, looking like laundry or parcels of meat. From time to time, one would cast off its covers and call—like any child in the night—for water.

As long as we were sky-high, the ceremony on the beach was beautiful—so many candles in their scooped-out sockets and pockets of sand, so many white-clad figures against the dark swell of the ocean. Even closer up, there was a strange kind of innocence— the white candles, white dahlias, white calla lilies, white daisies, "growing" in a sandy garden. But once we were really among the celebrants, among the priests and priestesses blessing their flock— and every half-inch *is* blessed!—seeing the black cigars and smelling their pungent smoke, observing the deliriums which, to me, seem self-induced, and in no way convince me of the "entry of a saint"— then the whole performance is not beautiful or moving or awe-inspiring, but disordered, ugly.

One group, as we watched, appeared to have been "taken over" by finger-sucking children, and one of our party gave cries of joyous recognition, recalling an occasion when the *macumbeiros*—she among them—were "taken over" by the same finger suckers. But to me there was no more semblance of a "takeover" than if I were to get up now and shuffle a bit and put my fingers in my mouth. However, I suppose it depends on what you want to believe. I remember years ago in Montreal when a group of us were interested in hypnosis and a friend who was a medical student tried to hypnotize me—told me to look at his ring, to close my eyes, to go to sleep; and I, willing to co-operate, did the first two. At which point he told me he had hypnotized me. When I protested that I was merely trying to aid the process, rather than resist it, he claimed that was exactly what hypnosis was—the difference between voluntary and involuntary evidently not existing for him.

I wish I knew more about *macumba*. It is a form of voodoo, of course, brought from Africa by the slaves. Today it has appropriated many of the symbols and artefacts of the Catholic Church—that Church having permitted and even, I believe, initially encouraged it as a way of bringing the Negroes into the "true faith" by easy stages. But the fact is, it is *macumba* that holds them—and steals from Catholicism to enrich itself. Most of the dancing women the other night wore crucifixes.

A Mrs. Omolulu, wife of a young man from the Gold Coast who is being trained in the British embassy—and whose...father? grandfather? was once a slave in Bahía but later returned to Africa—reports that at the *candomblés* she recently attended in Bahía, the words of the songs were in her language, although the Bahíanos no longer know their meaning. (Incidentally, the clay figures they sell in the market in Bahía are identical to clay figures photographed in a Pelican book on primitive art entitled *Clay Figures from the Gold Coast.*) And a book about *candomblé* initiation in Bahía shows a clearly marked ceremonial pattern—more revolting (living sacrifice of animals) but also more decorous than the examples we have witnessed. Interesting to see the initiate painted with spots, reminiscent of the aborigines in Australia—where, surely, there can have been no African influence.

The day after Christmas we went to the Maracanã football stadium, reputed to be the largest in the world. Seating capacity, 150,000. *Seating capacity* is absurd, but that's what the book says: "It has a normal seating capacity of 150,000 persons, distributed as follows: *standing room* for 30,000 on the first tier of the stand...." (Italics mine, as they say.)

Built of concrete without pillars, it is an enormous, two-tiered, elliptical amphitheatre—its major axis just under a thousand feet— crowned by a narrow fringe of overhanging roof which leaves the playing field open to the sky. The latter, incidentally, is surrounded by a deep moat to prevent spectators, in the zeal, from becoming participants. We were there to see the Rio championship semi-finals—if such is the term in football. I should think all 150,000 persons were present.

Pretty to see below us the immense oval of green grass, and above the oval of the night sky with the *Cristo* tinily and miraculously visible on the Corcovado. There was a kind of magic about sitting there, suspended by nothing—rather similar to what one feels when one can keep the hula hoop up—which, *graças a Deus*, I can now do!

Would so like to catch up on my journal, not only recording things seen, but some of my thoughts as well. Strange how I rarely write of things that distress me. Why? Because I cannot bear it? Because I try to forget? (I don't succeed.) "A Refusal to Mourn the Death, by Fire, of a Child in London"? I don't even know why.

Strange, too, how so many things come at the wrong time. For instance, Stephen Spender said in an interview that he considers me Canada's best poet. It's nonsense, but he said it, nevertheless. (There is *no* best poet, surely.) And the last *Tamarack Review* has an article that treats me, along with eight or ten others, as one of the serious and interesting poets. Would it have borne poetic fruit two years ago?

January 3

Notes for my journal read:

José—cook's clothes
Captain's clothes
Chocolate clothes
Blonde wife—son
Klaus—butterflies
d'Horta
Holy Ghosts

That was followed by a much more complex note, an attempt to understand my poetic silence, this translation into paint.

January 8

Have been using my crayons. Have done a Holy Ghost. Before Christmas, when I was shopping for presents, I found three Holy Ghosts—small—from old churches. All very baroque. All very expensive. One, after a five-minute hesitation, I returned to buy and found gone. *It* really must have been the Holy Ghost. The problem, of course, is that they all fail. How can they not? The first had the head of a goose. The one I nearly bought had the legs of a turkey. The third, more gothic, was too modest. I would still like to find a Holy Ghost at a price I feel reasonable. (And what would you think a reasonable price for a Holy Ghost, Mrs. Irwin?)

Have completed two crayon works—*Holy Ghost* and one other entitled *Stone Fruit*. But so little time!

The day before yesterday, Graciano complained that Klaus, the cook, was destroying the walls of his bedroom and that something must be done about it. "Very well," I said in some trepidation, "I'll inspect all bedrooms tomorrow." I found the walls of Klaus's room to be entirely covered with a collection of butterflies which he has caught while here. Hundreds of them. The immense blue ones, the soft dove-coloured ones with white or black "eyes" on their downy wings. Some with touches of red or yellow. Some white as if bleached and still rough-dry. Such ranges of whites and creams and snuff colours. All the night-flyers. And their daytime cousins—brilliant blues and yellows and deep orange. Beautiful against the white walls. Then to inspect Graciano's room. It contained two objects that were personal—the first a lightbulb moulded and coloured in the form of a flame, the second a large tinted photograph of himself.

Actually, at the moment our servants are pretty good. The oddest of them all is the cook's assistant, José. He is about thirty, small, and jet black. He is very, very quiet with the rest of the staff, often appearing to hear nothing. When alone he talks to himself just like Arara and just like Arara he laughs. He wears chef's clothes—tall chef's cap, kerchief around his neck. All very, very white. In the past whenever I have seen him in civvies he has worn a spotless and perfectly matched milk-chocolate suit, fedora, and shoes, however hot the temperature. But on New Year's Day, when I let him off, he marched down the drive dressed in what looked like an admiral's summer uniform—blinding white with gold braid and buttons. Very impressive. When I asked Klaus what it was all about, he said that José was a captain in the navy before he went crazy. But Klaus, of course, knows nothing. In Brazil, for all its liberalism, a coloured person cannot become an officer in the navy—in the army, yes; in the air force, yes—but not in the navy. For myself, I think he is another Jean LeNegre and has bought himself this nautical suit for his own pleasure.

After José had been here some time, I learned that he had a five-month-old son, Pedro, named after the Pretender to the throne of Brazil. So I bought a toy duck for this Pedro. Graciano told me—and I only believe a small percentage of what he does tell me—that José's son was purely imaginary. Klaus, on the other hand, claims that he exists. Fâtima, the upstairs maid, says José has a photo of a very glamorous white blonde who is his wife. No one knows the truth. If the son, Pedro, is not real, I had the pleasure of buying a real present for an imaginary baby. Shades of Marianne Moore!

Yesterday, went with A. to Santo Antônio. Saw not only the little gold chapel of the lay order, but the whole building—offices, crypt, and the store-rooms for the processional figures. Dating from 1800, they are kept in cupboards with glass doors through which they stare at you, "a skeleton with his clothes on". Outside on the terrace I felt the impact of Brazilian history as we looked across the old tiled roofs to a modern Rio of skyscrapers and poured concrete, heard a samba being played, saw bananas and cacti growing, and knew that people before us had stood where we stood, as far back as 1748.

Have been working with crayons. Strange how a hard point pleases me so much more than a brush. Painting, I am only really happy using the handle of the brush or a nearby nail file or the edge of the palette knife. I seem to lose all control of line and the capacity to dream when working with a flexible point.

This year we are really having a rainy season. Hot rain, which never stops. In a little over a week we'll be on holiday in Campos do Jordão—where it is said to be cold and dry. Hard to imagine.

January 19

Left in the scorching heat for Campos—roughly half-way between Rio and São Paulo. A hundred and ninety miles of good road led us to the foot of the Serra da Mantiqueira, where we drove onto the flatcar of a mountain railway. And there we sat—with, behind us, one lone horse for company.

Brilliant green rice paddies—a surrounding solid mass of green—became ruler-sharp green stripes alternating with ribbons of blue steel—or so the water appeared, as our vehicle climbed. Over it all, canaries embroidering. Ahead, looming jagged and purplish—the *serra*.

A light-hearted climb. It grew cooler. A. relaxed a bit. The country was glorious—little ferns and long tufted bamboos and pine trees and great banks and bushes of a kind of wild montbretia—flame-coloured flowers, the buds like bright beads. It reminded me of a trip in Tasmania, in a Chevrolet on rails, where the vegetation was very similar. As we passed the sanatoria, for which Campos is famous, I was suddenly swamped with the memory of *The Magic Mountain* and the feeling I had had as I read it, that I could contract tuberculosis from the pages of the book itself.

Campos do Jordão is a mountain resort and our hotel, the Grande, is set in groves of Paraná pines. On arrival we did a cursory tour of the town, which is so scattered it doesn't seem like a town at all.

Yesterday, our first full day, it rained and was bitterly cold. So much for the region's reputation for dryness! But we came mainly to escape the heat and that we have done. We also came loaded with painting equipment and if it remains as cold as this our fingers won't bend to hold a brush. I think that although my *skin* doesn't like extreme heat, my muscles and bones do. Also heat suits my kind of laziness. I am lazy about all things that bore me—dressing, for instance. In Rio you can dress in a tick, because you wear almost nothing.

January 21

Spent practically all of yesterday in bed, under a kind of marshmallow topping, cherry-flavoured. Never have I seen such a glistening and puffed eiderdown.

Today the weather improved and we explored. The town has a modern and very clean market. But its cleanliness seems to have pushed out crafts and folk art. The only thing I saw that interested me was a large green globular fruit with an intricately "carved" rind, called a *pinho* and said to be full of nuts, but not ripe yet. The surrounding country is much more North American than South American to my still uneducated eye. Lakes full of water-lilies, masses of ferns, many kinds of trees. We drove part-way down the *serra* to get a little sun and watched a man making bricks—or rather, setting them out in the sun to give them their primary baking. It is evidently a brickmaking area for we saw a number of little one-man brickyards. Roadside flowers—great salmon pink trumpets hanging on bushes as if to dry. Poverty terrible here and, because of the cold, it must hurt more than in Rio. So far, disappointingly, I see nothing I want to paint. Landscape doesn't seem to interest me in painting terms. Plants, yes.

Brought *Dr. Zhivago* and although I have been very eager to read it, I now feel I shan't like it and so put off the moment of discovery.

January 22

Went yesterday up a series of ranges to Pedra do Baú—a great square-topped mountain that can be climbed only by zigzagging. After the rains the roads were dreadful, ultimately impassable. But it was glorious country with strange wildflowers and a host of birds. One flower was remarkably like heather but its bell was a brighter pink and its stalk anything up to three feet tall.

January 24

Two days of sun. Really hot when it comes out. We are at 5,000 feet and when we climb—which is often—we go higher! The Pico de Itapeva is 6,600 and, according to our informant— an unshaven, unwashed, and very smelly gentleman in charge of a washbasin-and-meccano television contraption—it is the highest point in the state of São Paulo. And what a view—range after range of grass-covered mountains and drifting clouds. The wildflowers quite different from those on the way to Pedra do Baú. Such a lot of sky—stretching away in all directions and always in motion: piling up white castles, turning them pink, building flat-based black clouds, shifting, floating, blowing. And the country beneath them is wonderful too, underpainted as it is with the deep salmon, coral, cherry, and tomato of its soil—colours which jump out, raw, where roads spiral up the hills, colours which lie under the grass, giving it great vibrance. It is infinitely varied—here smudged by rain, there lit by sun, there plunged dark beneath the shadow of a cloud.

We get out whenever possible. It isn't the rain that stops us, but the roads. The other day when a road literally *did* stop us, we left the car and climbed quite high and came upon a great cave of bluish granite. A surprise as we've seen little rock in these parts. On nearby trees, I found some small yellow orchids—called, I think, *chuva-de-ouro* (golden rain)—and if they're not, they should be. We disentangled their roots from the tree and I am attempting to nurse them in order to take them home. Curious that they like so high and cold a climate. Found also, equally surprising, some violets growing wild. *Hortênsias* (hydrangeas) here are the size of blue cauliflowers. And today in the market, lemons the size of grapefruit. I asked the girl in the stall what they are called. "Lemons," she replied. "Big ones," I said. She conceded the point and added, "Sicilian."

On a curving road, ran into a whole collection of monks like something out of the Middle Ages. They were bearded, wore brown robes, rosaries, and immense straw hats of the kind we used to call "cow's breakfasts", when I was a child. One very old fellow in a beret talked non-stop in a high wheedling voice and told us they were Capuchinhos.

Have just finished Snow's *The New Men* and feel I've spent the afternoon in a men's club. Don't really know if I liked it or not. (When in doubt, the shirt is dirty!)

January 28

Took my *chuva-de-ouro* orchids to the Japanese who runs the local nursery and flower shop. He looked at them rather condescendingly and at the same time told me of the small red orchids which are rarer but obtainable in the region. I thought, when a Japanese and a Canadian talk to each other in Portuguese, the chances are "red" means "orchid colour". But it doesn't. It means red. Flame red. Because today we found them, high up on a tree. With the help of a vine, onto which I climbed and then, precariously, stood—and with A. pushing from behind—and aided by a long stick, I scraped the poor little things off. Covered with bark and lichen (the vine finally gave under my weight) but very victorious, we viewed our prize: two small flame-coloured butterflies. And then, almost as if they flew, we began to see them everywhere. Branches alight with them. Truly a red orchid (alas not letter) day. Why does one long for mail?

I now have two fibre flowerpots into which I have put my collection. The first contains the *chuva-de-ouro* and some shiny, dried-blood-coloured ones which look a bit evil. Into the second, those the colour of flame and a large clump of another small yellow orchid which looks rather like scrambled eggs. So all in all the orchid count is good.

Yesterday and today the weather has been clear and we have covered even more of this high country. Range after range of mountains stretch in whatever direction we set out in, and the red incisions of the roads lure us on. The roads are not without their difficulties. During rain they are thick mud, after rain like dried-out river beds, with deep cracks and furrows and a muddle of rocks. Often we have to turn back because of a combination of road and ignorance. Our ignorance is due to the fact that the tourist bureau, which has a whole building to itself in the public park and is manned by a full-time attendant, issues us maps that are three years out of date and artistic rather than topographical. Prominent landmarks are placed where they compose best and scale has not been considered. It makes every drive a surprise.

It is impossible to give any idea of the size of it all or the unexpectedness of it. Look across miles of ranges and there, on the topmost pinnacle, is a castle. The governor of the state of São Paulo has a palace here—enormous, turreted, and in some way absurd. Matarazzo, a wealthy industrialist, has another, entered through great gates we thought must lead to a cemetery because of their appearance and the legend over them: *"Quietude"*. Drive to the end of any road on which you have seen no sign of human life and you come to a summer house or a farm. Large amounts of money have been spent here—the houses complete with swimming-pools and stables. It all seems quite un-Brazilian. I have always felt that Brazilians like to be near their neighbours—really near—and making a noise and hearing the noise their neighbours make. But nothing about this part of the country feels Brazilian as we have experienced it. The birds sing with Canadian accents and the cattle are European—no sign of *zebú*. There is, however, something mighty odd about the horses, mules, donkeys, or whatever. One small horse must have been crossed with a zebra at some time for it has a clearly marked stripe across its shoulders and similar stripes on all its legs—black lines, drawn very exactly.

The people everywhere are courteous. They often look like brigands but if you stop a horseman, or draw up in front of a country store to ask the inevitable loungers about how to get somewhere, you are invariably treated with the utmost kindliness.

January 30

And yesterday was red letter day. Mail at last.

Weather still sunny and we are out all day long. Yesterday we were in butterfly country. One enormous, pale periwinkle blue one with saffron underside, and in its wake another blue—palest cobalt with black piping. The wildflowers are legion—a kind of climbing Canterbury bell, also periwinkle, and a small butterfly of exactly the same colour, so that every now and again a flower flies away. A hum of hummingbirds. Red banks down which vines throw their green ladders. Whole fields of flowers and, strangely, whole little forests of pear trees—old orchards, I suppose. But I would not have thought a pear tree would grow so tall. Plenty of small hard brown pears. Wild begonias everywhere, likewise wild fuchsias. I wish I had my North American wildflower book as I'm sure I could have identified many of the locals from it, although there are many that are totally different—the orchids for instance, and the enormous parasitic nests that cling to trees and thrust up great red spikes—bromeliads?

Some of the lower-lying parts of this country are parklike—the trees Paraná pines. Their cast-off old branches look just like monkeys' tails as they lie on the ground, and the piles into which they are raked are pure animal. It is really an extraordinary conifer. It is trying so hard to be a palm. An immense tree when mature, its dark grey branchless trunk could almost be a palm's. More remarkable still, it produces a fruit about the size and colour of a coconut. Odd how it has taken all the elements that make a palm and made of them its own image, so much more satisfactory than any copy. It is rather the same sort of thing Klee did in his *Plants, for Earth and Air.*

January 31

Yesterday was red parasite day! What a succession of "days". We drove out to Pico de Itapeva. The Paraiva valley, which the Pico overlooks, is the widest and longest of the nearby valleys, and beyond it, a succession of ranges. The last, we think, is the coastal *serra*. The entire stretch of the valley was palest pastel. I have sometimes seen paintings done with that palette and always thought the artist was trying to beautify and merely making the result sugar sweet. But in the *flesh* it was as remarkable as if your eyes had faded.

Gazing over a bank and down into a boggy kind of a glade, I suddenly saw the ground red with those bromeliads which normally grow in trees. These are tremendous plants with long lily-like leaves of bright clear green or deep maroon. As a rule they perch on tree trunks and along branches, giving a shaggy and Sleeping Beauty feeling to the landscape. Occasionally you see one in flower—high up—and I have longed, since arriving, to find one low enough to photograph. And then, there they were, at our feet—great red cones with strange stamens of puce and royal purple—as much like parrots as flowers.

But no sooner did we find them than the sun shot behind a cloud, it became nearly pitch dark, and hailstones sent us scurrying back to the car. From the look of the sky, we might have had to wait all afternoon for the storm to clear, by which time the very bad clay road over which we must travel would be impassable—and tomorrow it could still be raining. I suddenly remembered the tripod and so we took time exposures in the rain. Pictures completed, film used up, the sun came out as unexpectedly as it had disappeared. And so I began a painting and worked until sundown, when every biting, stinging, flying, and singing thing came out to plague us. But it had been heavenly. So quiet. Only the tiny thrum of hummingbirds and their creaking complaints.

On the way home the world had changed. The great valley was now dark—only the snaking river catching the light and shining like a grey satin ribbon. The clouds had turned blue and the pink light from the setting sun was staining the coral earth magenta. Occasionally, high in a tree, red parasitic flowers peered out of their green nests, like birds.

February 1

Returned to finish the painting, which I don't like. Far too literal. But it does have a kind of rhythm and the colour is clean and it may have taught me something so that one day I may do better. Odd how slowly I work in oil compared with the speed of my drawing. A. did a landscape—pointillist! He is much quicker than I when painting, while slower in other things—more deliberate. Also he's far less literal, whereas in other things he is more. And he can put his paint on in great gobs, which I cannot do—simply physically cannot, however much paint I load onto my brush.

February 4

Rain again—yesterday and today. Yesterday it rather had the upper hand of us but today we went down into the valley to get below the cloud. Even so, a thin rain followed us wherever we went. However it was warmer in the valley, and we took the turn-off to a boy's camp which we had heard of from an American diplomatic couple— a minister and his wife—who had deposited their son there and come on to spend the night at the hotel. Their assurances that the road was passable made us venture in on a wet day, and their information that the two priests running the camp were Canadians made us curious.

The valley was, I think, the Garden of Eden. Prelapsarian. It was about half the altitude of Campos—hills high and green, terraced by paths made by cattle, clumps of trees here and there. Rice, bananas, corn, occasionally coffee, grew in the valley bottom. Waterfalls like silver chains and silver dust; rivers; hedgerows bursting with flowers; one meadow full of flowers of forget-me-not blue. River banks sweet-smelling with enormous white flowers—a cross between an iris and a hydrangea—loosely arranged heads of large-petalled blossoms. Crops planted on the hillsides described green herring-bones or chevrons against the red earth. Here and there *pinheiros* in full bloom—towering trees covered with bright pink flowers like giant orchids.

Ultimately we came to São Bento do Sapucaí, a sizeable village with four churches (one Presbyterian) and a very Mineiran feeling about it—not surprising, really, as we are close to the Minas border.

One-storey houses made from brick and plaster with tile roofs. All the earth colours in the architecture—the red of the earth in the tiles and the whole range of ochres and siennas mixed in the "whitewash" for the exterior walls.

As I have had it in mind for some time to find some handwoven saddlecloths to use as small rugs, we stopped at various shops specializing in saddlery. Bought a charming cotton one with a grey ground with two white birds on white boughs, gazing at each other across a white heart. Still hoping to find woollen ones, we stopped at another store which was full of men. I explained what I wanted and an endless conversation ensued in which all the men joined— ah, yes, there were such things, but I would have to order them and it would probably take three to four months. Did they know anyone who might make one for me? Oh, it was the women who made them and the women were busy and besides, there was a shortage of wool. Everyone was interested in the conversation but it didn't seem to be leading anywhere and then the storekeeper said he had an idea, if I would just wait. So I joined A. in the car and we waited. We had all but given up, when the storekeeper returned with one over his arm— woven of natural wool in a design of brown stars, with tassels at each corner.

The three of us now drove to the woman who was prepared to sell it. We were ushered into a house past a small boy doing sums with the aid of a young woman, into a room with a round table covered with a lace cloth where we embraced the members of the family and were invited to sit down. We passed the time of day, paid the woman, learned who had made the *baixeiro* (literally, underneather), and were taken by the husband to meet the weaver. At a small house by the church he knocked on the door, and when no one answered he put his head through the window and called. A little thin old fellow in need of a shave welcomed us, showed us two more *baixeiros*, led us through the house to a dark, low-ceilinged room entirely filled by a loom of great age. As we returned through the kitchen A. drew my attention to the stove, which took up one whole side of the room and was fashioned in two steps. The top one contained the fire-box, the second—about twice the length of the first—was a kind of heated settee.

I arranged with the old man to buy one of the saddlecloths and then the wife—a sallow woman in unrelieved black—showed me her spindle. To operate it she sat on a low stool, held the unspun wool with her left hand, and twirled the rod with her right; the disc at the bottom of the spindle provided the inertia, and her right knee the balance, as the spun wool wound round the rod. So close to the ground, she reminded me of a child, and her movements were quick and graceful. She offered to teach me how to do it but I was a slow learner and my clumsiness was the occasion for much good-humoured laughter.

Continued up the valley to the boys' camp—a fine site on the green mountainside, with chalet-like buildings, immense playing grounds, and a natural swimming-pool. There we learned that the two Canadian priests came from the United States! So much for the U.S. minister's information. Interesting, this, because he hadn't told us about them casually, but had carefully written their names on a piece of paper which he gave to A. along with a lecture (he can't say "how do you do" without it sounding like one!) on the desirability of visiting one's countrymen, the responsibilities as a Canadian, etc.

February 5

Still raining. (I wrote that two days ago. Got two days ahead in my date. But the fact is, it *is* still raining.) Today we went into the valley once more and put in a couple of hours of painting before the rain really drenched us. I am working on an enormous canvas. A labourer's work.

Am well into *Dr. Zhivago* and liking it very much.

February 7

In less than a week we shall be gone. I have no wish to go.

Yesterday and the day before we returned to the valley to paint. My canvas is the size of the world, and now, after two days, I ache from the physical labour of it. Difficult to work in constantly changing light (I think of Monet), with sudden and violent storms driving us back to the car. A. worked on a very, very pale painting. So strange. To me the hills are all raw with the red earth and black clouds hanging full of thunder and throwing a kind of bruised light over everything. But A. saw an innocent blond landscape. Or did he? As I've noticed before, he is not the slave that I am. Before a canvas, he is God.

I would like to paint every day—six hours at least! I've never known such a madness.

Poverty here acute. The Japanese run shops and tend market gardens and look not too badly off, but the native Brazilians live in a pitiful state. Garden produce is carried to market by small *burros*. The drovers wear large straw hats and, in the rain—our main experience!—long capes made of dull, grey, army-blanket material which must weigh a ton when wet. Many of the houses have one unique architectural feature: they are rectangular and all the doors are at one end, all the windows at the other. I saw one with five doors in a row, quite close together, followed by four windows. My mind boggles at the indoor plan.

February 11

Today was bird day. Funny the way things go in "days"—almost as if the first specific is magnetic or in need of its own kind. Drove to the Parque Estadual—a quite lovely, abundantly treed area at the end of nowhere, with nurseries. We lunched, the only people in the picnic grounds, and were amused by a collection of chickens and their pecking order. From the moment we put down a glass jar with a little peanut butter in the bottom, one scrawny black bird proved herself hen-of-the-walk. She was mad about peanut butter. Never had there been such a taste! Thwarted by having to put her head in the jar, she tried to peck through the glass. Tried and tried again with that near-sighted, puzzled hen look. Finally, in frustration, legs bent, breast feathers pressed to the ground, she extended her neck and thrust her head in the jar. Bliss. Difficult bliss. Difficult, brief bliss. For now, from out of nowhere, the Dowager arrived—majestic, in full bosom and plumage. By a kind of divine right she simply took over. The peanut-butter jar, a sardine tin, and crumbs I swept from the picnic table were hers—incontestably so. Unhurried, regal, she circled her domain occasionally, made an authoritative, low, clucking sound, and finished off the feast.

In a farther valley we found a pair of woodpeckers—yellow and black and mottled; a pair of large, bluish birds—the male with a bright blue head, the female darker; and what I would guess must be a *bem-te-vi-do-campo*. It is very like the Rio *bem-te-vi* but with a black and white head and a brilliant yellow breast.

In a still farther valley, we heard what might have been a kennel full of puppies being attacked by a barnyard full of geese and saw overhead—flying two and two but in a great flock—dozens of green parrots. I would have thought Campos too cold for them, but then, I'd have thought it too cold for orchids, too.

It is our last day of holiday and I sit on the veranda on an incredibly bland evening, in a litter of moss and earth, having been tending my orchids prior to taking them home. A. is packing in the bedroom, and we both, I think, look at the accumulation of paints, books, thermos bottles, baskets, wet canvases, and we wonder. But it will fit in finally.

*"Almost totally preoccupied with drawing. It is like an illness
—anything beyond its radius is blurred."*

February 17

All well on our return. Duque to welcome us, a ceremonial leaf in his mouth—trotted proudly, like a show horse around an imaginary ring. Such a funny dog.

February 22

Very successful session yesterday with Schaeffer—that is, he claimed to be very much impressed by my *Stone Fruit* and a black-and-white drawing. I am pleased.

We are just back from a day in Petrópolis with a Brazilian family. It was enjoyable. Swimming-pool, cooler air, pretty house—much simpler than most Brazilian summer houses. I said this to our hostess, who replied that yes, it was true—her mother, for instance, could not live in such a manner, coming as she does from a generation that cannot dress itself. I know her mother. It had never occurred to me she was so handicapped.

Spent the morning with Helena the other day. We sat in the centre of their large, central hall, cleaners with polishers working around us, as Helena insisted upon showing me how to cut my own hair— "You never can tell when you'll need to know." She also told me that she had been driving all around the country in borrowed cars pushing letters into convents and monasteries asking the cloistered to pray for the priest who had killed his bishop. I saw the result of the trial this morning. The priest got off with two years and six months because it was found that the bishop did not die from the bullet wounds but because medical help had not been procured in time.

Have changed *mordomos*. Graciano has gone and Albino has taken his place. So far no household tremors register on our seismograph.

February 23

"...no one should compel himself to show to others more of his inner life than he feels it natural to show. We can do no more than let others judge for themselves what we inwardly and really are, and do the same ourselves with them. The one essential thing is that we strive to have light in ourselves." Schweitzer. A wonderful man.

I am working on a very large canvas which will probably be called *Woman's Room*. Funny how some works demand titles—in fact, the whole business of naming is curious. A person you don't know— one you see on the street, for instance—is quite complete without a name. Looking at him I may register his beauty or lack of it, his manner of dressing, his possible employment, even speculate perhaps about his nationality—but it would never occur to me to guess his name. Except in the case of caricatures. A real "Mrs. Gump" or "Mr. Diggle". But once you know a person, he *has* to have a name. He is incomplete without it. Certain of my pictures begin as known persons and therefore do not only need names but—as it were—have names. Come with them.

But back to Schweitzer for a minute. When he decided to be a doctor and go to Africa, all his friends knew what was right for him—and it wasn't that. "In general, how much I suffered through so many people assuming the right to tear open all the doors and shutters of my inner self!" In a small way, I know this too. One's own core forms, assumes weight, grows its lode. And where that points, one must go, even against the most excellent logic and arguments from one's friends.

February 24

A note on Aparecida—on the road from Rio to São Paulo. It rises out of the plain like the head of a tonsured monk—a ring of vegetation around the circumference of a clay-coloured town. It is famous for its Nossa Senhora and her miracle. First her body was found in a fisherman's net and then, sometime afterwards, her head. She is black, about a foot high, and owns more clothes and jewels than any other Nossa Senhora in Brazil.

We saw her, resplendent in satins and precious stones, in a glass bell behind the altar of the twin-towered church. In the shops around the *praça* you can buy her statue in any one of numerous sizes and in one of two colours—black or white!

We visited the *sala dos milagres* (miracle room) to see the testimonials to Our Lady—a shirt with a bullet hole and blood, bullet attached; a letter from a consumptive beside the five ribs which he had had removed; many graphic, hand-painted illustrations of doom averted—children on railway tracks, snakes coiled around women, etc. I was fascinated and repelled. Mostly the latter. Envious, too, in a way.

February 27

Painting lesson yesterday. I showed Schaeffer my *Woman's Room*, also *Sky Forms* painted on glass and some other smaller things. He told me that *Woman's Room* was an exhibition painting and that we would enter it in the next show.

Am reading a book about Klee and his ideas. Difficult but fascinating. He talks of drawing in detail from nature, then turning the drawing upside down and deciding upon its construction in abstract forms, then righting it and combining the two. An idea I shall try to adopt as this bending the "real" to suit oneself is something I find impossible. In fact Klee's ideas about construction are a comfort to me. Schaeffer, naturally, can only show me *his* way, which is to put your picture up like a building, according to plan, and this I cannot do any more than I could have written a poem that way. Just as one word draws out another, so one shape draws out another. In the book I am reading, the author compares Kandinsky and Klee: "Kandinsky stuck rigidly to his means and proceeded to apply them logically, calmly and constructively. He cast around for a structure, pinned it down and built up his picture from that basis. Klee proceeded from a germ of form within himself which he allowed to develop rhythmically. Direct construction seemed to him like a short cut, and he distrusted such procedures. Kandinsky took hold of the world but remained outside it. Klee sank himself in the world."

March 7

In my whole life I have never known heat worse than yesterday and today. Sitting naked, immediately following a cold shower, I am covered with a profusion of valueless pearls of my own manufacture, cascading down my neck, breasts, legs.

Last weekend we left for São Paulo to stay with one of the *deputados*. He is a wealthy banker-industrialist-farmer, and prominent in his party, the U.D.N. (National Democratic Union)—a former finance minister, in fact. He is one of ten children, his wife one of nine, and they have nine of their own—the oldest twenty-three, the youngest three. His *fazenda* is about a two-hour drive from the city, and blessedly cool by comparison with Rio. It is an old pink-and-white building which might once have been pretty—its dining-room, the only room untouched, still is. So large a family has made it necessary for him to add to the original house. It is now the size of a small hotel. Forty-two of us sat down to dinner—not counting the young children who ate separately.

The floors throughout the house are quite beautiful—wide boards that look oiled. The dining-room ceiling is made of three-inch boards running lengthwise, painted white, and in each corner and in the centre there are pieces of wooden appliqué, rather like the pastry rose and leaves on top of a pie-crust. The grey walls are covered with a series of paintings like medallions—charming, old-fashioned, and absurd. Bedrooms modest in the extreme and bathrooms likewise. Service excellent but informal. At meals we served ourselves, cafeteria-style, and sat where we wished.

At the end of the weekend I felt I had not spoken to the same person twice and never for more than a few moments. Everyone was flitting from diversion to diversion—creating the *"muito movimento"* so dear to Brazilians. Card games, tennis, swimming, riding. And the whole place in a state of flux—children bounding about or playing guitars and singing the inevitable sad songs of adolescence.

Our host has a very scientifically managed pig farm and he provides information for anyone wanting to start one (and those who don't!) For instance, we learned how to keep flies out of our sties by putting mounds of pig excrement on grids over pans of water at strategic spots. Why? Flies like pig excrement for laying their eggs in better than anything else. When the maggots hatch, they burrow away from the light and drown in the water. We also learned how to get the largest litters per sow. How? Import Swedish sows. They have been bred longer in the back and, miraculously, given additional teats to fill up the extra space.

I spent some time trying to draw chickens. Not easy. We toured the dairy herd and were introduced to some very strange indigenous animals. Two stringy-haired *capivara* in a pen reminded me of Thurber animals. Others with quills and long black snouts were *porcos de mato* (jungle pigs).

I cannot say I admired the pigs and their ways. One stood and urinated in the face of another that was lying down. The other just lay there, apparently unconcerned. But I *did* like the children—all bright, natural, with good manners, and seemingly quite unspoiled.

On our return to Rio I made a kind of picture from the poultry drawings—using them as patterns for stencils and combining the stencilled shapes with the original line drawings, to create a fowlyard. Also began a large oil painting of the stairwell. Called *The White Banister*, it looks as if it has been painted with the whites and yolks of boiled eggs. At Schaeffer's, worked to the Concerti Grossi of Corelli, and think it must have the same effect on me as music played in dairies to make cows let down their milk.

Went the other morning to the studio of a Hungarian who does monotypes. I have seen his work in exhibitions and always like it. He was a dear—very generous with his time and eager to show me how he works. Using a sheet of either glass or zinc for a plate, and very linseedy oil paint, he does a great deal of lifting and scratching with a razor blade to provide the form and definition. I have, of course, experimented with his method—unsuccessfully. Impatient, I haven't allowed myself a long enough period of time in which to work, nor have I paper with a tough enough surface to stand up to the razor blade.

He also lent me an immense book on Klee which I am devouring.

Open season for Canadians this week. A stream of them for dinner or tea. At home I always thought I liked Canadians but what I was liking, of course, was my own friends. I don't find myself invariably responding with the same enthusiasm to all those who travel abroad.

"...a hundred indecisions...and a hundred visions and revisions". That is the way it is, for "the week that comes", as the Brazilians put it, is to be full of the Duchess of Kent and her princess, Alexandra.

March 10

Am sitting stark naked in the heat, waiting for the time to put on my clothes and go to meet the duchess and the princess at the airport. She couldn't possibly have picked a hotter time for her visit.

Am amazed to find that both Schweitzer and Klee, the two men with whom I seem to be more than normally preoccupied at the moment, felt a tremendous affinity with Goethe. (I was going to quote but would have to quote half a book—*The Mind and Work of Paul Klee* by Werner Haftmann, published by Faber.) So now I must start reading Goethe.

Painting—but disappointingly. Started a largish canvas—*Room with Black Objects*—but can't stand its literalness. I don't understand why, if I have a model, I am so locked into it, as if I have taken an oath to change nothing. I don't want to paint that way. Want to be much freer. Wish it were Friday so I could talk to Schaeffer.

March 11

Met the Duchess of Kent and her daughter at the airport yesterday. The former very elegant, taller and thinner than I had thought, but with an ungainly walk and a raddled face with an icy eye. The princess looks like a thin-faced Philip. I wonder why a certain type of good looks goes raddled? Perhaps after fifty you have to choose between your face and your figure. You can't have both.

Painted all day today. But *so literal*. What if I were to work in a medium more given to accident—pen and ink, for instance, where you can mistakenly make blots? Pushed, forced, driven by Schaeffer, I draw more abstractly than I did. But what a fight. And do I want to paint abstractions?

March 19

No time for my journal—heat, royalty, and Canadians have all had priority.

Our luncheon for the duchess went well enough. I liked her better here than sitting one down from her at the Itamarity dinner where, in an unbecoming dress, she looked hatchet-faced. But I enjoyed the evening. After dinner we sat outside in the beautiful quad at little tables, the imperial palms like vegetable elephants against the old stone of the buildings. For entertainment, this year's prize-winning samba school—its members in a range of pale to dark greens, blues, purple-blues; and formal in knee-breeches and perukes—all jammed onto the floating stage on the ornamental pool, with their drums and *cuicas* (an open-ended drum with a stick inside which says *"cuic"* when stroked with a moist chamois).

But, back to our luncheon. No one fell while curtsying and I didn't address the duchess in Portuguese, which I was afraid I might do. I liked the young princess, who at close range is pretty—lovely eyes and voice. She was fascinated by Arara, who did his best to bite her—obviously longing for a royal mouthful.

In the evening we gave a buffet supper for the Canadians who were to be presented later at a reception at the British embassy.

Apparently, when the first Brazilian guests arrived at the British embassy they were presented, not only to the Duchess of Kent, but to Dom Pedro, pretender to the Brazilian throne. Brazil, of course, is a republic, and members of Brazilian society had agreed among themselves to curtsy or bow to the duchess out of respect for the British. They would not, however, bend the knee to Pedro. This, it is reported, greatly displeased the duchess, who claims that one bows to blood. Just as well we don't all have to wear placards around our necks proclaiming what or whom we are bowing to!

The week ended with a dinner and ball at the British embassy at which, in unbearable heat, the duchess removed her tiara to the indignant disapproval of those same Brazilians who would not curtsy to Pedro. "She didn't *have* to wear it, but once having put it on, she should have left it on." We all have our sense of the fitness of things.

The following morning went to the airport for the royal farewell and then, at last, I could see a doctor about my arm, which was behaving very strangely following two bites I had received at a picnic some ten days earlier. At first there was slight inflammation and then my whole forearm became swollen and inflamed. There was not much pain except occasionally, when it felt as if I were receiving a nasty injection. I had phoned a doctor when the swelling began and he had recommended a salve which didn't seem to do much good, but I hadn't time to do anything else. On the night of our buffet supper, the chiffon scarf with which I tried to cover it slipped and one of the guests happened to see the swelling. She said she thought I had *bicho-de-pé* (hookworm) and that I had better do something about it. Well, what it was was *bicho berne* (warble fly)—the fly that ruins cow's hide—and mine! The doctor was able to recognize it because he has a dairy. Apparently it rarely attacks humans—preferring cows and dogs. This gave my witty friends every opportunity to be witty. It is good to know I no longer have two warble-fly maggots making their dinner off me.

Have just learned of the sudden death of Sidney Smith. We are shocked, of course—it seems only yesterday he was here. Fear he may have died a disappointed man. One of A.'s colleagues wrote of him, "He was a very old friend of mine and he told me that he was afraid he had made a bad mistake when he left the university for politics. I'm afraid he did."

A bad session with Schaeffer. I took him a sketch with which he was very rough. Said it could never make a painting, that the composition could never be resolved, that I had merely put objects against a background and the canvas was nothing but empty spaces.

When I countered by quoting Fayga, a local artist with a reputation abroad—"In the past people have been concerned with filling space. I want to leave it empty,"—he said, "But her spaces have meaning. These haven't." Me: "Why not?" Schaeffer: "Because they aren't beautiful." Me: "Why are they not beautiful? It's just your opinion against mine, surely." Schaeffer: "Well, for instance, that space is bounded by a line which is neither a straight line nor a curve." Me: "What's wrong with that?" Schaeffer: "It's not beautiful." Me: "You find it in nature. Any tree has any number of such lines." Schaeffer: "But art isn't the reproduction of nature." This rather ends the conversation. I know that art is not the reproduction of nature. But I cannot see why every single natural thing has to be deliberately stylized, which is what he seems to want.

Trixie, my classmate and friend, has none of my troubles. She says, "Accept as truth what he tells you and later you will understand. That's what I do." "Like algebra?" I ask and she nods. "But art isn't mathematics. Schaeffer is not teaching me a science. And he might be wrong. I cannot accept it without understanding it." To which she tells me—and rightly— that I'd find it easier if I could.

Trixie, incidentally, is the wife of the Panamanian ambassador, and we take lessons together. She is roughly my age, and of mixed blood—Russian, Portuguese, and English, I think, but in looks she could easily be Panamanian. She went to school in Hong Kong with Margot Fonteyn, with whom she has stayed in touch. I must say, she is a very amusing creature and quite lovely—like a fruit, a stone fruit— a nectarine perhaps. We are good friends. Share the same tastes in reading as well as a wish to paint and, occasionally, loll about on the enormous brass bed which seems to constitute the living-room of their embassy—all the other rooms being taken up for offices— eating caviare and drinking champagne, two commodities they seem to have in endless supply.

Busy. Far too busy. Every night one or two parties. Emily Hahn at one with her husband, Major Boxer, who is a Portuguese scholar.

In between times I read *The Roots of Heaven* by Romain Gary and stare Klee out of mind.

March 29

Easter Sunday. The intense heat has broken. We have had three days of torrential rains. Whose ark tight enough to outride them?

Spent a morning recently with the Israeli ambassador—Arie Aroch—a very fine painter. Ever since he heard me say I have begun drawing, he has been rude to me about it, telling me I am a good poet, why chuck overboard all the understanding of one art form in order to begin another about which I know nothing? Logically, he couldn't be more right. The other night he saw my work for the first time and phoned afterwards to tell me he was impressed—he had not only liked it on seeing it, but had reseen it in his head afterwards. A good sign, he said. Also offered to show me how to handle oils in order to do in paint what I am now doing in crayon and ink.

For the first time I saw his work in quantity. Full of magic and fantasy. Objects as uncontrived and innocent as if they had been let fall from the hand of God. Surfaces as sensuous as polished stone. Subtle colour. It gave me such a new, fresh feeling, as if I'd just washed with remarkable soap. A happy contrast to the previous afternoon class when we had solemnly painted fish on red canvases. I had been so bored by it, so bored; nothing coming from anywhere inside me to help.

Well, Arie showed me how to mix the tempera of the Old Masters—egg, oil, and water—and how to use this as a surface to scratch through. He also showed me how, in oils, to paint wet on wet without getting the colours dirty. An exciting morning.

Went last week to the Museum of Modern Art to see a show of neo-concrete painting and poetry. Lygia Clark, one of the artists, escorted Trixie and me past a series of her black and white squares. On reaching one that was totally black, totally square, and minus frame, she said, "This is my latest phase." Did she mean last? Did she mean final? Where can one go from there? Can she not see? Is it her statement about what she sees? I was depressed by it all. I suppose it is post-bomb painting.

April 14

Back last night from a trip to the Amazon—arms full of monkeys, alligator skins, pottery, fruit, *cupuaçú* jelly—hot, drenched in black coffee, and tired.

Wakened this morning to the kapok tree covered with "cucumbers" and full of birds—the *saí de sete côres* (seven-coloured skirt), the *saí-azul* (blue skirt), canaries, wrens, tiny birds with red breasts, and—singing like all the rest but, alas, not a song of joy—Benjamin Fledermaus, in his little box.

Benjamin is one of the wonders of the trip. He is a *macaco-leão* (lion-monkey), according to the Benjamin who gave him to me in Manaus yesterday. I would call him a marmoset. At dinner at the palace the previous night, a dinner companion told me he would like to give me a *macaco-leão*, and yesterday morning, as good as his word, there he was at the airport in his striped pyjama-like clothes, with a small round cardboard box in which holes had been punched with a pencil or some blunt tool. Inside, complaining, was lion-monkey. I didn't dare open the lid for fear the little creature might escape. But I did push bits of biscuit through the holes in an attempt to offer him, if not food, some kind of communication. And I chittered and chattered back to his non-stop complaints.

It was a bumpy trip—many air pockets. We hit the biggest bump just as we had been served coffee. A disaster. Not scalded, but nearly so. Uncomfortable. And the box flew from my hands, the lid jerked off, and there was Benjamin, flying around the plane.

Just who was most upset by the incident, I don't know. Women were yelling, people scrambling to catch poor Benjamin, and Benjamin himself—well, who can imagine the thoughts of a lion-monkey from the jungles of Brazil flying frantically around the interior of a Constellation? Poor little frightened thing—six inches from head to tail-base, tail another six inches, face the size of the top joint of my thumb—and such a look! He nearly broke my heart. What comfort could I possibly give him? All I could do was stuff him back into his small round box. And until his cage arrives, there he will have to stay. Already Duque's nose is out of joint. He knows there is something in that box that he doesn't like. I shall probably keep Benjamin on the balcony outside our bedrooms and forbid Duque the run of the upstairs. The only way to avert murder.

But back to our three-state visit to Amazonas, Pará, and Maranhão. Although we flew more than five thousand miles, we saw only fragments of the immense basin Brazilians call Amazônia. It stretches from Peru to the Atlantic, from Venezuela to central Brazil: two million square miles of it, two hundred rivers—half of them navigable—and the world's largest continuous forest, known to geographers as the *inferno verde* (green hell). Population: two per square mile.

We left for Belém, Pará's capital, two weeks ago, in a thunderstorm at eleven o'clock at night. Slept fitfully, sitting up. Arrived at five. Belém, which squats approximately sixty miles from the sea on the southernmost channel of the Amazon's delta, was awake. And hot. Not surprising, as it is only a few miles off the equator.

Were met by the mayor and other dignitaries. A. went straight to the hotel—and bed, in the hope of getting a couple of hours' sleep before tackling what looked to me like a formidable schedule. I, with no morning programme, was free to head for the market with the mayor.

It consists of a series of buildings and outdoor stalls on the bank of the Amazon—a wide expanse of surprisingly muddy, yellow water. The nearby port, chock-a-block with brightly painted sailboats, is a jumble of interlacing masts and ropes. The mayor led me on an exhaustive tour, pushed strange fruits into my mouth with his fingers, insisted that I drink *mingau de milho* (corn gruel) from a *cuia*. I returned exhausted, hot, with bags of tropical fruits I have never seen nor heard of before, an embalmed tortoise, a painted *cuia*, two pipes with clay bowls and long, slim reed stems, some mother-of-pearl jewellery, and "the real *guaraná*". This last has been used by the Indians over time. It is said to be good for you—unlike, I suspect, the very sweet synthetic version made in Rio, a favourite with Brazilian women as a substitute for cola. "The real *guaraná*", dark maroon in colour and made from the seeds of a tree, powdered and pressed into paste, is sold with the dried rough tongue of a river fish with which to grate it into water.

Fell into bed at eight a.m.—just as A. was getting up—in an old hotel with wide floorboards of alternating dark and yellow woods and deeply recessed windows. There I stayed until it was necessary to dress for luncheon with the mayor and his wife and the governor's *chefe de gabinete*. The governor himself is dying of leukemia. The talk, among other things, was of water buffalo—a possible answer to the problem of cattle in the tropics.

In the afternoon to the Emílio Goeldi Museum, set in a garden with many specimens of Amazonas flora and fauna. Wondered at the *peixe-boi* (literally fish-ox, which we call sea-cow—thought to be the origin of the mermaid myth!) Belém reminded me very much of British Guiana—the same kind of heat, the same vegetation, the same muddy waters, enormous water-lily leaves, mermaids. We saw one small rodent which, when awake, went round and round in circles, chasing its tail—it should surely be let loose—and in the aquarium, a tank of small fish which keep their heads permanently lower than their tails and another of small fish which keep their heads permanently higher than their tails. It really does make one think.

The Indian pottery in the museum was extraordinary—burial urns of rather Martian figures squatting on their haunches. The curator told us that very little anthropological or archeological research has been done recently. Digs have been begun but abandoned for lack of money. We also saw the blow-pipes, known to all readers of boys' adventure stories. I had expected them to be small, something you could conceal on your person. But they were great long things, taller than the Indians who used them. Saw, too, a shrunken head from Ecuador, dressed shimmeringly in parrot feathers. It was smaller than my closed fist, not in the least wizened or wrinkled as I had imagined it would be, but quite smooth-looking, as if alive—its thick lips sewn together with coarse string and the string left dangling. The curator could shed no light on the process. Did they shrink the bones or remove them? How could a head be made the size of my fist? How could the skin remain soft? And why, with everything else achieved as if by magic, was the mouth sewn—if it had to be sewn at all—with such crude stitching?

The rest of the trip was hot and frantic. As to how hot, nobody knew, not even we—for we are Brazilians now and the temperature and the humidity are matters Brazilians ignore. So we changed our clothes and went to receptions, changed our clothes and went to dinner, went off in the morning to agricultural colleges, changed our clothes and attended luncheons. Bands played and one even accompanied us on a boat trip upriver to Mosqueiro, the noise of the brasses making the day hotter still. I attended an "ice-cream" offered by the mayor's wife—great trays of ice-cream of every flavour, mango being the only one I had ever tasted before.

We learned about a breeding programme to improve the water buffalo—the tropics' answer to the cow—which crops grass under water, useful in a country where the major river periodically inundates the land. If pressed, the animal will even eat the leaves of trees, like a giraffe.

And we were presented to our first brazil nuts in their original cannon ball—an incredibly hard shell which must be broken before one gets to the equally hard-shelled nuts inside. Nature was certainly protecting that nut meat. Now if *that* had been the fruit of the Tree of Knowledge....

April 16

Benjamin Fledermaus turns out to be Benjamina. Her cage has arrived, equipped with straw for her bed. And I have acquired a tiny leather belt for her to wear above her hips to which one can attach a chain.

Her first days here she was very unhappy and scolding constantly like a squirrel. If I put my hand into her cage she tried to bite it, but however great her rage, she could barely break the skin. I was desperate over her. I couldn't keep a miserable lion-monkey. If I couldn't make her happy...what? Then yesterday, in a frenzy of sympathy, I picked her up despite her protestations, and held her against my side, thinking that perhaps animal warmth would comfort her. I was wearing a dress with a pocket and the moment she saw it she dived into it and came up again, head over its edge—her complaints changed to a song of joy. How could I have known that it was a pocket she wanted? I have now made her a white piqué hammock for her cage and she adores it and sleeps there uncomplaining. We are already good friends. As I type, she is on my shoulder, "de-fleaing" my hair with her tiny fingers, occasionally watching me type, just as if she could read.

But back to my travel notes. São Luís, capital of the state of Maranhão, is a coastal city (population 130,000) about three hundred miles east of Belém. It was founded by the French in 1612 and named after Louis XIII before it passed into Portuguese hands a year later. The whole area once boasted wealth and style, and São Luís was known as the Athens of Brazil because of the number and quality of its writers. The old Portuguese buildings are beautiful—lovely lines, lovely grillework, and glazed *azulejos* the colours of pale sherbets. Today, these are all that remains of an elegant past.

The small airport was almost colourless in the blinding sun when we arrived and a military band struck up "O Canada". Following the usual greetings and ceremonies, we proceeded to the palace with Governor Matos Carvalho—a physician turned politician—his wife, Dona Ada, and small daughter. As we drove through the city, I was appalled by the poverty and realized a vast change had taken place in my attitudes since I had gone to British Guiana when I was twenty-one. Then I had thought of the people as "natives", living in conditions natural to a primitive people. Here, seeing similar conditions, I am shocked by how poverty-stricken the north-east is, and how deplorable it is that these Brazilians are deprived of adequate housing and adequate diet.

The palace, by contrast, was an impressive, long, low, white building in a street of elegant buildings faced with *azulejos* which shone softly in the sun. Its interior, however, was considerably less attractive—red carpets, and carved furniture varnished with molasses to resemble carved toffee which would, you felt, be sticky in the heat and might melt. Sky-high on the walls a "collection" of paintings, all more or less toffee-coloured too, and hanging very crookedly. After being formally received, we went to a large banqueting hall for a meal of local dishes—a kind of hard custard and a very salty bread with a tough crust made from sago.

As A. went off to official calls, I was shown upstairs to an immense bedroom full of more carved-toffee furniture and there, watched by Dona Ada, her small daughter, and a friend, I unpacked. Dona Ada lost no time telling me that she and her husband had been married sixteen years, that their daughter was born after six years, and now their second child was to be born after another ten. She was having considerable difficulty with the first, who was already consumed by jealousy of the impending baby.

The governor, his wife, and aides quite obviously use the formal rooms only ceremonially, and ceremony now being over, we foregathered before luncheon in a small room off the kitchen which was equipped with two telephones, a large white refrigerator, a table covered with a heavy patterned plush cloth, two more or less comfortable chairs, and various hard ones. The palace overlooked the harbour with its sails of sky-blue and earth-red, but alas, this small room had no view.

After a luncheon of mammoth proportions—one always eats two meat dishes—we rested a short time and then drove through the city and out to the shark-free beach. There, in a sudden rain, we took photographs of row after row of colonial tiled houses. Such a variety and combination of tiles. Each house different—blue, green, or pink with contrasting trim—and shimmering like trout in the rainlight. On the way to the beach we stopped at a Baptist mission—three hideous stucco houses without light or water, in a muddy yard. Even the beautiful tropical vegetation was cut back as if it were a product of the devil. In a slither of mud we reached the governor's beach house, but we couldn't see the sea because of the rain, nor get to the beach because of the mud. Drove home in the dark, listening to the frogs which sound like birds—not peepers such as we have in Canada, but real whistlers.

The palace was staffed entirely by the military, and Dona Ada, of whom I grew very fond, evidently made no attempt to supervise her endless stream of orderlies, for our bathroom was dirty when we arrived and stayed so during our visit. Also the clothes cupboards were so full of dust and old magazines and disorder that there was almost no room for our clothes. This is one of the most baffling aspects of Brazil. These people, with very high standards of personal cleanliness, often live in conditions which to me seem less than clean. (Even Helena—sophisticated and travelled—walking about our house one day said, "How lovely it must be to live in a house as clean as this." And when I remonstrated, "Yours is every bit as clean," she replied, "No, it's not. My servants don't know how to clean. Not like this.")

Next morning, very early, we pulled hot clothes onto sticky bodies and set off to the airport to fly, via Cessna, a distance of ten miles across the bay to Alcântara—one-time city of 20,000, prosperous seat of a prosperous colonial captaincy—now an impoverished village of 1,100 where a group of Canadians from Quebec have, at the request of the Vatican, established a Catholic mission.

There were four of us in the plane: the pilot, the governor, A., and me. As we circled the narrow grass landing strip, a gash cut in the forest close to a straggling cluster of red-tiled roofs, we could see puffs of grey against the green—the burst of welcoming rockets—and a gathering of people waiting at the edge of the clearing to receive us.

The plane landed. We stepped out into the broiling heat, and the thin sound of "O Canada" in French rose from the throats of a hundred children. Then the Brazilian anthem, followed by a greeting to A. as ambassador, to the tune of "Roll Out the Barrel"—composed for the occasion, we later learned, by Alcântara's mayor. Then the introductions: the composer himself, tight blue suit, waiter's bow tie; the other local dignitaries; the beaming bishop, an elderly and charming Italian in black soutane with flamboyant cerise sash; Father Picard...Nicolet; Father Tanguay...St-Hyacinthe; Sister

Tereza...Nicolet; Monsignor Cambron...Sherbrooke; Sister Lucilla, Sister Romulus...one by one, twenty or more—white-clad, a little shy, a little questioning, but all obviously happy to see faces from home.

From the Canadians—with whom we speak Portuguese, to the great amusement of the Brazilians—we learn that this community, which must be one of the poorest in Brazil, is entirely without industry. The people throw a small net into the sea and catch small fish when they are hungry and they plant and grow a handful of *mandioca*, one of the staples. Fruits? No, they don't like fruit. Rice? No, only the few "wealthy" can afford to eat rice. Meat? Good gracious, no. Do they not suffer from malnutrition? But, of course.

The Sisters put up black umbrellas against the sun and look like cool ivory under their large black haloes. We walk in procession over the grass-grown cobbles of the old streets between ruins, tiled houses, wattle huts.

The day is a day of emeralds, sapphires, topazes—startlingly bright, terrifyingly hot. There are no roads to Alcântara so there are no wheeled vehicles to transport us. We walk past the Slaves' Church and come at last to the partially restored Nossa Senhora do Carmo, the church of the nobles, on a high point overlooking the sea. Lining the path to its entrance are dozens of small children in uniform—who sing "O Canada" in French—and two tiny girls with flower petals, which they are meant to throw on us, but they are too tiny and too stunned to do so.

The church is on a green square, the elegant falling-down tile palace of Dom Pedro II across the way. Our procession has now become formless. A. and the governor, well in the lead, are greeted at the main *praça* by an honour guard of convicts, themselves guarded by khaki-clad warders with fixed bayonets—for here in an old building, beautiful but hardly fit for human habitation, is the State Penitentiary. At a discreet distance, more children—in neat blue and white—are lined up on the square. One of the most classical of the tiled buildings has been converted into a school.

The children sing again and then the mayor makes a speech. It is so impassioned a speech that we are left breathless. Sentences roll out of him, mount and mount in great crescendos, break, begin again. His is the rhythm of the true orator—and all spoken without notes. You can see him so carried away with himself that you wonder if he will be able to stop. Small children faint and are carried off. Finally, of course, the mayor *does* stop but that is only the beginning. Speeches are self-generating.

Next, one of the Fathers speaks, first in French, then in English, then in Portuguese. His English is just like what A.'s French is going to be in a few minutes. He calls me the "flower of Canadian womanhood". Then the bishop's turn—his rather frail grey head, his eccelesiastical coat embroidered from neck to shoe with a row of tiny buttonholes all done in "cherry-coloured twist". He is Italian but he speaks in Portuguese. Next, a small boy, evidently trained by the mayor, declaims in full voice the glory of everything Canadian, everything Brazilian, especially the Canadian mission and the Canadian embassy and the governor. It is most impressive. Still more children faint. Then the governor speaks, and finally, A.

We go into the hospital, another thick-walled, eighteenth-century great house with beautiful tiled exterior, and sit down and rejoice in the shade and the chairs. The missioners are so full of things they want to tell us; we, so full of things we want to know. There is neither time nor common language enough to cover them all. The mission has been in Alcântara three years. One of five centres in the state, it is the poorest. It provides the children with the rudiments of schooling, gives evening classes in sewing, reading, and writing to adults, does what it can with health and nutritional problems. The members of the mission themselves have difficulties adjusting to this equatorial climate and, like the entire north, they too suffer from shortages of meat, fresh vegetables, flour.

There are no medical services in Alcântara so the Nursing Sister finds herself dentist and surgeon as well as general practitioner. She shows us her dentist's chair and her operating room and her best pulled teeth, kept as trophies to her prowess. Her great problem is obtaining the necessary drugs. Customs authorities can hold things up as long as six months and, without *mordidas*, they have been known to hinder delivery of essential supplies. (It is interesting to learn that the governor has been to none of these missions before. He could not fail to be impressed by what he saw. Perhaps he will be able to help them although nobody, I suppose, likes charity even when it is dispensed at the suggestion of the Vatican.)

The Nursing Sister says malnutrition is general, there are many fevers, various types of worms in addition to all the other ills mankind is heir to. We are given Nescafé in glass cups, glasses of *maracujá* (passion-fruit juice), and cookies. We eat and drink guiltily.

Through the french doors on the second floor of the school, we are led onto balconies which accommodate two, and we sit—A. with the governor, I with the bishop. We lean on the wrought-iron balustrades and look down on the grass below where four jet-black old women with drums, three girls in white with white flags, two in pink with pink flags, and a youth with an Espírito Santo on a stick pay homage to the visiting party. The old girls beat tattoos on their drums and call the names—"DA da-da DA *goVERNaDOR*. DA da-da DA *emBAIXaDOR*." Then, still beating, they all do a slow turning back-to-back dance to celebrate the Holy Ghost. And it is over. *Terminado*.

I am sitting talking to the bishop when suddenly I am assailed and assaulted by silk flags—pink and white, white and pink, a smother of them, swishing all over my head and shoulders. "They are giving you the Holy Ghost," the bishop says. (Ah, could I but receive it.)

We are now invited to the *prefeitura* so that the mayor and the municipal authorities can greet us officially. Accordingly, the governor, the ambassador, the bishop, the missioners, "Uncle Tom Cobbleigh and all" march out into the sun again and across the square and past the penitentiary where the prisoners who made up the honour guard are now back in their cells.

At the *prefeitura* the governor unveils a coloured photograph of himself—hung at the only height they hang pictures here—ceiling-high. The mayor makes another resounding speech; the governor and A. both reply. Then the mayor asks the governor to cut the tape so that we may gloriously enter the Municipal Museum of Alcântara, which we gloriously do. And while we stand in the centre of a small and mediocre collection of artefacts, the speeches begin again, this time on the subject of history, tradition, and art. But if mediocrity can be elevated by high thoughts, this collection is beyond price, for the mayor, in his third speech, really hits his stride. We are humbled by his eloquence, and any critical thoughts we may have entertained about the poverty of this museum are quickly put to rout by the loftiness of his concepts and we sign our names to the municipal by-law read by the town clerk, proclaiming the museum open.

On our return to the airport, I am accompanied by one of the young priests—white-robed, serious. He is eager to show me the interior of a wattle house. At his knock, two nearly naked men greet us at the door. They use the customary Brazilian welcome—*É sua casa* (It is your house). I have not lived here long enough to hear the phrase the way I hear "How do you do," and am always moved by it, but in this context I find it unbearable. Their *house*. It is all they have.

Inside, an uneven earthen floor—were it a road you would say it had pot-holes—a hammock, a few calendars (for the coloured pictures, I suspect, rather than last year's dates) and on the windowsill, some *cuias* to use as bowls. There is a back lean-to where we have interrupted them in the process of binding branches together to make a broom. They are courteous, smiling, grave. I am overwhelmed, horrified by the plenitude of our lives.

We stop at the Slaves' Church with its naively and charmingly painted altar and church furnishings ruined by defecating bats.

At the airstrip, green as shamrocks, the four old black women from the dance fling themselves on our bosoms like desperate children, full of *saudades* and flattery. Then back in the Cessna across the fat, slow, mud-coloured sea where sharks lie, and over the bone-white city blanching in the sun—in our minds, the still-vivid images of Alcântara, and *os canadenses* in soutane and coif.

After cold showers and lunch we tour the factories and faculties of São Luís. We see a plant where oil is extracted from the fruit of the *babaçu* palm to be used in cooking and soap-making; a cotton mill where the cotton fluff pours in foaming white falls and spreads out into a milky stream; the library (new) and the law faculty (old) on the Praça Gonçalves Dias, named after an early romantic poet. *"Minha terra tem palmeiras/Onde canta o Sabiá."* (Does Portuguese lend itself to trochees?) Finally, almost dropping with fatigue and heat, we arrive at the new medical faculty—an immense pink building, only recently opened—a goat tethered at the front entrance and two very young doctors more than cock-a-hoop with the premises and equipment and anxious to show us every last test-tube and catheter. We follow, wordless and worn, barely able to comment let alone enthuse until, entering a room, I am suddenly shocked into speech, A. into total silence, by two human legs lying on a table. This is immediately followed by one of the doctors lifting the lid of a large bath-shaped container in order to let us see a naked black cadaver floating in liquid. It is some time before I can think why the body is black or what the liquid is.

As A. is continuing on for a Commercial Association meeting, I return to the palace and seek out Dona Ada to consult as to what she is wearing to the official dinner. Find her eating a turkey leg in her fingers and looking slightly guilty. Were it anything but a leg she offered me, I would probably have joined her.

For dinner the dining-room is arranged with a table running around three of its sides. Outside a band is heating us up with rousing marches. Now all the men of São Luís begin to arrive, dark-suited, formal. I join A. and the archbishop and discover I am the only woman in the room. The others—what few of them there are—are hugger-mugger in the pantry with Dona Ada and the refrigerator, sitting around the plush-covered table.

In the morning, the dining-room is full of dirty plates and dead flowers and so we breakfast in the pantry, where we really should have been all along. Dona Ada tells me she couldn't get over the English guests bringing their wives. Invitations are sent to both, of course, but only Brazilian husbands come. We exchange gifts, pay a farewell visit to their *japiim* or, if you prefer, *xexéu* (there's a word!)—a crazy black-and-yellow bird which whistles the opening bars of the Brazilian national anthem, just slightly sharp. He has the reputation of being able to reproduce anything he hears. Later, up the Amazon, we saw his nests—the nests of a real artist—long, untidy, hastily constructed and stocking-shaped, hanging like windsocks from the trees.

Farewell, farewell, past the tiled and beautiful buildings in the stifling heat, to the airport to catch the plane back to Belém en route to Manaus.

May 23

I realize I have never reported the flight of Benjamina, or, in detail, her charming and tiny life with us. Or the small but real tears I shed over her loss. How describe her delicious smell or record her habits? Another day, perhaps, when my head is sufficiently clear to think in miniature terms. Today, I feel more at home with the larger forms of the northern trip.

We arrived in Belém from São Luís about midday, had lunch, and grabbed a cab to see the sights we had missed before—three churches (one sixteenth-century), tiled houses, and the harbour with its painted boats. An enchanting small boy asked me to take his picture. When I enquired why, he said he would like to have it. I explained that if I took it, I couldn't give it to him immediately, but he waved my words aside, saying that we would meet again one day walking down that same street and I could give it to him then. I wonder what was going on in *his* head?

Back to the hotel where I was to meet a group of Canadian women who had asked me to tea. They were mostly young wives from small towns in Canada, their engineer husbands employed in looking for oil. Many from Alberta.

At dinner ate a turtle served neatly in his little shell.

Up at six to catch the plane to Manaus—capital of Amazonas—where we arrived at 8.30, Manaus time. Were greeted in the usual fashion: A. inspected a smart guard of honour and we watched a march-past of very trim troops.

The city (population 160,000) sits on the north bank of the Rio Negro a few miles above where it joins the Solimões to form the Amazon. Once the rubber capital of the world, it is still struggling to recover from the collapse of the turn-of-the-century boom. (London rubber price, 1910—three dollars and six cents; 1932—five cents; today—thirty-four cents.) A. compares it to a faded, middle-aged woman living in genteel poverty in a sagging mansion built by *nouveau-riche* parents on the edge of a jungle.

The river here is copiously indented—the creeks or *igarapés* (canoe paths) pushing their long fingers inland. And squatting on them, like the early river-dwellers, modern man in long-legged houses with thatched roofs or in clustered houseboats—the water his plumbing and his highway. Almost like going back in time.

Although it is nine hundred miles from the sea, the port can dock ocean-going shipping. A cruise ship from New York came in while we were there, and a 15,000-ton oil tanker was anchored in midstream. All the docks float, to accommodate the river's seasonal rise and fall—which may be as much as fifty feet.

My memory of the city, with one or two exceptions, is a memory of grey. Grey and straw-coloured. Grey and mud-coloured. Yet, in the main streets, a very pretty small-leafed tree, its trunk painted white, spread a lacy shade on the sidewalks. And large Victorian buildings, relics of the rubber boom, impressive by virtue of their size rather than their style, towered like multiple Gullivers among the Lilliputians.

After showering and trying to fit ourselves and our bags and clothes into what is really a very small hotel room by any standards—and a good deal smaller when you are hot—we set off to call on the governor, escorted by a military aide—a thin, wiry little colonel covered in gold braid, who claims to have sired seven pairs of twins, with twins on neither side of the family. The palace, full of red, white, and black plush chairs, was like a bad cubist painting. The governor, Gilberto Mestrinho, looked a little like the traditional movie tough guy—or such was my initial impression—but he is, we are told, the first Amazonas governor in memory with a passionate concern for his state.

To refresh my memory of the trip by referring to our official programme is no use. Our call on the governor was the only thing that went according to schedule—for a small, green-eyed, brown-skinned man with an imitation leopard-skin tie was the official programme arranger and he took his job so seriously that he arranged, rearranged, and disarranged hourly.

We *did* visit the golden-domed opera house, capacity 1,500, built at the turn of the century at the height of the rubber boom—where Patti once sang. Today it is empty. Its four galleries, governor's box, marble, chandeliers, elaborate paintings, moulder in the steaming heat. One immense canvas shows the theatre itself surrounded by jungle and "life primeval" and, flying from it as from a great Pandora's box, the myriad creatures of fantasy, taken from a Brazilian opera.

Arranged or rearranged, a local pianist—a middle-aged woman in a print dress, with a soft face and untidy hair—played Chopin for us on the incredibly out-of-tune Steinway concert grand. It sounded as if it had not been tuned since the last "renovation", in 1929, when the marble steps of a stairway were replaced by wood. "Tropics-tortured," A. called it. There we sat, on two kitchen chairs, on a stage larger than Covent Garden's—in that vast, dimly lit space, surrounded by all that past splendour—and did our best not to look at each other. Our hearts ached for the pianist—a simple, pleasant woman who may well have known just how incongruous and pathetic it was. Our military aide, however—full of pride—whispered that she was playing "The Polonaise in A-flat Major" and made it clear to us that culture is something that Manaus has had, rather as if it were an evolutionary stage to be transcended.

Three factories: jute, brazil nuts, rubber; and a refinery. The jute factory was interesting. Saw the original raw jute move through a series of "jutefalls" and the fibre become progressively finer and finer. The finished product is a very superior product—as I should know who have used jute for curtains in the past. At the rubber factory we saw latex just arrived from the forest in two forms— as "milk" in barrels, mixed with ammonia to prevent coagulation; and in blackish lumps—coagulated and smoked. The former was put through a machine built on the principle of a cream separator which removed the "milk". The latter was cut up on a circular saw by a man putting the pieces through by hand. (The company guide who showed us around had only one arm!) The pieces were then put through a roller and stretched into sheets for shipping.

In the brazil-nut factory we saw row upon row of empty nutcrackers (the nuts are all cracked by hand!) It's not the season for brazil nuts, nor for crocodiles, come to that, although we saw a crocodile tannery.

Everything steamed.

Rio Negro water, in bulk, is tar black—hence the name. Yet a glassful taken from it is a sparkling, crystalline, pale urine. Where the black waters of the Rio Negro meet the yellow waters of the Solimões, they are strangely slow to mix. The sharp line of demarcation between the two persists for an astonishingly long time. "No one understands why," they tell us, exactly as if the best brains had studied the subject and given up, baffled. When you say, "Different specific gravities, perhaps," they shake their heads and repeat, "No one understands it."

An old man, at a party, gave me three orchids of a dark blood colour and about the size of the palm of my hand, curiously anatomical-looking. He asked me to touch a particular spot and I was promptly attacked by a small yellow object, like a miniature heron, which attached itself to my finger. "The penis of the plant," they explained to A.

Escorted by our military aide, we visited the historical museum, where the curator and a priest took us on a detailed tour of exhibits so dust-covered that it was impossible to see them. Did the museum staff no longer notice the dust? No longer remember there were exhibits under the dust? However, we did see a coin collection claimed to be the largest in the world, which contained some very old coins indeed; but as an electric drill had dislodged them from their places, it was impossible to determine just which one was "the earliest known coin in existence".

Perhaps most interesting of all was our visit to a large convent which houses a school for some two thousand children and directs many missions among the Indians in Amazonas. An Italian Sister, bursting with indiscriminate enthusiasm for us, the school, the children, the missions, the Indian artefacts, as well as a new and ghastly saint in cellophane, led us through the classrooms.

Upstairs in four large rooms was the best collection of "Indiana" we have seen yet. The Tucanos—a highly developed tribe of handsome people, hair cut pudding-bowl style—make dishes of a mixture of clay and bark (the bark for strength), and have devised a kind of glaze. Their basketwork was elegant, likewise their musical instruments—bone flutes and strange stringed instruments made from gourds. One room was filled with ceremonial masks—black, clay-coloured, and white—which cover the whole body, not only the head. Another entire room was a reproduction of one of their huts, complete with all utensils. There was even a seat for baby, hanging from the ceiling.

A. blew a blow-pipe. The "arrow" is about a foot long with a metal shaft and its base bound with some soft fibre which makes it fit the pipe barrel tightly. A sharp puff sets it off at terrific speed. The Sister told us that the art of curare arrow-poisoning was developed by a tribe of small, stunted, ill-formed people, slaves to the Tucanos. Something curarious here.

We spent one dreadful morning sloshing our way along wet clay roads in pouring rain to see the Japanese market-gardens which supply Manaus with vegetables. Never managed to get there. The outing gave us a good idea of the difficulties of transportation and a small idea of the country—slightly rolling and bleak—in the rain anyway. No real sense of rain forest but any number of different palm trees, each with its own edible nut or bean. A few bright flowers in the roadside scrub and occasionally a *caboclo*'s thatched hut and naked children staring at us. (A *caboclo* is part white, part Indian.)

We found the hotel grim, its food ghastly, and the general feeling of decay depressing, but the locals love Manaus. The mayor and his wife, not many years from Rio, adore it. There was an optimistic, governor-inspired belief that Amazonas would go ahead. One couldn't help wondering, however, about a people who lived so much in the past. A nice people, heaven knows, cheerful and gregarious like all Brazilians, with no sign of the dissipation usually associated with tropical outposts. The British consul, with whom we dined one night, was a quiet man who had lived there thirty years and whose hobby was cabinet-making. He said life had changed since the war, his wife had gone home because she was no longer happy there—it was too hard to run a house when you couldn't buy the simplest foods in the shops. The shops I saw seemed to sell mostly hammocks and luggage—for sleeping or leaving. But the Brazilians didn't complain. When you asked them why they liked Manaus they said it was because it was still a small town, you knew whom you were talking to, knew who was good, who bad. And you could still choose your friends.

Courtesy of the governor we spent two days afloat on the Amazon—our destination Itacoatiara, an isolated lumber centre a hundred and twenty miles downstream from Manaus. Our ship: the *Terezina*, a ninety-ton, flat-bottomed, shallow-draught, wood-burning sternwheeler—vintage 1910. Two decks. Upper deck: wheel-house and a dozen cabins forward; a roofed open space aft, which served as dining-room; kitchen and lavatories in the stern. Lower deck: one firebox and boiler, one steam-engine, a large woodpile, and six cows and one pig—not quite an ark—the vessel's on-the-hoof milk and meat supply. At full speed we made six miles an hour with the current.

We went aboard at ten p.m. to be startled by a quarter of beef, two sides of pork, and ends of entrails hanging from a dining-room stanchion. The crew were loading bananas.

An odd assortment of passengers: the mayor's wife and her small daughter, our military aide—who turned out to be a very clever sleight-of-hand artist—the city's most prominent dentist and his wife and her sister, the Columbian consul and his daughter and a friend, two photographers, a young female reporter, a professor of languages, the chief of police and his three small sons, and sundry others.

By the time we had played "twenty-one or bust" until two in the morning, we were all friends. Then to bed—we in our deluxe quarters, a small four-bunker with a minute wash-basin. Straw mattresses and pillows on top of short, narrow wooden bunks. Many cockroaches.

We had no sooner undressed than the *Terezina* drew into the bank to take on a load of firewood. Eerie in the black night, the torchlit procession of fuel-carriers. Refuelling—repeated every few hours—made for little sleep, but we would probably not have slept much anyway as it was stiflingly hot and our cabin was over the boiler. Stops to cut grass for our lower-deck passengers began with daylight.

Breakfast at six. Informality ruled, for as we ate we watched our fellow-passengers cleaning their teeth—detachable or fixed—and washing their faces and hands in the row of public wash-basins along the dining-room wall. Two toilets—one for men and one for women—and two showers. The first day I managed a sloppy and none too successful spongebath in our tiny basin, but by the second I was brazenly walking the length of the vessel in my lacy négligé.

Arrived at Itacoatiara about three in the afternoon to be greeted by salvos of fireworks. The welcoming committee was still in mid-rehearsal. But what matter? More salvos followed, and the dignitaries, led by an enormous *prefeito*, trooped merrily aboard to escort us ashore.

Well attended by the tricycle brigade, we set off on foot, in indescribable heat, for the sawmill and the factory for cracking brazil nuts. I am unable to describe what I saw, with the exception of a number of half-naked workers, for the heat had melted my eyes and my brain. It was almost as if one had a serious illness.

Down dale and up hill we paraded to the *prefeito*'s office, sat on office chairs lining the walls, drank the "real *guaraná*", made a shot at conversation. And the heat stood all around us, stood solid like pillars, like walls. Then heaven took pity on us, opened its sluice gates. The town hall became a drum for the downpour, its tattoo deafening. It glazed the open windows, made rivers of dry streets.

With great excitement, the one truck in Itacoatiara was commandeered to relay us back to the boat. The mayor's wife, her small daughter, and I piled in next to the driver and as the door slammed the small child said, "*Somos aquí. A Senhora Embaixatrix, a Senhora do Prefeito, e a Prefeitinha.*"

The rain ended as suddenly as it had begun and when we set sail it was clear again, if muggy can be called clear, and *caboclos* in little light canoes, diamond-shaped blades to their paddles, offered us tropical fruits and fish. We passed small farms with their fields of jute, *mandioca*, bananas, sugar-cane, and were told that no one plants more than the bare minimum on which he can get by. Who would, in such a climate? As to fruits, they don't plant; all they have to do is gather. A., interested in what the Amazon could grow, was asking questions: "Can it grow tea? Can it grow coffee?" etc., etc. But it became clear that he and the man he was questioning were on different wave-lengths when he asked, "Can it grow peanuts?" for the man replied with a note of impatience in his voice, "Yes, if you *plant* them it can." In his mind, if one went to the trouble of putting the seeds in its soil, the Amazon was capable of growing anything at all.

We saw few birds—one variety of large kingfisher which flew in flocks and lived in holes in the river banks; no monkeys, no crocodiles. And we saw nothing that I think of as jungle—lianas and the dark green foliage of Rousseau. Just a wide yellow river and a scraggy shoreline of grey trees. But we did get a close-up of the battle of the Solimões and the Rio Negro. As the Rio Negro came in sight, it was as if the yellow water on which we floated was a great sand bar or beach and, ahead, was the black line where the water began. But when we arrived on top of that seemingly sharp division, we saw that the two rivers were not mixing gradually, molecule by molecule, dissolving into each other. Instead, great balls of our sand bar were breaking off and floating like dumplings in a black soup. The Brazilians on board were delighted and pointed, and told us again that the two waters won't mix and nobody understands why.

Food on the trip was good, monotonous, abundant: oranges and *mamão*, bread, butter, coffee, and milk for breakfast. Platters of fish and green peppers and rice, meat and green peppers and rice, *mandioca* flour, oranges, *mamão*, and fruit juice for lunch. Much the same for dinner. And always someone cleaning his teeth or washing his hands nearby, endless talk, friendly banter, laughter.

Back in dock at Manaus, we lined up with the captain and his crew for a photograph. Their round black faces, the blinding white of their "whites" in that light—fresh as Pep-o-mint Lifesavers—and we, dishevelled and sticky, like gumdrops pressed together.

That night, overwarm, my hair untidy from the trip, we attended a state dinner at the governor's palace. In the black night the street lamps gave off so pale a glimmer that we were barely able to see them. Then, like a blazing beacon, the palace itself led us in, dazzled us—festooned as it was with lightbulbs and drawing so much power that the city's streets were in darkness.

The women were very friendly, and, to my eye, very overdressed, in their long gloves. I must have looked like a milkmaid in my cotton. I sat between the bishop and the soft-spoken governor, whom I liked better at dinner than when we had first met. He was so genuinely concerned about his state—all 601,000 square miles of it—the largest in Brazil and the least homogenized, with parts totally undeveloped, others in decline. He lists its problems as hostile Indians, wild jungle, disease, laziness, ignorance, and—as if those aren't enough—Rio seems the other side of the world away, and Brasília won't seem any nearer. He feels Amazonas will never get the help it needs from the federal government. "We are Brazilians too," he says, but, desperate, dreams of secession.

Back in the hotel I remember *Green Mansions* which I haven't read since my late teens. Where was it set? Venezuela? Brazil? No matter. Not that we have seen any signs of Rima. But I vaguely recall that the English boardinghouse-keeper whom Hudson married had been a friend of that very Adelina Patti who Amazonians pride themselves once sang in their domed and doomed opera house.

All in all, a most wonderful trip.

June 8

Between one thing and another, it has taken me weeks to get the Amazonas notes written. We have all been flu-ridden. And the weather cold.

I go on with my drawing which shows signs of becoming surrealist. Odd how little we know of what is inside us. Would like to be able to solve my paint problems. Shall I concentrate solely on drawing?

Have read two of the "angries" lately. John Braine's *Room at the Top* I disliked but *Lucky Jim* by Kingsley Amis was really very funny. Also read *The Borrowers*, a children's story by Mary Norton which I adored. But very little I read satisfies me. What *do* I want?

June 21

One part of me doesn't exist when I don't make notes. So for about two weeks that part of me has been missing, but I did manage to get some clay dolls which I have wanted for a long time. Perhaps they will make up for it. They come from Bananal Island, in the Araguaia River which separates Mato Grosso from Goiás, and they rarely arrive unbroken. They are made, as toys, by the Javaé Indians, from clay and beeswax. I was lucky enough to be on hand when a shipment came in and was able to buy as many as I wanted. I have one or two standing figures, a woman having a baby, one grinding something in a dish, and one, remarkably, with three heads. I am told they model what they see!

It is cold. We actually have a heater in the library. Have been to a show of engravings by Isaac Friedlander. Extraordinary technique but—but what? Too whimsical? I don't quite know. Also to Martin Bradley's show of large oils handled almost like watercolour—glowing and loose.

I go on drawing and trying to paint. My relationship with Schaeffer seems as binding as marriage. Every week I mean to leave him and every week I can't bring myself to do it. The fact is, I like him personally, very much.

Arie Aroch here yesterday telling me not to give up on paint.

A young architect from the University of Manitoba on a Canada Council grant, discussing Brazilian architecture, says, "Well, there is Niemeyer and then there is Brazilian architecture." He finds Niemeyer fabulous, inventive, generally marvellous. When I told him how difficult most of his buildings are to live in, he looked as if he could have hit me. "But his forms...!" he exclaimed.

Apropos Niemeyer and Brasília, I am reminded that when a guest at dinner complained to Kubitschek about the Congress building and asked why so much of it was underground, he replied, "You don't understand. My Michelangelo has the soul of a mole." (*"Tem alma de tatú."*)

Attended the première of the prize-winning film about Brazil—*Orfeu em Carnaval*. Quite wonderful. The *favelas*, carnival, the views—marvellous. But it was long. Carnival seemed as long as it is in life, and that is *long*. The *macumba* was rather dragged in, I thought. But the death scene among the stationary *bondes* was extraordinary—the *bondes* like the skeletal remains of giant caterpillars. And when the small boy picked up Orfeu's guitar and played the sun up while the minute, five-year-old girl danced, my hair was on end.

The artists took a bow as the film ended, stood against the silver screen—the black boys handsome in black-and-white dinner jackets, the black girls in tight-fitting black dresses and rows and rows of pearls.

The audience was almost entirely café society. Fascinating to see the women whom I've not seen since last season when they wore their hair in pompadours, now all wearing it in elaborate ram's horns.

-1959-

July 10

The day before yesterday, A. phoned to say he had received a wire from Ottawa that we are to return in August, that his next appointment has not yet been decided, and that they will be sending the name of his successor soon. I was so tired when he told me that I barely reacted.

But I'm reacting now. Am desolate that the dream is ending—this beautiful, tropical, golden dream.

Sorry in a hundred ways to leave. Sorry to leave Helena, who has struggled so doggedly and obliquely to make a Catholic of me. She is appalled by my godlessness. "Do you believe there is a higher part of yourself?" she asks. "Then, pray to *it*." And she has given me a prayer to the Holy Ghost, written out in her elegant hand: "*Divino Espírito Santo, Alma da minha alma, eu Vos adoro....*" How could I possibly say that in English? "Soul of my soul, I adore you." I couldn't. But in Portuguese...?

Sorry to leave Trixie with whom I have shared so many hours of painting, argument, laughter. To leave...but I cannot name them all. To leave the servants and Arara and Duque. Sorry, too, to leave my Brazilian self, so different from my Canadian self—freer, more demonstrative.

It will be hard to turn my back on luxury. I expect never to have so much again. Hard to leave so much beauty, so much sun, so sweet a people. And to leave this house, which I have come to feel is mine.

A. has bought me a Martin Bradley. Very beautiful. Two pomegranates on a white chair. The chair so rosily white. Eagerly await its frame.

July 29

Thanks to Trixie—and despite the frenzy of getting packed and partied and off—I spent part of yesterday with Margot Fonteyn and Michael Somes. In order to express her thanks to Brazil for giving her husband political asylum during the troubles in Panama, she has come to dance with a Rio company. And she has brought Somes with her.

Disconcerting to be confronted informally by someone who has, in the past, moved me so totally. And, of course, I *feel* I know her. Rather how you feel when you meet someone you don't know very well, after having dreamed about them.

She is smaller than I had thought, and spare, almost taut, in the way she holds herself from the waist up—head, neck, back, too straight. Recognizably a champion. And there is another quality, hard to describe—a kind of total self-awareness, as if she is on guard for leaks. Somes is good-looking and a dear, but rather out of focus beside her.

August 1

Saw them dance this afternoon. Where does her tautness go? And he comes into sharp focus on the stage. Trixie says it's as if he puts on a vital part of himself with his costume.

They are wonderful. Danced *Giselle*. Oh, what madness. Those mad feet.

"... have painted all day. Began by doing the grand piano with the chandelier over it."

-1959-

August 21

Aboard the S.S. *Brazil*. It is exactly a week ago tonight that we left Rio. And what a night! One of Rio's wildest storms. I thought we should never get to the ship—that trees would be down, or power lines. But we said goodbye as if we were going—to Klaus and Fátima and Albino and José. They became suddenly shy, spoke formal goodbyes, *"Dispense-me por alguma coisa."* And me, and me. Forgive me, too.

We walked out into the wailing night. Albino and Nildo put our hand luggage in the trunk of the car and Nildo for the last time slipped in under the wheel and, with our headlights dim, as if for a funeral, we slid forward into the black wind and down under the wildly waving palms, through the beautiful city—hidden now, but glistening here and there under a street lamp—and, finally, to the docks.

The great white liner, half wedding cake, half toy boat, loomed above us. Numb from the pressures of leave-taking, from parties and packing, we climbed aboard—there to find almost everyone we knew. We called for champagne and more people came, wet from the whistling rain, with presents and *abraços*. So very Brazilian, so generous, so bitter-sweet. And Albino and José arrived—Albino impeccably suited and José in his best milk-chocolate brown with fedora to match. How had they travelled that dark wet distance without a car and only able to set out after we had left? But they drank champagne with us and looked delighted when A., reversing the usual procedure, passed glasses to them.

Hard to believe Brazil has gone, that if Duque picks up a leaf or a twig as his ceremonial present for us, when he hears our car enter the gate, we shall not be in that car; that Arara will go on, mindlessly, calling to A. in my voice; that A. and I, returning from some function or other, will no longer look at each other and decide whether to have a swim now or before bed, or both.

Already it is part of a past which will blur more and more, until it is as pale as the aquamarines and topazes and beryls mined from Brazilian soil. Already the very special quality that was "Brazil" for us exists only in our memories and no words can recreate, for us or for anyone else, what was golden, perfect, complete.